SPRING

AN ANNUAL OF
ARCHETYPAL PSYCHOLOGY
AND
JUNGIAN THOUGHT

1981

SPRING PUBLICATIONS
P.O. Box 222069
Dallas, Texas 75222

CONTENTS

I. Archetypal Imaginings and Reflections

Psyche's View
Gilbert Durand
(translated from French by Jane Pratt)..........................1

Silver and the White Earth
(Part Two)
James Hillman...21

Archetypal Topography
The Karma-Kargyudpa Lineage Tree
Peter Bishop..67

Stopping: A Mode of Animation
Patricia Berry..77

The Academy of the Dead
On Boredom, Writer's Block, Footnotes and Deadlines
Stephen Simmer..89

II. Arts and Fictions

Six Approaches to the Image in Art Therapy
Mary M. Watkins..107

Art Education and Archetypal Psychology
Howard McConeghey..127

Shadows of Eros
Notes on Dorothea Tanning's Surrealism
Norman Weinstein..137

The Benzene Uroboros
Plastic and Catastrophe in *Gravity's Rainbow*
Michael Vannoy Adams..149

A Soul's Journey
Albert Camus, Tuberculosis, and Aphrodite
Michael P. Sipiora...163

Socrates and Stories
David A. Kolb...177

III. Jungian Thought and Therapy

How Jung Counseled a Distressed Parent
William McGuire...185

Schopenhauer and Jung
James L. Jarrett..193

Coupling/Uncoupling
Reflections on the Evolution of the Marriage Archetype
Robert M. Stein...205

Fragmentary Vision: A Central Training Aim
Andrew Samuels..215

* * *

Book Reviews
Bailey, Weinstein, Roll, Donat, Moses.......................226

ACKNOWLEDGMENTS

To Princeton University Press for quotations from the *Collected Works* *(CW)* of C.G. Jung (Bollingen Series XX), translated by R.F.C. Hull, edited by H. Read, M. Fordham, G. Adler, and Wm. McGuire, and published in Great Britain by Routledge and Kegan Paul, London. Other quotations have been acknowledged throughout in appropriate notes and references.

Manufactured in the United States of America for Spring Publications, Inc., P.O. Box 222069, Dallas, Texas 75222 by Arrow Graphics, Plano, Texas, and Sheegog Printing Co., Inc., Dallas, Texas.

PSYCHE'S VIEW

GILBERT DURAND
(Chambéry)

> Among the Fideli d'Amore vision is proportionate to the degrees of love, the faculty of finding proportionate to the heart. It is love that *makes* us see; the object seen is not the cause of the love.
>
> Henry Corbin

This year the question posed by the University of St. John of Jerusalem is formulated in two ways: first as a contrast between symbolic images: "Eyes of fire and eyes of flesh"; then as a comparison of philosophical methodologies: "Science and Gnosis."

After the steering committee had enthusiastically chosen this question for our annual program a certain discomfort came over me. This may have been primarily because I am a specialist in symbols, and "fire" is never symbolically opposed to "flesh"; rather, all classical literature testifies that the vital impulses of the flesh are comparable to the heat of fire, and that probably—as Bachelard's[1] reveries have it—the primitive tinderbox was modelled on the hot rhythms of intercourse. Then I was led to enquire whether this unusual and symbolically erroneous opposition between flesh and fire did not overlie an identical misunderstanding of the opposition between knowledge and knowing, Science and Gnosis.

So in the first part of this paper we will ask when and in what way profane science became separated from the kind of knowledge that is integrated and salutary, since that is the definition of gnosis. Then we will quickly show the immediate consequences of this insupportable "splitting apart" of consciousness.

Gilbert Durand, one of the most eminent thinkers in France today, is Titular Professor of Sociology and Cultural Anthropology at Grenoble and after founding the Centre du Recherhe sur l'Imaginaire at Chambéry was its director for many years. His writings appear in the Eranos Yearbooks as well as in many articles and books in French. In English, his work has appeared only in *Spring* (1971, 1976). This paper was translated by Jane A. Pratt (and somewhat revised for this printing) from a paper delivered in honor of Henry Corbin at the annual meeting of the University of St. John of Jerusalem in June 1978 and published in *Les Yeux de Chair et les Yeux de Feu: La Science et la Gnose. Cahiers de L'universite de St. Jean de Jerusalem*, 5 (Paris: Berg, 1979).

In the second part, by the light of "Psyche's view"—as this is revealed to us in the tale of Apuleius, in its relatively modern seventeenth-century prolongations, and recently through its resurgence in contemporary therapeutic psychology—we will examine how a recovery of gnosis may be glimpsed today in the great crisis of values affecting the scientific West during the past two hundred years.

*

I will not delay over the process of "secularization,"[2] but for some time, this process has been producing what—to maintain the imagery of sight—we will call a divergent "strabism" in Western consciousness. We will leave to contemporary theology (called the theology of secularization) the responsibility for those fantasies which in the wake of Karl Barth along with Harvey Cox or Peter Berger have made even "desacralization" into an eccentricity of Judeo-Christianity![3] The only result of theological fantasms of a bad conscience, like these, is a response such as Carl Amery's ecological neo-paganism.[4] Neither will we go back—seriously this time—to the reflections of the historians and philosophers who have meditated on such questions as whether it was with Guillaume d'Auvergne or Siger de Brabant that the strabism in question began to show in a practical way (that is, to manifest itself in what the civilization did)[5] or to ask whether, as one famous thesis holds, it was the ethics of Protestantism and the spirit of Capitalism in the sixteenth century that occasioned the divorce.[6]

No matter. But it is certain that by the seventeenth century, and particularly in France, the moment of divergence had blatantly occurred.[7] The secularization of scientific knowledge had already been accomplished in 1620 when Bacon's *Novum Organum* appeared and in 1637 with Descartes' *Discours*. The splitting off of anthropological knowledge had already taken place in 1690 with Locke's *Essay on Human Understanding*. Barely seventy years separated Bossuet's *Le Discours sur l'Histoire Universelle* (1681) from the *Discours préliminaire* (1715) with which d'Alembert opened the century of the Encyclopaedists. In fact as early as 1697 Bayle had produced the famous dictionary that had such ambiguous ideological results.

But what always matters more than the bickering of scholastics—or scholars—is the way the intellectual sensibility (a term I prefer to "ideology" which is too dry) of a whole epoch is impregnated, or better, the way a myth is incarnated in a whole epoch. The Century of Louis

XIVth was the majestic preface to the "Siècle des Lumières" (Century of Lights). The Enlightenment and positivism flowed from it.

Mythically a whole network of images made up what would become a Promethean torch as the eighteenth century ended, the mythology of the Sun King, or the Apollonianism of the Classic Ideal. The Apollo theme, particularly when joined with the theme of Daphne, emerged again and again in counterpoint with the solar thought of the seventeenth century and at the beginning of the eighteenth. Bernini returned twice to this theme, in a painting and a sculpture, Poussin devoted a canvas to *Apollon amoureux de Daphne*, Tiepolo also took up the theme; d'Assouçy made an opera ballet out of it, as did M. da Gagliano. Claude Lorrain put the figures of Apollo and Mercury into a landscape...and so on.

The paradigm of this Apollonianism—aside from its culmination in the realization of the Palace of Versailles (1670-1682), marked with the theme of the Victorious Sun—was certainly the basic project of Descartes forty years earlier when he wrote his treatise *Du Monde et de la Lumière* (On The World and Light),[8] which was to provide a cosmogony and cosmology (observe the total comity of the scientific "method"!) starting with the phenomenon of light. Certainly one might suppose oneself to be concerned here with an entirely Biblical or Platonic metaphor issuing from the *Fiat Lux* of Genesis or the well-known myth of the cave in book ten of the *Republic*. But no! This was a century of opticians: it opened with Galileo's telescope and closed with the philosophy of Spinoza, a maker of lenses.[9] Descartes' treatise *On the World and Light*, like his *La Dioptrique*, was obsessed by the phenomena of vision.

In the great philosophical disputes that now began, Cartesian dioptrics, model of all the mathematical physics that would come, stood for the reduction of the world, of matter—and that is what Leibnitz held against it—to geometrical and finally to algebraical laws of understanding. The dualistic cleavage between spirit and matter, so often denounced by Henry Corbin, and the conjuring away of the soul (or its reduction to rational spirit) were achieved. The absolute monarchy of the future Sun King (born a year after the publication of the *Discours de la Méthode* in 1638) was prepared for by Descartes' absolute method which in its "clarity and distinction"—both optical qualities—rested upon "evidence," "simple seeing," the bare fact of sight without mediation. After that, by way of Malebranche and Spinoza—and possibly through all

3

the thinkers of the seventeenth century who were seemingly most opposed to each other: the Molinists and Jansenists, Bossuet and Fenélon—this absolutism of clear reason led to the emergence of the "Encyclopedic spirit."[10]

An important thing to note here is that the myth was stronger, and more pregnant with effects upon this century than the disputes which would be called "ideological." It mattered very little that Bossuet fulminated against the quietism of Fenélon, Boileau against the modernism of Charles Perrault; whether Molière attacked Visé or Boursault and Descartes attacked Gassendi, or whether the Uranists led by Mme. de Longueville opposed the Gobelins led by the Prince de Condé, the fact remained that they all spoke the same language which was an Apollonic language of Classical Idealism. It was Boileau in 1674 in *L'Art poétique* who formulated the rules for this language: "Nothing is beautiful except truth... therefore love reason...." To everyone, truth, the evident, the commonsensical seemed "natural."

*

The price of this Apollonianism was a split in consciousness, and first as a split between science and faith, so evident in Pascal's *Pensées* and Bayle's *Dictionary*. But the faith was more and more distant and nameless. Already the consuming flash of the *Lumières* (lights) had little by little reduced the God of Abraham and Jacob to the "God of learned men and philosophers." Then, finally, the vague deism of men like Rousseau and Voltaire evaporated when triumphant Science no longer needed even that well-known "chiquenaude" (snap of the fingers) to explain the mechanics of nature. Psychology too was conjured away just after the birth of its name by the very people who would make use of that name later.[11] In turning his attention to the soul Descartes had cut it in two; one part, entirely abstract and empty, would become the famous *ego cogito*, and the other, falling back to the level of neurology, would constitute the seat of modern psychophysiology.

After this reduction of consciousness to a single science and a single analytical and geometrical method, no choice remained to Western thought other than one between split consciousness with its distressing and inescapable dualisms and blindness. The West is one-eyed. It is blinded or half-blinded as the greatly punished figures in mythology always are: Tiresias was blinded for wanting to see Athena; Erymanthe, son of Apollo, for having seen Aphrodite; Ilos for disobeying Athena;

Vesta blinded Antylos, and so on.

Like the familiar cyclops, the West sees everything with *the same eye*. Thus the distress of split consciousness was succeeded by the malady of one-dimensionality. And this last is what led conscienceless Western science, as though by the crematories' glow, to the lightning blast at Hiroshima. I will not dwell on this picture: it is the picture that follows all attempts to escape the unhappy Kantian split by reductive philosophical thinking. Such a view is characterized by a century-long reductive myth which from Condorcet to Comte or Hegel has given if not a Cyclopian tone at least a Titanic[12] one to all modern philosophy. The cyclopian philosophy resulting from this movement flattens out the nuance of difference by calling it *antithesis*. In wiping out differences it levels the hierarchies. The morality of our science is egalitarian, a leveling which is of service only to the half-blind Cyclops who confuses ends with means. Thus the theological and the metaphysical are reduced to the "positive," the thesis to the antithesis, and the antithesis to the synthesis. In this way all knowledge (*gnosis*) is brought down to a science of the instant, to a method of knowing the here and now. The one-dimensional language of Classical Idealism has set a bad example: for it is upon its reductive system, its flattening out of signs and defiance of symbols that our whole despairing pedagogy and all our disoriented information are presently based. This one-dimensional language has assimilated all romantic, symbolistic, and Freudian advances and bifurcations. It is as universal as a Latin without lexicon or Roman syntax. It levels all nuances—that is to say, all values—its inadequacy being equally "translatable" from Los Angeles to the Latin Quarter, and from there to the Unter den Linden. Altogether inadequate for the expression of soul, one-dimensionality constitutes the essential symptom of a sickness in our civilization which, beneath its linear logic and its wrinkleless future, is brooding a gigantic titanomachy. As Ricoeur said in criticizing structuralism, sophists are kings when language no longer makes any sense but "the sense of non-sense."

*

These disputed matters and reflections gain precision when one reads my friend James Hillman's presentation of them in *The Myth of Analysis*.[13] The whole first part of his book is devoted to the modes of psychological creativity—and refers back to the Apuleian legend of Eros and Psyche, while the second part is given over to a violent criticism of the "language of psychology" which he says "insults the soul" and sterilizes "metaphors into abstractions."[14] The language of psychology has died, it seems to me, of the lethal illness that has overtaken all language in Western culture. Indeed the angry question of this psychotherapist may be generally applicable when he asks, "What has happened to this language of psychology in a time of superb communication technics and democratic education?"[15] That is the whole problem also for us who are philosophical anthropologists and to resolve it we must make use of the same solutions used by Hillman, as he continues on from Jung.

To begin with we must denounce the academic language of communications technics and mass education. The familiar Freudian-Marxist-Saussurian language blocking the entire system of knowledge with which the industry of our universities now pleases itself—the language of textbooks, diplomas, organized contests, and the media—must be repudiated on pain of that "death of Man" upon which Foucault insists. To counter a sterile and inadequate dream-language truthful procedures have to be used. And truthful procedures oppose the axiological leveling of saying "nothing is true." A philosophy claiming to be new because yesterday's philosophy is worn out should have a correspondingly new *organon*.

Without delaying here over the psychological specifications for an adequate philosophical language, let us merely point up the methodology of the "New Psychological Spirit" that Hillman illustrates so well. This means abandoning the dualism, so tenacious in our Indo-European languages,[16] in favor of a language that is "more discontinuous, now this and now that, guided as much by the synchronistic present as by the causal past, moving on a uroboric course, which is a circulation of the light *and* the darkness."[17] This language is therefore not antithetic as philosophy from Socrates to Hegel has believed; it is at once *metaleptic* (guided by the aims of desire, present synchronicity and past causality) and *metabolic* (that is, repetitive and differentiating). But *metalepse* and *metabole* are really the style of myth.[18] The new language uses *meta*—not *anti*. This change of course has primordial importance: in the game of dialectics the antithesis is *as good as* the thesis and only the Titanic *deus ex machina* of historical becoming introduces the value of truth. By posing the problem as "meta" one reintroduces an internal hierarchy that escapes the Titanism of history. Seen in this perspective those who have been conquered by history and counted for lost are no longer necessarily in the wrong. Truth is reestablished as transcendent in relation to the world and as immanent in relation to the Man of Desire.[19]

We will not redefine myth here, I will just refer you to other places where I have given such definitions. We will not go back over that philosophy of ours where—in the wake of the greatest surrealist poetry, and of Jung and Henry Corbin—we can affirm along with Walter F. Otto[20] that "Speech and myth are the same thing. Initially myth means *the real word . . . speech about what is.*" Thus, to honor Henry Corbin, we may certainly say that myth is the "language of the Imaginal." Ordering dilemmas, as it does through its structure, myth is the center of hierarchy formation, the model by which values are established as neo-Platonism and Hermetism were well aware. That is why myths call for the intervention of those instances of supreme values: the Gods.

This language, at once "metaleptic and metabolic," constitutes a dynamic source of multivocalism opposed to the strabismic univocalism, that linear language of the classic ideal, of mechanism and positivism. Moreover the procedures of truth in imaginal language permit more pertinent and comprehensive readings, and are more 'enlightening,' than the Cartesian analyses of the manifestations of the human soul.

The procedures of mythical language are agents of truth. Let me show this in a non-dialectical way, for, in one and the same language, and in an ideology which appears on the surface to be homogenous, another language can arise in the chiaroscuro of myth; another ideology, and another myth can come to birth that nourish the depths of the first. And I insist that this has nothing to do with the dialectic succession of antithesis, but rather with the metaleptic and metabolic hollowing out of the hierarchic levels of the thesis.

*

Let us return now to our historical example, the "Century of Louis XIV" so well prefaced by that of Richelieu.[21] That period from the Revolt of the Princes in 1614 to the death of Louis XIV in 1714 is characterized by the classical ideal and the myth of solar luminaries. Nietzsche was the first—thanks to a truly scholarly philology—to show that cultures live only through the depths of their contrasts and that in the end the Knowledge which really enables us to escape from nihilism is the Joyful Wisdom of the depths. Apollo shines only during the nighttime of his brother Dionysus. It is the same with the seventeenth and eighteenth "Siécles de Lumières" [Centuries of Lights]. Considering the first only, we may ask what kind of night-time hollowing out occurred during this century of Apollo *redivivus*. René Huyghe demonstrated that it was the "false unity of XVIIth-century France"; Pierre Brunel speaks of "an apparent triumph of order,"[22] saying that the proud device *"Post Tenebras Lux"* should, to the contrary, be *"In Tenebris Lux."* Nothing is easier to see than the actual ambiguity of the "Lumieres": illuminism—*"alumbrados"* in the Spain of St. John—meant in the XVIth century, as it did also in the XVIIth and XVIIIth exactly the opposite of the *Aufklärung* [Enlightenment].[23] Its inverse, not its antithesis. For the shadow of a century is more like a mirror image, as though behind the paintings of Lesueur, and Poussin, and Champaigne, a Caravaggio-like "luminism" was preparing to appear, like that of Georges de la Tour, a chiaroscuro like Rembrandt's, crepuscular paintings like Lorrain's, and even the unwonted realism of the Nain brothers. Behind the century of the Sun King a whole night was waiting watchfully.

And there was a myth that would organize this night, one that had been reborn in the very soul of Raphael's, Titian's and Correggio's paintings during the previous century, a century at the end of which Goclenius (1590) and Casmann (1594) had for the first time used the term "psychologia,"[24] a century where in the wake of the *devotio moderna* all the mystical orisons of St. John's followers were concerned with the "deep center of the soul": *"de mi alma en el mas profundo centro...,"* this myth is none other than the myth of Psyche.

When we consult the list made by Le Maître[25] we find that between the *Psiche* of L. Geliot in 1599 and, to set an arbitrary date, Sériey's *Amour et Psyché,* 1780-90, we can count not only twenty-four Latin translations of Apuleius' tale but also fifteen French translations and about fifteen translations into other languages. In addition, we find twenty-six operas and French novels, six cantatas, and fifty-five paintings or sculptured works. It is true that the mythical figure of Psyche would continue to haunt the romantic century with this same intensity. We must, however, strenuously assert that no train of reasoning—not even a negative procedure like dialectic—can deduce the resurgence of Psyche from the classic ideal. Logically, that ideal, and its century, were more likely to seek for the soul in the pineal gland or Gassendi's atoms, or as they did later in the *tabulae rasae* of Condillac's marble statue. With such linear deductions one risks becoming trapped oneself in the unidimensionality of 'classical' discourse. (Not even Michel Foucault, with all his subtlety, has been able to escape that in what he says about the "representation" and "speech" that characterize classical epistemology.[26] Faced with the dictatorship of this representation, with the language of *mathesis* and *taxinomia* Foucault could only assert that outbursts of "madness" put an end to its totalitarianism. His subtlety has become the victim of his formative academic background, so geometrically and precisely dependent on classical language.)

What hollowed out the depths of the *Siècle des Lumières* [Century of Lights] was no more a pathological "counter culture" than what happens in any other century; it was the whole somber nocturnal support underlying the culture. For this century excited itself shockingly less about the nascent sciences and the politics and economics that the social sciences were outlining than about religion. Paradoxically, the seventeenth century marked the highest point in the "flight of modern spirituality."[27] It was the century of "extraordinary Catholic renewal": churches multiplied, new orders flourished. Its Christianism was fundamentally Augustinian. And whereas the "Lights" monopolized all the glamour, theology and religious feeling emphasized the misery of fallen man...[28] No religious fermentation of this kind had ever so greatly animated France before, and the names of the most illustrious thinkers were as much, or even more, associated with religious passions as with the discoveries and stylistic characteristics that we remember them for today.

We too often forget that the seventeenth century was also the century of the mysterious Rosicrucian[29] brotherhood, with which Descartes had some contacts. Descartes did not launch his philosophy until encouraged by the mystic Berulle, and his correspondents were often eminent religious persons: Father Charles de Condren, General of the Oratoire, Father Gibieuf, Father Mersenne. Nor may we forget the less usual Descartes of the *Olympiques*, the famous dreams, the glowing visions and the vow made at Notre-Dame-de Lorette.[30] Louis XIVth linked his name and his solar prestige with the Gallicanist principles and practices of the French Church (*Declaration des quatre articles*, 1682). Pascal is more celebrated for his *Provincial Letters* against the Jesuits than for his treatises *On the Vacuum* and *On Conic Sections*. Special mention should be made of Fénélon and the doctrine of Pure Love which returned in the middle of the Century of Light, via Mme. Guyon, to the Alumbrados' "inspiration of the heart." Behind the light of the geometrical spirit that was then coming to a focus, "reasons" of the heart were rising along with a spirit of finesse [subtlety].

Racine, in his Jansenism and his plays, is certainly most representative of the style demanded by the classical ideal in both the elegance of his presentation and the preciosity of the rhetoric with which he overlays the "essential motivation of his tragedies which is love." Love as passion and religion—*Phèdre* and *Esther*—are linked in counterpoint in the classicism of Racine. Moreover with Racine—as with Melle de Scudery *(Chart of the Tender,* 1648) and Margarite Marie *(Alcoque of the Sacred Heart,* 1673)—this Love becomes a perilous and painful quest, the psychic interiorization of the passion known to the Spanish mystics in their ascensions of Mt. Carmel or Mt. Zion.

During this nocturne of the seventeenth century the myth of Psyche with all its perennial meanings was reborn. Also, as noted earlier, with the century the term "psychology" came to birth. Indeed this century was studded with the flowering of works all bringing the drama of Psyche explicitly to view. Let us recall a few dates.[31] In 1623 there was Marino's *Adone,* a strongly colored allegory in which Love, as the Soul's Desire, opposes the bad advice of Psyche's sisters, representing liberty and the carnal temptations. Then in 1665 in an *"autos mitologicos," Psiquis y Cupido,* Calderón allegorized the legend in a more religious way by personifying Faith as Psyche and Cupid as the Charity incarnate in the Eucharist. In 1656 Benserade's *Ballet de Psyché ou de la Puissance de l'Amour* was danced before the future Sun King. In 1669 La Fontaine devoted two books to the *Amours de Psyché et Cupidon,* and in 1671 Corneille composed a "tragic ballet" about Psyche in five acts. Finally at the end of the era of the Lights, in 1780, William Blake illustrated George Cumberland's story of Eros and Psyche.[32]

That this myth did not lose favor after the Great Century is certainly evident in Victor de Laprade's famous *Psyche* of 1821 and in 1823 in the description of the Psyche story that figured on the cup in Lamartine's *La mort de Socrate.* But it was the greatest writers of the seventeenth century who seem to have been suddenly struck by the legend that they inherited directly from Apuleius' novel, the *Metamorphoses.*[33]

*

So we must ask, What does this celebrated story contain? Jan Ojwind Swahn[34] has showed that Apuleius' scenario is an integral part of a definite group of stories found all over Europe and that it is made up of a series of motifs: a *prohibition is violated by a young wife* (against seeing her husband in the light, destroying his animal skin, going back for too long to her family, opening a forbidden door, etc.); punishment by separation ensues and a *search for the lost husband* begins through *a number of trials* (wearing iron shoes, filling a jar with tears, crossing deep rivers and inaccessible mountains); some of these *tasks are impossible* (carrying water in a sieve, sorting an enormous pile of mixed grains, cleaning a stable to the bottom); and during these trials the searcher has *encounters that help her* (with her husband, with animals, objects, etc.); then finally a last task (the descent into hell whence something must be brought back) occasions the *return of the husband and reunion with him.*

Swahn's study demonstrates how pregnant with extensions this myth scheme is, as witness our own *Beauty and the Beast,* collected in 1757 by Madame Le Prince de Beaumont.[35] We must keep in mind, however, that all the authors were inspired by the novel of Apuleius and that the significance of that novel was reinforced by the framework of initiation in which it is set. Apuleius knew all the mythographic traditions of the second century: a native of Africa from Madura—like St. Augustine, his illustrious 'neighbor' a century and a half earlier—there was nothing he did not know about Neoplatonism and Asiatic mysticisms. He took his inspiration from *Lucius or the Ass,*[36] a little Greek novel by Lucian, in which he enshrined the Eros and Psyche story. Actually what we find in the *Metamorphoses* is one initiation story embedded in the heart of another: the story of Lucius changed to an ass for having practised magic and restored to the human condition by Isis, to whom he dedicates himself after "eating roses" as he was advised. Indeed all stories with the mythical theme, detected by Swahn, of a quest—or actually a reconquest—no less than Psyche's explicit adventures in the *Metamorphoses,* are tales emphasizing the initiatory character of the misfortunes that befall the Beauty, the wife, and Psyche. The Soul (Psyche), Love (Eros, then Tlepolemos disguised as the brigand Haemus), and Initiation are the constituents of this mythical tale.[37] Or better said, it is a tale of the *Soul initiated by Love.*[38] Just here we find the answer to this problem of the separation between science and gnosis, to this intolerable strabism we have inherited from the Enlightenment's "immediate" light of sense-evidence.

Because opposed as it is to the famous "Method" and to the immediacy of evidence, the myth of Psyche is a myth of metamorphosis, but of the *metamorphosis of perception.* Corresponding with the transmutation of language to which psychology invites us there is a transmutation of awareness. Hillman expresses this in a masterly way when he says, it is a matter of passing from the "Enlightened man, who sees" to the "transparent man...who has become transparent through self-acceptance."[39]

We will not linger long on the trials that mark the course of Psyche's quest for initiation; according to Swahn they are highly banal. One need only remember that in Apuleius[40] there are four trials: one consists in sorting an immense heap of mixed seeds before evening, this is the trial by earth; another in bringing back wool from the sheep with golden fleece who are fierce so long as the sun's ardor communicates its heat to them, this is the trial by fire; then comes the trial by water to go and draw some of the icy water that feeds into the Styx and Cocytus rivers. In these three trials Psyche is helped first by ants, then by a verdant reed growing in the river, and finally by an eagle who comes to bring her water from the Styx. As for the last trial, it is the most fearful: to go and ask Persephone, queen of Hades, for a bit of her beauty. Then a high tower from which she was intending to throw herself—trial by air as invisible and impalpable as Orcus—comes to her aid and gives her the means to make the terrible journey. Here we have a classical scenario of the course of an initiation by the four elements. It is an initiation of the soul, painful, slow, and endlessly recommencing.[41]

Most significantly, this scenario is framed at its beginning and end with two interdictions against seeing, interdictions that I have elsewhere called complexes, the *"spectaculaire* complex" (Bachelard) and the "Psyche complex."[42] These two sequences are absolutely symmetrical: the first has to do with being forbidden to look at Amor, the husband, who is foreshadowed to be a monster; the second with being forbidden to see the beauty of the death that Persephone gives. This interdiction and this consent to a certain "blinding," a certain limitation of simple seeing, is also found in a number of other myths, the myths of Orpheus and Eurydice, Izanagi and Izanami, and those about Odin or Horatius Cocles who have power only because they have sacrificed part of their sight. This also occurs in happenings (that Jung calls synchronistic) where the historical event confirms the meaning of the sensory happening. Was not the seventeenth century also the century of Milton, a blind singer, like the blind Homer whom Rembrandt would paint, and would not Milton be able to say—as Greco had said a century before—that Paradise regained surpasses human clairvoyance, that it is the pure view of the poet, the elect? We know how popular the theme of blind Belisarius was to become in the eighteenth century and that in 1760 Macpherson would successfully create from nothing the mythical story of Ossian, the blind and inspired bard who was inspired because he was blind.[43]

What profound meaning has this initiatory restriction upon 'seeing,' for the immediate, the evident which was the touchstone of the Cartesian Enlightenment? Psyche's restrictive view is certainly connected with the mystical night, that constant theme with spiritual people. This night is the opposite of the clear and distinct evidence from which the analyses, syntheses, and meticulous listings of the classical ideal proceed. Besides this spiritual aspect, could the restriction not also be one way of expressing the *modesty* of Psyche's way of viewing things.

Let us just say that the simple view of science which is pragmatic and technical—"accidental" in Aristotelian terms—stands apart from the profound, total knowledge that constitutes destiny or the meaning of human existence from cradle to grave. Between the instantaneousness of the object and the compulsive instantaneousness of the subject is situated the *durée concrete* [concrete duration] that Bergson mistakenly sought in the latter and that Hegel mistakenly thought he could construct with distinct theses and antitheses. The "modesty" of Amor, that "holding back" from viewing which Amor recommends twice to Psyche, is indeed imperative for mediation. The temporal maturation that it introduces is certainly the antipodal opposite of time in the old, so-called Newtonian physics that Bergson denounced. The holding back from viewing that Amor teaches is, to begin with, just educational. Amor—often represented as a child, even a little angel—does not educate the soul in a stern Promethean manner but by leading it back to the first movements of infancy. Maturing a plant consists precisely in bringing it to produce its fruit, *its own initial seed:* this is the meaning of the famous Platonic definition of Amor as "childbirth in Beauty." "In Beauty," Socrates says,[44] but not in the unveiling and objectifying of that Beauty. For Beauty is made more beautiful by her veils.

Let us not forget that holding back from viewing is called for twice in this myth: the first time before the living beauty of the husband in the nuptial chamber *(thalamos),* and a second time before the casket containing and veiling "the beauty" of the Goddess of the dead. And here again with Hillman[45] we must denounce the scientific insufficiencies of Freud: Eros is not the opposite of Thanatos. Furthermore all Western poetry from Tristan to the Romantics runs counter to such an opposition. With his torch reversed, Eros is himself Thanatos. He is the supreme proof and promise of a triumph "stronger than death." And this because Eros' knowledge goes 'beneath' and 'beyond' the simple view. This is well expressed by the twice repeated interdiction of our myth: in the *thalamos* (and it would be tempting to Latinize the word as brain neurology has done; the *thalamus* being the localization of infra-rational sensory knowledge) the simple view is forbidden to illuminate intuition.

If Psyche haunted the nights of consciousness when Cartesianism was becoming established and expanding, it was because the simple view is not enough for knowledge. The initiation of Psyche shows that this view is not the whole of knowledge: there is a night time of the senses, and knowledge comes finally through a sixth sense, very much like the penetration of love. The *Vulgate* integrates these two meanings of the verb *cognoscere* beautifully. It is what Bergson foresaw although he confused the original data of knowledge with the immediate data of consciousness. Similarly, when faced with the mystery of the Beyond *post mortem*, the simple view gets no further than the corpse, it cannot see the Beauty. When the Psyche figure in the tragic ballet of La Fontaine/Corneille opens Persephone's casket her face turns black. Beneath and beyond is that kind of inclusive knowledge portended by the prefix "meta" of which we spoke in the figures—*metalepse* and *metabole*—of the new language. For this *meta* knowledge is what unites the beneath of Eros to the beyond of Thanatos: Eros endows life with meanings that only death confers upon the soul. And that is where the hierarchy supporting truth becomes established: contrary to both the immediacy of the simple view, the obvious, and also to Bergson's amorphous duration, the initiatory maturation concretized by Eros somehow makes the prohibition, the discipline, the condition *sine qua non* for possessing truth. The prohibition plays a major role in establishing the truth; it constitutes the stages, the "degrees," in the hierarchy.

Thus the new language inspired by the object of these reflections leads to a new logic which is neither the logic of identity nor of antithesis (its inverse), but that of antiphrasis by means of which—as Hillman[46] says antiphrastically—"the blind eye of love sees through into the invisible, making the opaque mistake of my loving transparent." Gnosis is neither the linear product of positive science—reached through an analytic procedure—nor its antithesis in an impossible counter-culture which is U-topian in the bad sense of that term. Gnosis is the antiphrasis of science just as Amor and the reasons of the heart are the antiphrasis of the objective simple view of geometry, just as second birth is the antiphrasis of death.[47]

The same process of initiating the Soul (Psyche) through the search for Love (Eros), which occidental tradition rediscovered in its seventeenth-century reactivation of Apuleius' tale, was promulgated by the entire initiation process of the Fideli d'Amore who proclaimed themselves emulators of "Joseph and Zulaykha."[48] "The inner pilgrimage"—to repeat a title of Henry Corbin's—which stresses Joseph and Zulaykha, Majnun and Leyla, in the manner of a deepened *Carte du Tendre* goes back over the stations leading from the exile to the exodus: Beauty, Love, Sadness. Even the condition of Majnun, "absorbed" by Leyla, implies the transmutation of human love to divine love and the ending of duality in a *unique* duality: Majnun as "lover" of Leyla is the "mirror eye" with which God contemplates himself.[49] The whole doctrine of theophany in Beauty, of Ruzbehan of Shiraz who wrote the famous *Jasmin of the Fideli d'Amore,* "tends toward the transubstantiation of the contemplative lover into a pure mirror, as such he then subsists as witness of the Absolute, as the very eye with which the Absolute contemplates itself." Furthermore among these mystics death is inseparable from the absoluteness of this experience of love. But certainly it is the same Platonic spring that gives rise to both this oriental mysticism of the gnosis of love and to the misadventures in the Amor and Psyche story. And it is not without importance that in the depths of the Western Enlightenment the finest spirits of the seventeenth century should have recalled Amor and Psyche. In concluding, however, let us ask ourselves—returning to our meditation on the Century of Lights and its psychic night—who in our time is antiphrastically connecting modern science with the gnosis.

*

I do not know if the notorious 'Princeton gnostics' exist. But theoretically the antiphrastic reversals undergone by our mathematics, our logics, and our physical and cosmological theories would authorize such a gnosis. Did not *Le Nouvel Esprit Scientifique* and the upsets proclaimed by Bachelard forty years ago in *La Philosophie du Non*[50] provide access even then to alternative ways [an *altérité*] of knowledge, and at that time to the poetic in particular?

But I am certain that in my field of human studies there has been a movement for thirty years—despite the myopia, even blindness, following the laborious birth in the middle of a positivist century of psychology, sociology and history—toward an anthropological gnosis.[51] Jung's whole work confirms the antiphrastic transmutation of contemporary psychology. The recent book in French translation of my friend Hillman, which I have frequently referred to here, is the outcome of just such a circuit turning psychology back to the myth of Psyche and bringing the myth back to the archetypal realities, back to the Gods.

Thus, although I do not know if there is any gnosis in Princeton[52] or Pasadena, I am sure there is a gnosis in Ascona, Switzerland, because through a life work such as Jung's and Corbin's, through the work of Hillman, and the whole of contemporary anthropology (as I have shown elsewhere) there has occurred a gigantic reversal of the epistemological values set up by the classical "luminaries." Since then, laboriously, like Glaucus overburdened with the scoria of a millenium of submersion, our theory of knowledge has been brought back to what it was before the divorce, before the tearing apart of distressed consciousness. Paradoxically the extreme progress of our profane sciences is leading us back to a recurrence of the point—an imaginary point—just before the West abandoned its culture for the vertigo of its civilization.

What about the hard work, the impossible initiation tasks, the lessons of the Psyche myth? What about the night side of our culture, hidden first by the Apollonian and then by the Promethean triumphalism of our civilization? We are tempted to ask ourselves if there are no short cuts, if "elsewhere" than in the West the language of the birds may not have escaped alteration by the language of the philosophers of the Enlightenment; if there is somewhere an Orient of Luminaries where the light of the eyes of flesh has not wounded the night and the secret of the soul; if "elsewhere"—in a radical u-topia—the hierarchic difference of rank is respected between the inwardness *(intériorité)* of the modest view and the pragmatic view of the world. How many departures for Khatmandu, how many vulgar pursuits of Zen or Sufism, how many onslaughts on fragments of ancient knowledge are seen in our time, occurring before the astonished eyes of our lost clergy and our bewildered churches, astray in the obvious of the day before yesterday!

Yet the monumental life work of Henry Corbin is there also to serve as a sure guide for the enthusiasm of young orientophiles who can be easily confused by the exploiters of Western bankruptcy. His work is there in all its scholarly rigor to attest that a direct cultural way does indeed exist to assure ourselves that gnosis—that of the Fideli d'Amore, for example—does embrace and justify the wholeness of the human view. It is there to attest that there is something that "views" or "regards" me when I enter upon the stages of the passionately faithful and contemplative regard. I have alluded in the course of writing this article to Corbin's four volumes, modestly entitled *En Islam iranian* which constitute the most significant sum of material to which a New Philosophy in the West can turn.

Now that our deepest scientific certitudes seem to be oriented again to a knowledge in which the known, the knower, and the method of knowing are all constituents of the same reality, we can see the long detour that Western thought has taken from the way pursued by other ardent seekers who have neither blinked nor hesitated in searching for the Absolute. It is this witness of faith in the existence of a gnostic process of thought that Henry Corbin's work brings us. So we can say that although we do not know whether a gnosis exists in Princeton or Pasadena, we do have the certainty that it exists here now through the presence of Henry Corbin at the heart of the University of St. John of Jerusalem.

Translated from French by Jane A. Pratt.

1 Cf. Gaston Bachelard, *The Psychoanalysis of Fire*, trans. A.C.M. Ross (London: Routledge, 1964) and James Hillman, *The Myth of Analysis* (New York: Harper Colophon, 1978), pp. 45, 67, 71.

2 Cf. my "L'Occident iconoclaste," *Cahiers internationaux de symbolisme*, 2, 1963, and as revised in my *L'imagination symbolique* (P.U.F., 1977). Also: J.P. Sironneau, *Sécularisation et religions politiques* (Thèse d'Etat, Univ. de Grenoble, June, 1978), I:2, 4; II:2, and bibliography.

3 Cf. Harvey Cox, *The Secular City* (N.Y.: MacMillan, 1965); F. Gogarten, *Destin et espoir du monde moderne* (Casterman, 1970); J.B. Metz, *Théologie du monde* (Cerf, 1971); Peter L. Berger, *The Heretical Imperative* (N.Y.: Basic Books, 1979).

4 Cf. C. Amery, *Fin de la providence* (Paris: Seuil, 1976).

5 Cf. Henry Corbin, *Avicenna and the Visionary Recital*, Willard Trask trans., Spring Publ. 1980 and G. Mathieu's *Cérémonies commémoratives de la seconde condamnation de Siger de Brabant*

(Paris: Galerie Kleber, 1957). Cf. also "Entretien avec Georges Mathieu," *Paradoxes* 29, October 1978.
6. Cf. Max Weber, *The Protestant Ethic and the Spirit of Capitalism*, trans. Talcott Parsons (London, 1930).
7. Paul Hazard, *La crise de la conscience européenne, 1680-1715* (Paris: Fayard, 1961).
8. The treatise, although published in 1664, was written in 1633 before the famous *Discours*. The phenomenon of light and vision obsessed Descartes all his life; he went back to it constantly in the physiology of the *Traité de l'homme* and of course in the *Dioptrique*, which is an application of his method where he devotes the first discourse to light, the fifth to the eye and the sixth to vision.
9. Cf. Spinoza, *Ethics*, 1677.
10. Cf. F. Brunetière, *Etudes critiques* IV, 1895.
11. Cf. J. Hillman, *The Myth of Analysis*, op. cit., p. 127f.
12. Cf. V. Czerny, *Essai sur le titanisme dans la poésie romantique occidentale entre 1815-1850* (Prague, 1935).
13. *Myth of Analysis, op cit.*
14. *Ibid.*, p. 121: "We are made ill because *it* is ill."
15. *Ibid.*, p. 123: "Is the soul abandoning speech altogether? If so, the very root of human culture is withering."
16. Cf. Jung's interest in the Chinese language of the *I-Ching*, and the works of my friend Rudolf Ritsema on the import of this language for the imaginal in *Spring* (1970, '71, '72, '73, '76, '77, '78, '79).
17. *Myth of Analysis*, p. 184.
18. *Metalepse:* "a rhetorical figure that consists in introducing something by expressing what brings or follows it." *Metabole:* "a rhetorical figure that consists in repeating the same idea in different terms in order to get it assimilated."
19. Cf. my article "Linguistique et métalangage" in *Eranos Jahrbuch* 39, 1970 (Leiden: Brill, 1973) and revised in my *Figures mythiques et visages de l'oeuvre* (Paris: Berg, 1979).
20. Cf. W.F. Otto, "Die Sprache als Mythos" in *Mythos und Welt* (Stuttgart: Klett, 1962). Italics mine.
21. My friend P. Brunel in his *Histoire de la littérature française* (Bordas, 1972) even discerns a "Louis XIII century."
22. Cf. R. Huyghe, *L'Art et l'âme* (Flammarion, 1960), pp. 273-300 and Brunel, *op. cit.*, p. 227.
23. Cf. A. Faivre, *Mystiques, theosophes et illuminés au siècle des Lumières* (New York: G. Olms, 1976). We are aware of the confusion that would occur in the XVIII century regarding the "illuminés de Bavière" (enlightened ones of Bavaria).
24. For the first use of this term, cf. Hillman, *Myth*, p. 127 & n.
25. Cf. H. Le Maitre, *Essai sur le mythe de Psyché dans la littérature française* (Imp. Person Beaumont, 1939).
26. Cf. M. Foucault, *The Order of Things* (N.Y.: Random House Vintage, 1973). A. Malraux was the first to give a bad example of this kind of one-dimensionality in *Le Musée imaginaire*.
27. Cf. L. Cognet, "La spiritualité moderne, I. Its Rise: 1500-1650" in *Histoire de la spiritualité moderne*, vol. III (Aubier, 1966).
28. Cf. Brunel, *op. cit.*
29. Frances Yates, *The Rosicrucian Enlightenment* (London: Routledge, 1972). This sound scholarly work opens new perspectives on the beginnings of the XVII century.
30. Cf. Descartes, *Oeuvres philosophiques, op. cit.*, p. 213 & n. 8.
31. Cf. R. Perche, *Les myths poetiques (Oedipe, Narcisse, Psyché, Lorelei)* (Paris: Soc. d'Ens. Sup., 1962).
32. Kathleen Raine, *Blake and the New Age* (London: Allen & Unwin, 1979).

33 Cf. M.-L. von Franz, *A Psychological Interpretation of the Golden Ass of Apuleius* (2nd ed., Dallas: Spring Publ., 1980); also E. Panofsky, "Blind Cupid" in *Studies in Iconology* (N.Y.: Harper Torchbooks, 1962).
34 J.O. Swahn, *Cupid and Psyche* (London, 1955).
35 Ch. Perrault certainly must have known *Amor and Psyché* since he speaks of it in his 1695 preface to *Contes en vers*.
36 Cf. *Romans grecs et latins*. Texts presented by P. Grimal (Paris: Gallimard, 1963), pp. 141ff.
37 *Ibid.*, pp. 263-68.
38 *Myth of Analysis* exposes this central idea of the tale, but see also the collection of essays on the subject gathered by Gerhard Binder and Reinhold Merkelbach, *Amor and Psyche* (Darmstadt: Wissenschaftliche Buchgesellschaft, 1968); E. Neumann, *Amor and Psyche*, trans. R. Manheim (N.Y.: Pantheon, 1956); M.-L. von Franz, *op. cit.*; also C.C. Schlam, *Cupid and Psyche: Apuleius and the Monuments*, Amer. Philol. Assoc., University Park, Pa., 1976.
39 *Myth of Analysis*, p. 92.
40 Cf. Apuleius in Grimal, p. 248.
41 *Myth of Analysis*, pp. 93-96 where the torturing aspects of the initiatory tasks are emphasized.
42 Cf. my *Le décor mythique de la Chartreuse de Parme* (Paris: Corti, 1960).
43 We should note that in some modern initiations the candidate is blindfolded.
44 Plato, *Symposium* 206b.
45 *Myth of Analysis*, p. 77.
46 *Ibid.*, p. 91.
47 Cf. H. Corbin, *En Islam iranien*, III, "Les fidèles d'Amour" (Paris: Gallimard, 1972).
48 *Jasmin des Fidèles d'Amour*, p. 25, quoted by Corbin, *ibid.*, p. 75. *Ibid.*, II, p. 373 on the "Histoire de Joseph."
49 *Ibid.*, III, p. 141.
50 G. Bachelard, *Le nouvel esprit scientifique* (Paris: Alcan, 1934); *La philosophie du non* (P.U.F., 1940).
51 Cf. my *Science de l'Homme et Tradition* (Tête de Feuilles, 1975).
52 Raymond Ruyer, *La gnose de Princeton* (Paris: Fayard, 1974).

Creative Man
Five Essays
Erich Neumann
Translated from the German by **Eugene Rolfe**

This selection of essays by C. G. Jung's favorite and most creative student explores important avenues between analytical psychology and the study of literature and art. Written over a span of years about diverse personalities—Kafka, Trakl, Chagall, Freud, and Jung—these essays have a common theme: the relationship between the personal and the transpersonal, the ego and the archetype.
"Fascinating reading."—*Library Journal*
Bollingen Series LXI: 2. Illus. $13.50

Now in Paperback
Psychology and Alchemy
C. G. Jung
Translated by **R.F.C. Hull**

"[This book] presents the gold that Jung believes the alchemists *did* produce from baser metals, and it consists of their guarded, confused, heretical anticipations of modern psychology."—*The New York Times Book Review*
Bollingen Series XX:12. Illus. $8.95 (Cloth, $20.00)

Princeton University Press
Princeton, New Jersey 08540

SILVER AND THE WHITE EARTH
(Part Two)

JAMES HILLMAN
(Dallas)

> "Writing wants to go on."
> Gertrude Stein

IV. Terra Alba, the Whitening, and Anima

Albedo is another alchemical term for luna and for silver. In alchemical color symbolism white is the principal stage between black and red, a transition of soul between despair and passion, between emptiness and fullness, abandonment and the kingdom. Albedo is also the first goal of the work; it is like the *unio mentalis*, coming after the nigredo has divided the world into mind and matter, yet before the rubedo restores the subtle body to its carnal keeper. Because of alchemical warnings about the "reddening coming too fast" and about the black crows creeping back down into the nest, the *albatio* or "whitening" is essential to slow the reddening, on the one hand, and on the other to raise the blackness from its inertia. As a state between, the albedo is referred to as bride, Mary (as intercessor), moon, dawn, and dove. As a state between, it is both closely attached to what it joins and yet is distinct from them. It thus corresponds with that middle realm and mediating attitude we speak of as "psychic reality,"[1] so that the descriptions of the albedo and of the white earth teach about the nature of psychic reality and the operations of the albatio teach how reality becomes psychic, and psyche, real.

Beware here! There are at least two sorts of white (*Spring 80*, p. 24):

The first three sections of this article appeared in *Spring 1980*, p. 21-48 where the occasion of it (p. 21) and abbreviations in it (p. 46) are explained. An additional section, "Alchemical Blue and the Unio Mentalis," is being published concurrently in *Sulfur* (ed. Clayton Eshleman and Robert Kelly), California Institute of Technology, Pasadena, and distributed by Spring Publications, Dallas.

"conditions which often look alike/yet differ completely" as Mr. Eliot says in "Little Gidding." There is an original white, the primary luna or virgin's milk, pure virgin, smoke, cloud, the lamb, spittle of the moon, urine of the white calf, summer, white moistures, lye, syrup—all names for the primary material,[2] all names for those early and repetitive miseries of the soul: the syrupy nostalgias and over-eager kisses, tender calf love, the mouth of salivating desirousness (Freud's oral phase), the days under the cloud, summertime, the agenbite of introspective lye, the smoke that neither clears to fire nor dissipates, and above all that psychic innocence of self, world and others that psychology has renamed "unconscious." This primary white is pre-black. It appears in figures of speech, behavior, and in dreams whether made up at night or by ad-men: the toothpaste smile, spot removers, milk shakes and ice cream, white flannel trousers and Mr. Clean, ski resorts (the resort to skis), aspirin-consciousness, "jes fine, jes fine."

Primary white is immaculate (without stain or blemish), innocent (without hurt, harmless), ignorant (without knowing, disregarding), unsullied and unsoiled. This condition cannot be the *terra alba* because there is no earth to whiten. So the work begins on these original white conditions, blackening them by scorching, hurting, cursing, rotting the innocence of soul and corrupting and depressing it into the nigredo which we recognize by its stench, its blind impulse and the despair of a mind thrashing about in matter, lost in its introspective matters, its materialistic causes for what went wrong. Our white, the second white or albedo, emerges from that black, a white earth from scorched earth as the silver from the forest fire (*Spring '80*, p. 32). There is a recovery of innocence, though not in its pristine form. Here innocence is not mere or sheer inexperience, but rather that condition where one is not identified with experience. Virginity returns as impersonality. Or let us say memory returns as image, the evening with the photograph album and you are not the person there on the film and maybe not the person turning the pages. Experience and experiencer no longer matter as the "images that yet/fresh images beget" release one from the nigredo of personal identity into the mirrors of impersonal reflections.

This second whiteness is also not mere ignorance, a disregarding insouciance of the world and its ways. Rather it is that casualness with the world and its ways, which results from psychic realities taking precedence over more earthbound perception that attempts to resolve psychic difficulties either away from the world or into the world. *Albedo* prefers neither introversion nor extraversion, since the differences between soul and thing no longer matter, that is, are no longer imagined in the material terms of *nigredo*.

These two whites combine in anima, one reason that anima is such a complex psychological affair. She is the White Goddess[3] and also Candide/Candida, the little innocent. The two whites shadow each other, so that latent in innocence and its seductive stupidities is the yearning of Candida for the whitened mind, while shadowing the sophisticated White Goddess is both the snowblindness of purity and the blindness of lunatic imaginings, being "out of it," which delude one again and again into that same uncaring ignorance which was the primary material. Because of these white shadows, we must take pains in this section to differentiate the sophisticated white from its fall into the primary condition.

Transitions of color in our moods, tastes and dream figures reflect alterations in the material of the soul. Inasmuch as alchemical psychology equated change in color to change in substance, the albedo is not only a state between but a condition per se. It is, however, difficult to speak from this condition: either one tends to feel it as betterment, as rising from the dark, greeting whiteness in the Christian symbolism of baptism and resurrection or one tends to feel it as a not-yetness, a silent potential (Kandinsky),[4] an absence, that has still to become the color of fire itself (Corbin).[5] We shall try, nonetheless, to stay in the middle ground speaking of white as if we stood in its earth.

*

When the word earth appears in most psychological contexts, it weighs us down: earthy rituals and earthen pots, mother earth and earth sciences, gravity and the grave. Psychology assumes earth is material. As Patricia Berry[6] has written on Ge, Demeter and the archetypal mother, "earth" is that projective device by means of which we unload ourselves of matter, an elemental dump for the modern mother complex. We imagine earth only with a material imagination, that naturalistic fallacy which identifies the element Earth with natural dirt and soil: to be earthy, we must be dirty and soiled. Psychology insists Earth be our red body, brown mother, black madonna. Open the *Whole Earth Catalogue* and there amid the concretisms of bedrolls, ridgepoles, herbs and canoes you will search in vain for the material ways of the mind and the qualities of *psychological* soil, inscapes of arid plains, muddy swamps, hidden banks where green lovers entwine, where there are also bedrock faults and islands, whole continents of the mind, an imaginal geography whose catalogue covers the whole earth, as Gē is also a region of soul, white earth.

Although the modern naturalistic earth of psychology is a supportive element, it mainly supports heroic spiritual fantasies. Even Bachelard lumps earth together, not only with supportive repose, but with the fantasies of will (forging, cutting, conquest, work, and action).[7] The dumb and supine materialization of earth, as well as the fantasy that it needs attack (mining, plowing, moving) insults Gē, as Berry says, buries her under our dirt, forces her to bear our misplaced concreteness, depriving her of her own inner sky, Uranos, her own luminous and celestial possibilities. As a Goddess, Earth is also invisible. She generates immaterially, unnaturally. She supports perhaps most where she is seen least, in psychic territories of repose, like the void in the vessel that is the vessel, like the rest within all rhythms, the hollowness in the drum,[8] working her will within the intangible forms of things into their visible matter.

The gross notions of earth in contemporary psychology betray its materialism; this psychology is so heroic and spiritualized that mother must carry its grounding. No wonder that modern psychology cannot leave its philosophy of development, its laboratory concretism and reliance upon measurement, its reductive explanations. It has not found another earth that would give support and yet not be materialistic.

This other earth is described in Henry Corbin's book *Spiritual Body and Celestial Earth*. There is a marvelous Earth, an imaginal place (or placing in the imaginal) whose "soil is a pure and very white wheat flour" (p. 156). It has a physics, a geography, climates and fertilities. This too is a ground, the earth our heads touch just as our feet touch this earth here. Our heads are always reaching up and out to the celestial earth. And the problem of head trips is not that they are trips or that they are heady, but that they are not grounded. To ground these flights of fancy and ideational excursions, psychology sends the head down again to the material earth, insisting it bow down to the dark madonna of tangible concrete existence. Psychology fails to grasp that spacey head-trips are in search of another ground way out, an attempt to reach the u-topic, placeless, farfetched terra alba of anima inspiration.

It is as if psychology hasn't even read the Bible, page one, reminding of two firmaments, above and below.

Corbin's work opens a radically different perspective toward grounding and earthing: the firmament above is an archetypal, angelic ground of the mind. The mind descends from archetypal configurations; it is originally in converse with angels and has this angelic originality forever possible, so that all terrestrial and material events can be led back by the act of *ta'wil* (return) to the original ground in the white earth. If we ground ourselves in the upper firmament everything is turned around, so it is precisely by turning everything around (seeing through, metaphorizing, *ta'wil*) that gross matters become subtle. To make the terra alba, one must start in the terra alba. Anima consciousness, or the albedo in alchemy, offers a different mode of perception. Seeing, listening, attending all shift from the gross attachments of the nigredo to a new transparency and resonance. Things shine and speak. They are images, bodies of subtlety. They address the soul by showing forth their souls.

What is here presented in the subtle language of Corbin and alchemy, can as well be stated in the gross language of our usual psychology. The phase called whitening in alchemy refers to the emergence of psychological consciousness, the ability to hear psychologically, and to perceive fantasy creating reality (*CW* 6, § 78). As long as the psyche is struggling in the nigredo, it will be emotionally attached, stuck in materializations, fascinated by facts, grinding away. It will sense psychic "material" mostly as dense and difficult: (she has such long dreams; I get confused listening; he's a hard case; the hours drain me, exhausting, depressing—a long mortificatio). The gnosis of the nigredo is mainly diagnostic and prognostic. Its eye is on the materialization of predictions, fascinated by the various forms of putrefactio which clinical psychology calls "diagnoses." (The DSM diagnostic manual is a catalogue of materia prima becoming nigredo states, like one of Ruland's lists.) The nigredo eye looks for what's wrong, the *caput corvi* (raven's head) of foreboding prophesy. It is caught by *physical* questions whether in etiology (is it an organic, neurological problem?), in transference (touch or not to touch, bed or not to bed?), or in treatment (pills, body work, or maybe dance therapy?). Grossness casts a cloak of physicality over the subtle body of the patient.

The grounding of mind in whitened earth is what I have written about at other times as the poetic basis of mind, consciousness—not the product of brain matter (left or right, it's still matter), society, syntax, or

25

evolution—but a reflection of images, an ongoing process of poesis, the spontaneous generation of formed fantasies. So, for the deepest comprehension of mind, we are obliged to turn to poetry. We must go to the moon people, the lunatic poets, who say, like the poetic clown in *Les Enfants du Paradis*, "La lune, c'est mon pays." Poetry gives us chunks of whitened earth, moon rocks, which when seized upon with Apollonic mission prove dead and worthless. (Imagine! the greatest deed of our age's heroic quest was to capture and bring home to actual earth a tangible souvenir of the physical moon. The insanity of literalism.) But when the moon rocks are turned over in the imaginative hand, then ideas, songs, dreams, dances—essences of mind—emerge. For these ores of the moon, these mythopoeic materials, are the primordial seeds out of which soul life comes. Platonic psychology says that souls originate on the moon, which means nothing less than psychological life begins in the places of our lunacy. Of course, Hegel insisted that lunacy was necessary to the soul's development.

The lunar ground, and therefore silver, whiteness and anima, assume a favored place in a psychology that begins in a poetic basis of mind, *i.e.*, in an imaginal or archetypal psychology. The tradition of this psychology, such as we find in Medieval and Renaissance accompaniments to alchemy like the *Picatrix* or Ficino's *Book of Life*,[9] "start on the moon." The moon, says Ficino, rules the first year of life and every seven-year cycle thereafter; the moon is *primus inter pares*. All prayers to the planets and all influences from them pass by way of the moon, according to the *Picatrix*. The moon is intercessor, the landing place between outer space of the spirits and the mundane world of the natural perspective. What passes by way of the moon becomes lunatic, that is, enters imaginal reality. The direct prayer from us to them and the literal planetary message from them to us become fantasy images, metaphorical. It is this sense: that all occurrences must first be imagined, that they begin as images, that the very cycle through which anything turns, including ourselves, is a psychological process, that soul fantasies are the ground and seed in all we think and do, want and fear—this is the terra alba.

The terra alba is a climate and geography, with palaces and persons, a richly imaginal place, not mere abstract wisdom. In Corbin's accounts the celestial earth is full of spiritual bodies; or let us say that the subtleties of soul are embodied in the *mundus imaginalis* by primordial persons, eternal archons, angelic essences who offer human consciousness a grounding in hierarchical principles, enabling a human being to recognize what is essential, what comes first, and what is of lasting worth. It is a place of truth. Its orientation toward truth, however, is eastward rather than up or down, toward the orient, dawn's early light, glimmer of silver, hard to see by and declare.

This hierarchical sensitivity to values, truth and first things, coming as it does via personified forms who are these firm subtleties themselves, brings us to truth psychologically—in vision, dream, fantasy dialogue—and so we gain a *psychological* apprehension of truth. We are instructed by the silvered mind (*Spring '80*, pp. 34, 41) rather than by spiritual enlightenment; this truth evokes reflection and the illumination of the senses, especially the ear, else we could not hear the messages (angels), angels who are not only there in that other earth, but here in this earth that can be whitened by a mind which perceives whitely, metaphorically. Although silvered perception of truth may be polished to hard and cool sophistication, it is nonetheless glancing, oblique, a poetic truth which includes poetic license—even truth as fantasy and truth of fantasy—so that it may not seem truth at all in the rational eyes of reason alone. Ray (of the sun), radiant (bright), radius (of the circle or a straight measuring rod), *ratio*, and rational are etymological cousins—archetypal descendants of the Sun.

We cannot hold Corbin's accounts of the lunar earth in our solar minds, in our usual hands, any more than our usual ears can get anything from poems. They are so remote from daily consciousness, so farfetched and arcane. ("The moon is the arcane substance," *CW* 14, § 154.) Even if alchemy says that "earth and moon coincide in the albedo" (*ibid.*) they feel miles apart, like death and life. How can they be co-present and how can we be real and imaginal, sane and lunatic at the same time? The answer is closer than we realize: the "white brain stone" (another term for the white earth and the arcane substance, *CW* 14, § 626) is an actual experience any day. Poems, dreams, fantasies are wispy, haunting, elusive, arcane, calling for petrifaction by definite fixation techniques (memorizing, recording, depicting). At the same time these shimmering gossamer psychic materials are dense and impenetrable: "I had this powerful dream, but couldn't keep it." "I can't see through it; it escapes me." "I had it once, but can't get it again." Little tiny things, yet so hard to crack—poems, dreams, fantasies. And, full of impact, shocking us, hurting us, driving us to the far corners of lunacy, unforgettable, possessed by beauty, by anima, a mere whim or poetic phrase. The substantial language about matters that supposedly have no substance at all shows the subtle body in the solar world. These experiences that so annoy our everyday awareness are the apprehension in the mind of the white earth dawning.

What is this dawning? How is it felt? Precisely, as feeling. What dawns is not a 'new day' but the day in a new way. Rosy-fingered dawn, as Homer called her, touches all things aesthetically. It is as if the world had a new skin, imagination become flesh. There is an erotic hue, an Aphroditic cast, pleasure. The Goddess of Dawn (Eos) is both daughter of the Sun (Helios) and sister of the Moon (Selene). She holds together silver and gold and is engaged in multiple affairs of love. The consciousness that dawns now awakens into the world as into a rosy-armed embrace, the white earth inviting with smiles because it is a lover.[10]

*

The white earth shows in dreams, but not necessarily as snow fields, white sands, or azure-silver celestial scenes. What shows rather is the whitening of tangibles, common familiar objects: painting the house white, a white jacket, silvered things. When a blade, needle, thimble, dish or dress is silver, then silvering is occurring *to* these activities (one's knifing, fingering, stitching, serving) and silvering is occurring *by means of* these activities. That is, by means of knifing, sewing, robing, the psyche is being silvered or whitened. Things themselves are becoming psychic; the psyche's thingness, and its thinking (Heidegger), are beginning to show reflection: things as images, images things; the *dinglichkeit* of psychic phenomena.

Those silver containers of which the Grail is the classic example refer us back to the etymologies of silver as shining, glistening, glancing (*Spring '80*, p. 23). A silvered or white chalice, cup, bowl, spoon, jar, or mug present containment, shape, and reflection in one and the same image. Shaping is a mode of reflection, and reflection is a way of holding things and putting them in definite shape.

A silvered container differs from an earthenware pot, wooden box, leather bag, glass bottle. Each permits and prevents certain kinds of holding; each depicts attitudes to psychic contents. When the cup is silver, then there is swiftness in our holding mode, a keen quick grasping—for silver and white mean flashing, swift and light. The silver receptacle shows mental intelligence, a rapid understanding. But silver tarnishes, clouds over, so that it tends to lose the insights that once shone clear. At the same time, silver as the precious metal of money *values* what it holds, or rather it holds by giving worth, dearness to events.

Of course the silvered container is usually thought of as the chalice for the blood. The rubedo first requires a receptive soul and a comprehensive understanding, else it streams in the firmament, reddening the world with manic missionary compulsion, the multiplicatio and exaltatio as conversion, moneymaking, and fame. But the nigredo too requires a silvered vessel. ("Take the black which is blacker than black, and distil of it 18 parts in a silver vessel.")[11] It seems that the best way to hold the blackest of the black—that irremediable and inert pathology—is again with a silvered soul, that quality of understanding appropriate to the holiest of essences, that enlightened and compassionate mind which belongs to the white anima. Only she can distil from the utter blackness some trickle of possibility.

Silver may also appear in the sky: airships, white forms, missiles. If the airy element is the ground and place of mental life, then the mind is projecting out new directions, shaping new forms, exploratory speculations. It may be reaching for the moon, not merely escaping the earth. Whether or not the waking personality can follow its night soul in these directions is a therapeutic question, but silvering in the realm of air is a process as regular as natural dawning, dew, starlight and the throat of larks, and appears in dreams as well as nature.

The white ladies in dreams and sickbed visions (in a silver gown, head in light or white cloaked, a dead beloved, the man with the silver badge or instrument) are figures of the white earth calling one to another inscape by sounding music, shearing away, opening passages, instructing, beckoning. They are 'calls' away from life who signal the death of one's embeddedness in the body of the world. So we fear them and are wonderfully impressed when they ask us to come across the border. But what border? I think it is less the simple, literal line between life and death and more the one we've drawn around love, holding it from death. The white lady or the silver man makes the passage easier by bringing one's love to death, a loving death, moving Eros to Thanatos so that we may follow more easily into deep unknowns, ready to go, anytime mount the stair, all aboard for White City.

Although the remarkable phenomenology of white figures has been examined by Aniela Jaffé,[12] there is something further to be said about white animals. They have been called witch, spirit, ghost, or doctor animals, but what really is happening to the soul when a whitened or silver-blue-gray animal appears? First of all, the animal is now a shade of itself, "dead" or psychized. The figure is now both a psychic presence as well as an animal presence. Its body is now subtle. Second, by virtue of its color, it belongs to the albedo. It is an animal of the anima, an anima animality. The animal is no longer a terrestrial natural figure, what psychology calls "instinct," but this animal, this instinct, appearing in white, shows that the *terra alba* is also a place of vital life. There is animality in whiteness; there is instinctual body in silvered subtleties.

A whitened animal is one that reflects itself; animal action hearing itself, knowing itself. Reflex and reflection joined in one image, desires that self-respect, the sulphur whitened to surefooted awareness, an animal faith. No wonder that such animals are doctor animals; they are the guides of soul, image-guides who can sense their way among images. Their territory is the white earth, silver land where the mind and voice of the soul's intelligence rule. They bear intelligence, bring reflection in their white forms. So the best way to keep them near is to treat them with the food they live on: intelligence, speech, words, thoughts. Speak with them: Doctor Dog, Frau Doctor Cat. Talk is their soul-food.

Of all these phenomena—silver vessels and instruments, white missiles and animals, perhaps the most singular event of the albedo is the puzzlement of consciousness. The mind as it was is baffled by the paradoxes of its whitening, a paradox expressed even in the term "white earth." Ludwig Wittgenstein's little book on color[13] shows an excellent mind struggling, during the last eighteen months of his life, with white—the anima? We may read his questions and statements with a metaphorical eye as if they came from an old alchemical text having to do with the whitening of consciousness. Even more: as if white were the color of psyche, and of psychology.

> But what kind of a proposition is that, that blending in white removes the colouredness from the colour? As I mean it, it can't be a proposition of physics. Here the temptation to believe in a phenomenology, something midway between science and logic, is very great. II.3

> What then is the essential nature of cloudiness [*Truben*]? For red or yellow transparent things are not cloudy; white is cloudy. II.4

Isn't white that which does away with darkness? II.6

"The blending in of white obliterates the difference between light and dark, light and shadow"; does that define the concepts more closely? Yes, I believe it does. II.9

If everything looked whitish in a particular light, we wouldn't then conclude that the light source must look white. II.15

The question is: is constructing a 'transparent white body' like constructing a 'regular biangle'? III.138

Nor can we say that white is essentially the property of a—visual—surface. For it is conceivable that white should occur as a high-light or as the colour of a flame. III.145

A body that is actually transparent can, of course, seem white to us; but it cannot seem white and transparent. III.146

But we should not express this by saying: white is not a transparent colour. III.147

'Transparent' could be compared with 'reflecting'. III.148

We don't say of something which looks transparent that it looks white. III.153

We say "deep black" but not "deep white". III.156

Consider that things can be reflected in a smooth white surface in such a way that their reflections seem to lie behind the surface and in a *certain* sense are seen through it. III.159

What constitutes the decisive difference between white and the other colours? III.197

What should the painter paint if he wants to create the effect of a white, transparent glass? III.198

White seen through a coloured glass appears with the colour of the glass. That is a rule of the appearance of transparency. So white appears white through white glass, i.e., as through uncoloured glass. III.200

This much I can understand: that a physical theory (such as Newton's) cannot solve the problems that motivated Goethe, even if he himself didn't solve them either. III.206

Why do I feel that a white glass must colour black. . .while I can accept that yellow is swallowed up by black? III.208

We often speak of white as not coloured. Why? III.210

Is that connected with the fact that white gradually eliminates *all* contrasts, while red doesn't? III.212

I am not saying here what the Gestalt psychologists say: that the *impression of white* comes about in such and such a way. Rather the question is precisely: what is the impression of white, what is the meaning of this expression, what is the logic of this concept 'white'? III.221

The logic of the concept white is precisely what we are working on in this paper, in order to show it to be a psycho-logic, "something midway between," and something both transparent and cloudy, a strange third that cannot be made into a "regular biangle." This psycho-logic also attempts to account for feelings such as Wittgenstein's that "white does away with darkness," "that a white glass must colour [stain, lighten, tincture] black," and that "white eliminates all contrasts" [the albedo as relief]. Moreover, as consciousness moves from the darkness of the materialistic perspective toward the white earth, we can understand why Wittgenstein finds Newton's physical approach cannot answer the kinds of questions set by Goethe.

*

Despite the intellectual puzzlement, whitening frequently comes first as an experience of emotional relief, a lightening after blackness and leaden despair, as if something else is there besides; within the misery, the tremor of a bird. Burnout cools; the *ida* stream of Kundalini (*Spring '80*, p. 38) showers the exhausted and bitter soul with gentle dew. A mood dulcet, a descending grace. Traditional symbolism speaks of white as the color of pardon appearing after the black of penitence. We say: "It's lifted"—not so heavy, not so frantic. "I feel I'll make it." All the while there is a new sense of trust in what's going on. For Dante, white was the color of faith. This faith, however, is not adamantine as a credo, or an iron anchor, and feels rather like sweet anticipations of another chance, a second coming, and that one can go on because somewhere down the line there is a holding place (that same gray ash, dry sand, sere leaf now white earth).

A whitened holding place must be imagined with a whitened mind. For the *terra alba* is not merely rest after struggle; it is not rest at all in the sense of surety. In fact, "white is motion, black is identical with rest" (according to that same twelfth century text which concludes with the famous "emerald tablet").[14] So the albedo is experienced also as the *motion* of psychic reality, what we have come to call "psychodynamics" and "processes"—so long as these are not literalized into systems with which we can rest content. For, when motion becomes a *system* of motion, rather than the actual moves the psyche makes, then we are again in a nigredo, that is, densely unconscious that our language (of psychic energy, process of individuation, development and psychodynamics) is stifling actual movement in concepts about movement. The nigredo must speak in the past tense as part of the mortificatio and putrefactio, whereas the white abjures reports of "what happened" and how it got this way, in order to move with the actual images. Albedo talk speaks rather of "what's going on," this move and that: how the psyche is moving and what moves the patient and the analyst make in response.

Another sense of the turn to whiteness is shelter: less exposed, less raw, less delivered over to the fires and floods. Wounds swathed in white dressings; untoiling lilies; milk, flowing and coagulating[15] into the more solidly putrefied culture of cheese. The soul has now a tabernacle; Mary as refuge. There is some structure and a place where it can tend to its motions; it finds itself placed within itself and not driven "out."

We also find ourselves easing off, no longer purging the bowels of *putrefactio*, no longer guilty. Complaining gives way to recollections in tranquility: the memories are there but no longer hold one to their rack. The sense of sin is washed, *ablutio*. The material has sweat itself into moistening, and we may even find a sense of humor. Ironic chagrin relieves shame. The voice now speaking in the inner ear and the words now coming from the inner figures of imagination tell us "it's all right," "take it easy," "let it be," "give yourself a chance." The white lady brings peace. She sits in the garden with a wide lap.

*

"Putrefaction extends and continues even unto whiteness," says Figulus;[16] yet "Matter, when brought to whiteness, refuses to be corrupted and destroyed."[17] When does the putrefaction finally cease? Is the soul's resistance to destruction ever accomplished and when is its own capacity for corrupting and destroying overcome? Evidently, even after whiteness is there, the putrefactio extends and continues in some manner. One text speaks of "a white vapour, which is a soul that is whiteness itself, subtile, hot, and full of fire."[18] Other texts refer to a "white ferment," and we have already discussed the affinity of silver for sulphur as silver's inherent tendency to corruption (blackening, tarnishing, quick heating, etc.), its "phlegmatic leprosy" (*Spring '80*, pp. 27-29).

We must therefore amend our notions of the white earth as place of repose. Something else goes on in these anima states, despite the comforting whispers in the inner ear. Silver is copper within, says Rhasis.[19] Within the whiteness lie the former stages. As whiteness emerges from blue, from black, and from great heat ("White medicine is brought to perfection in the third degree of fire"),[20] so these prior conditions are there within the albedo itself. It *must* tell us of itself as sweet, soft, and cool, just because it is always threatened by its own red copper, its propensity for sulphur, its hot and black inner nature. It is precisely this inherent putrefaction that distinguishes the albedo from the primary states of whiteness (innocence, purity, ignorance) and guarantees the soul against its own corrupting effects. Thus whitening gives the anima an awareness of its innate power, which comes from shadow that is not washed away and gone but is built into the psyche's body and becomes transparent enough for anyone to see.

This brings us to four major *dangers* in the transition to white.

1) Transition as conversion: the black all gone, born again, a new love, cure as loss of shadow. As clinicians know, the danger of impulsive suicide may be greater when coming out of depression into a manic phase or defense than when in the depths of melancholy itself. Thus every whitening needs clinical inspection. Conversion, as regression to innocence, to the garden before the fall is the eternal seduction. There had to be killing at once on leaving Eden to make dead sure that all of them—Cain, Abel, Seth, Adam, Eve, and maybe the Biblical God too—wouldn't be tempted back. In the garden the serpent is the tempter, but once out in the vale of soul-making, it is the garden itself that seduces. Whenever whiteness—white lights, white ladies, white knights, white pages for a new leaf—draw us to them, keep the clinical eye. Remember your alchemy: the albedo must always be distinguished from the prima materia.

Just here the difference is hard to discern. The urge to white is so close to the escape from black. Then the ablutio can become simply whitewashing, and candida can mean only a clean breast, a frank and open discussion, candid. "Albation," says the dictionary, still means dusting (off, away, over) with a fine white powder. Here the whitening converts back to primary innocence and the opus is back where it began.

Bonus offers a way through this danger. "When the Artist sees the white soul arise, he should join it to its body in the very same instant; for no soul can be retained without its body." "Now the body is nothing new or foreign; only that which was before hidden becomes manifest...."[21] And what is this "body"? Bonus says: "body is the form." Elsewhere: "The Ancients gave the name of body to whatsoever is fixed and resists the action of heat."[22]

I understand this body that resists heat and stays as it is (does not convert) to refer to those hidden forms within each of the manifest emotional changes that have led to the albedo. The occurrence of white can make us feel we are wholly in a new place because we are identified with the whitened condition. If however the white is fixed in its own body of images, that is, its attention fixed upon the "hidden" forms that shape experiences (rather than the manifestations of those experiences), then we are less subject to conversion. For conversion here is nothing else than a consciousness caught in its own white phenomena. Anima-enthused, anima-inflated, as the Jungians say. The soul has lost its body, the hidden form or image by which it can see itself.[23] So the whitening can simply mean being unconscious in a new way, which is baptized (whitewashed) by the exalted name of "conversion experience."

Now, we do not gain anima-awareness (whitening) only by examining manifest experiences: remembering what happened and how it felt. Anima comes to its knowledge by an imaginative process: by the study of its own images. That's one reason why my kind of analysis spends so much time on dreams (and less on reports of what happened)—to awaken the soul to imagination by the study of its images. "If the study of his images/Is the study of man, this image of Saturday,/This Italian symbol, this Southern landscape is like/A waking, as in images we awake,/Within the very object that we seek,/Participants of its being. It is, we are."[24]

Anima wakens in its images—of Saturday, Italy, landscape—becoming what it is by virtue of those forms, those bodies. Notice that the "body" of which Bonus speaks is *its* body—"nothing new or foreign." The whitening is present in any object that we seek once we seek it *as image.*

of the albedo is already there, the earth whitened, as the formal pa... which shows itself to the imagining anima as images. The lines of Wallace Stevens add to Bonus the further idea that these image-forms are participants in each being, including that being we consider to be ourselves.

2) Transition as "premature cooling." The term is von Franz's interpretation of a passage referring to fearing "the cold of the snow."[25] Von Franz sees this as an inflation in which "feeling, relatedness to one's fellow-men, perishes and is replaced by an intellectual form of relationship."[26] I have discussed the potential silver that lies in coldness (*Spring '80*, p. 38f.) and the innate coldness of the soul itself at some length elsewhere,[27] also showing that the very word *psyché* is cognate with many words signifying cool and cold. Furthermore, coldness works in different ways at different times. For instance, "Digestion is sometimes quickened by outward cold....For cold drives heat inward and increases its action," says Norton in his *Ordinal* (HM II:43).

Since coldness is familiar to the soul and intrinsic to the whitening (as in Kundalini, *Spring '80*, pp. 37-38), why *just now* the fear of snow? I think the danger to the work has less to do with feeling relationships than with a benign neglect of the alchemical fire which can occur at this moment.

Because the albedo brings relief from the tortures that instigated the process in the first place, we forget that the soul, whose body (its images now fixed) is better than ever able to bear heat, now requires a higher intensity than before. Bonus writes: "When the Alchemist...has reached the end of the first part of our Magistry in which is seen the simple white colour...then he must straightway set about the second part of the work, and this is the ferment and the fermentation of the substance."[28] By ferment, Bonus refers to "seething or bubbling" which makes the soul substance "swell and rise, exalting it into a nobler condition."[29] Premature cooling stops before the ferment. As things improve—and after all, the albedo is a betterment according to every text—there is less urgency. The whole work may go into the freezer, the baby abandoned in the snow. We forget that the long point of the opus is not resolving the nigredo nitty-gritty of our personal neuroses, but an exaltation, a multiplication of the soul's vermilion nobility to its full-blooded and manifold realization. Thus at this moment the analysis itself, as instrument of the fire, may have to turn up the heat deliberately in order to prevent cooling, which separates body and soul. "So long as the substance is volatile and flees from the fire, it is called soul; when it becomes able to resist the action of the fire, it is called body."[30] In order to keep the body, we must keep the heat.[31] We may have to invite new aggressions and passions; summon up the furies; force confrontations with essential questions that the white lady might prefer to cool. Active imagination, for instance, may now begin grappling with the angels of one's destiny, angels who are cores of fire. Now, "therapeutic support" means feeding the fire. The fire is the guardian angel and guards the angel from cooling. Analysis: place of fire. "The Spirit is Heat," says Canon 94 of Figulus.

3) Transition as premature calcining. This is the caution against "burning the flowers." "Premature drying only destroys the germ of life, strikes the active principle on the head as with a hammer, and renders it passive" (*HM* II:188). Yes, the opus needs intense heat to dry up the personalized moistures: sobbing collapses, longings that flow out, sweet dopey confusions. These are dried in the soul-making process. But these conditions cannot just be hit over the head, taken to the (dry) cleaners, caustically scorched. For in them there is a germ trying to flower. The flowers are burnt when anima seizures are blasted with scorn, with desiccating criticisms or abstract analysis. One of Figulus' canons states: "Those who...use sublimate, or calcined powder, or precipitate, are deceived, and err greatly" (134). So do those who "resolve Mercury into clear water" (135). What is wanted, as the pressure rises and the heat intensifies and anima infuses herself into everything, are not clear and distinct reasons. No dry powders. These kill the germ of life.

This is a curious warning. Though calcination (drying in heat) is essential for whitening, this same process can lead to analytical burnout. When the therapeutic base in moisture, in permanent underlying humor, gentleness, and mercurial slipperiness (*aqua permanens*) is forgotten; then calcination blackens with mutual accusations, disappointments, exhaustion from too intense a heat at the wrong time. We are back to the nigredo, cynical, bitter, burnt. Analysis failed.

Instead, like cures like—even while calcining is the main operation, responses to anima effusions can be in kind, i.e., feeling-toned images and reflective speculations, but only if held in the right mirror. We remember (*Spring '80*, p. 26) that mirrors catch images because they are "moist," like the anima effusions themselves. But the mirroring moisture is cool and *limited* (idem), contained by the act of mirroring. A modicum of moisture, humourful mirroring helps then, and personal effusions that start off by flowing out everywhere hysterically will achieve a more objective telos: the white earth flowering, a sense of Flora in matter, the whole earth alive with her.

4) Vitrification. This is the sudden solidifying of the soul-work into glass. Bonus says, "If by calcination a metallic spirit becomes vitrified, it is not capable of any further change."[32] Unlike cold metals, he goes on, "on which one can either engrave or stamp any image...and it will retain that image; but glass will do nothing of the kind." Vitrified materials have lost their "metallic humour" and can no longer amalgamate with the perspectives of other metals.

We find several specific dangers. The vitrified soul can no longer receive an image. It cannot imagine and so it cannot change. What isolates, then, is the lack of imaginative receptivity. (Conjunctions take place when subtle bodies join, that is, when fantasies open to one another, take each other in.)[33] Here, the isolation results specifically from the soul's loss of insight into itself as an image in a "metallic" process. The "metallic humour" in alchemical psychology may refer to the realization that all personal events are objectively produced by the basic metals. What goes on in the soul is not of your or my doing, but refers back to the germination in us of the Gods in the earth, the seven metals of the objective psyche or world soul. Vitrification closes us to this awareness; we become glassed into our personal individuality.

Vitrification "may happen at any time from the middle of the Reign of the Moon (into) the Reign of Venus" (*HM* II:194). It is a danger in the anima process. As the sweetness of the albedo passes into a venusian love of life, a copper-greening of the material (*HM* II:194), the heat can rise beyond the capacity of the material. It glazes, fixes, and petrifies. The intensity of the psychic process, fused by desire, creates an *idée fixe*, a globular obsession or glassified idol. "...be on your guard against the danger of vitrification; too fierce a fire would render your substance insoluble and prevent granulation" (*HM* II:195-6). No longer can one release the psyche from the form in which its passion is cast; no longer can one deal with it in particulars, piecemeal.

Silvering as granulation needs special comment. During the Reign of the Moon while the substance coagulates into the many shapes of silver, dissolving and coagulating "a hundred times a day," then "you see it all divided into beautiful but very minute grains of silver like the rays of the Sun.... This is the White Tincture" (*HM* II:193). Vitrification prevents the particularization of awareness, the tininess of insight, analytical precision that *divides* reflection. Not the large mirror reflecting broad vistas and whole perspectives all at once, but rather a granulated, gritty, grainy consciousness that picks up "very minute grains," each spark, the little intensities, "a hundred times a day."

The passage from "An Open Entrance" (*HM* II:194) continues: "Do not irritate the spirit too much—it is more corporeal than before, and if you sublime it to the *top* of the vessel it will hardly return... The law is one of mildness, and not of violence, lest everything should rise to the top of the vessel, and be consumed or vitrified to the ruin of the whole work." We tend to forget that work on the psyche (soul-making) does indeed make the spirit more embodied. We forget that what goes on in the mind is gaining more and more substantial reality. If these newly made psychic realities rise to the top, they tend to take on a life of their own, up and out, in behaviors "glazed and unsusceptible to any further change." Evidently, the body that is gained through the work is to be substantiated lower down in the vessel, as the body of the images themselves rather than as sublimed into hard truths, real values, factual persons and hot projects. Ideational inflations, highs, "that's the tops" can be vitrifications which, at this moment of anima substantiation, spell "the ruin of the whole work."

Glass is an ideal analogy for psychic reality: it mirrors, warms and cools with its content, becomes transparent, appears like its contents though is untouched by them, and it forms them according to its shape. It is the material par excellence for the opus. It both contains and allows seeing-through, or seeing-through events is a way of containing them, as containing events is a way of seeing them as psychic images and processes. But glass is *not* itself the substance of the opus, and when it becomes so, vitrification has occurred. When the vessel becomes the focus of the work, when we take psyche itself substantially, when we literalize containment or seeing-through, then we are vitrifying. Psychology as a subject of its own, rather than a mode of seeing through, reflecting, shaping and containing other substances, is simply a vitrification, a glazed and fixed consciousness without humour, without imagination, without insight. Psyche has become Psychology. The paradox here is that seeing-through, as an act that makes any substance transparent, puts it into glass, and so can tend to vitrify the act of seeing-through. When an insight coagulates into a truth (because of too much heat, because it is compelled by Venus, because it rises to the top), this is vitrification.

*

Let us now turn to three alchemical versions of the whitening in order to grasp better what goes on in this process.

The first is a statement from Mary the Jewess: "If the two do not become one, *i.e.*, if the volatile does not combine with the fixed, nothing will take place. If one does not whiten and the two become three, with white sulphur which whitens (nothing expected will take place).''[34]

So we are told that nothing happens to the soul unless its gaseous state becomes solid, and its solidities mobile. All the scattered flying about and lofty arrogances of the spirit need fixation. At the same time, those certainties that we feel unquestioningly shall find wings and take off. To volatilize the fixed is to realize that things as they are are not as they are. Nothing takes place until we can see through the fixed as fantasy and coagulate fantasy into forms and limits. The precondition for whitening is simply this embodiment of spirit and inspiriting of body. Until this simultaneous action occurs, we do not feel psychic reality. We perpetuate the "realm of the two" (body vs. spirit, inner vs. outer) and are vexed into every sort of "difficult decision."

When we recognize that all these hard matters are in the mind, then a whitening is happening. We are now in a new, third place where both being scatty and being stuck, being in the world yet not of the world, being volatile and being fixed, are reflected as *psychic* realities necessary to each other, setting each other up within the retort of an alchemical attitude. The two have become one, as Mary the Jewess says they must. But not by joining them, not by living them as oscillating alternatives, not by compensating one with the other.

They have become one because they have lost their literal pulls. And they have lost their oppositional tension, because our attention is on their relations (rather than on their substantiality), the movement between them, how they resound or require each other, and how we have required them. Realizations dawn; insights, illuminations; the sulphur active and whitened. The whitened sulphur here is not so much a purified will power that can hold the opposites and hold from acting them out (cutting off the green lion's paw). Rather this white sulphur i coagulation of psychic reality as a third place that holds, a sti..., a gum or mucilage,³⁵ that keeps the doer in the soul, making a third place between "the two," *esse in anima.*³⁶

One finds oneself standing on a new ground, the white earth. But the earth does not necessarily come before the standing; the standing may make the ground. To stand one's ground, in the soul and for the soul, helps make the very ground one stands on.

Here is another discussion. It is a tale told by John Trinick,³⁷ whom Jung called "one of the rare alchemists of our time."³⁸ (I remember meeting him while he was working on his version of Eirenaeus Philalethes' text, Introitus Apertus or An Open Gate, a text which Jung examines in the *Mysterium Coniunctionis.*)

Trinick describes the white earth much like a pale young English lady, a virginal spirit, who is in love with a slim, aristocratic, but distant and winged youth. Trinick's vision shows two white 'spirits' attempting to join: the dried white earth waiting to be released from salty encrustations and the refined white sulphur wanting to fecundate. But—the white lady is also being pursued by another sulphur, "the red thief," vile, coarse, active, and smelly, and so she cannot escape her imprisoning room.

We must note in passing that *salty* whitening is not sufficient. "Luna is never fixed... having only been washed, and fixed (as they call it) with Salt.... O foolishness! O blindness of mind! can common Salt be the Soap of the Philosopher?"³⁹ The lady's tearful pining, the soul locked into its private introspective room, is not enough to fix the white earth. The ablution is not performed by tears alone; nor by memories, repentance or remorse. Not salt; sulphur.

But which sulphur? Who will break through the door and open the space, white puer or red thief?

In Trinick's account (p. 38) it is the lady herself, in a moment of negligence, who unbolts the door. At the same instant the white sulphur, forgetting his anxiousness and resorting to his own style, enters on a rush of wings, and the sulphuric thief is left on the other side of the threshold to vanish gradually away. Notice that the two come together in a double unconsciousness: neither reason nor will bring this pair together. The scene, says Trinick, is tumultuous and dark, which describes the state of consciousness as one tosses tensely looking for what is wrong, yet that very upset signals the opening door, the sulphuric wings. The alchemical process of whitening happens *to* sulphuric consciousness, but not necessarily *in* consciousness.

To go on: The two white lovers within—the virginal anima whose imagination is caked in fearfulness and the crusted images of childlike knowings, and the white puer spirit of sulphur—have no vital instinct. They do not know what to do, how to conjoin. Slowly, the white lady, delivered from her fear of the red thief, its fat, its smell, its violation of her timing, comes to life through melting: "the pores of the Earth will be loosened," "the youth enters easily through the pores."[40] What was passivity and immobility of the salted condition becomes a receptivity, a capacity for fusion. This conjunction is not a sexual penetration—a juxtaposition of dissimilars—but a fusion of likes, a gentle exchange through the pores as windows in and out of the body, the interchange of subtleties: the conjunction here a flowing conversation of images.

The substance in question (the "medium" of the conjunction) Trinick writes (p. 80) is a "vapour—unctuous, yet highly subtilized—a smoke, or fume; that is, an exhaled matter.... It is exuded—as milk from a nipple; or exhaled—since it is usually described as a 'thick white vapour.' "[41]

The crucial white "medium" occurs concomitantly with the " 'dissolution' of the two 'bodies.' " Another text[42] says: "at last you must see that nothing remains undissolved. For unless the Moon or Earth is properly prepared and entirely emptied of its soul" it will not be fit for the conjunction. Now what is going on here?

The Moon or Earth becomes whitened when its own identity as Moon or Earth is emptied out, dissolved, losing its old ground in order to enter the new middle ground. Anima is now no longer defined by its own feminine principle. With the dissolution of the two bodies goes also *the dissolution of gender*.

This conjunction unlike many others in alchemy is not described in sexual terms where gender represents extreme opposites which opposition is solved by the apposition of these (sexual) extremes. This conjunction teaches us something about gender thinking: it derives from the opposites, maintains them, and prevents the formation of the middle ground. Both feminism and male chauvinism are inherently unpsychological; the imagination remains trapped in the oppositions of gender. The dissolution of the two 'bodies' (substantiations) does not occur and the white earth of psyche cannot seem to dawn out of the nigredo of physical naturalism.

Now we can understand why in this paradigm the "red thief" is the wrong lover. His vision is bodily; he emphasizes the opposition in natures of male and female, red and white. The white sulphur, however, joins the anima at that place where they are most similar: the mutual experiencing of fantasy and feeling. An imaginative conjunction is a conjunction in imagination.

But what happened to the red sulphur? Is it enough to say with Trinick (p. 39) that "the young lover...recognizes...that his own evil shadow is departing from him, never to return"? Here we must recall the "wateriness"[43] of the sulphur within silver, its latent copper, the potency of the white ferment, how suddenly silver heats—themes discussed in *Spring '80*.

As an Artephius text says: "a white vapour, which is a soul which is whiteness itself, subtile, hot, and full of fire." "It is whiteness itself which quickeneth...."[44] The red sulphur is no longer thief when he is already 'within,' as that liveliness which sulphur brings to soul. His activity gives images their sense, their palpability and musk, their sexual attraction as well as our delight in being seized by them. He remains a thief only when the psyche remains like a lady in a small space, door closed against the visitations of clamoring images. These she then must see as dirty (fat and smelly), as a moral problem which divides the sulphur into good and bad kinds, and as literal demands on her for carnal actions. Fantasy then seems like an assault, a red thief, demonic and compulsive.

We learn from this text that imagination does not come into life directly. The anima of fantasy does not find its way to the world unless mated with sulphur, and yet the red phallus is not the answer to the maiden's prayer—though the puer's wings are. She meets the spirit side of sulphur first from which the body later comes. The maiden here of course is not a woman, but a soul, *i.e.*, that condition of psychic inability, of waiting in boredom and fret for something just beyond the threshold to come in, when tears are no use, nor is hope, only a sense of being threatened by life and knowing it would be too direct and too concrete to bear. That it is *white* sulphur which does the job of releasing the soul points to the operations upon desire itself: it must become white to be effective. This sulphur is like the image of Pan, white as snow, mentioned in Vergil (*Georgics* 3:391), a sense that the sulphuric fulminate generating within all nature is the imaginal force of the world soul. Sulphur too is soul, as

Figulus says. And sulphur whitens when it is seen not as will or compulsion or desire only, but as soul; or, when we recognize soul in the compulsion, the will and desire. This recognition releases the imprisoned soul from feeling itself cut off from life since life too has now become whitened as a sulphuric aspect of soul, *i.e.*, life fused with *psychic* reality through and through.

Trinick's account has come from a young man's text: Philalethes is said to have written it at twenty-three. The problem and resolution are mainly sulphuric. But this is not the only method of whitening. For example, the text of Artephius is by an old man over eighty. It insists that "without antimonial vinegar no metal can be whitened." This antimony "is a mineral participating of Saturnine parts." It is "a certain middle substance, clear as fine silver" which receives tinctures so that they be "congealed and changed into a white and living earth."[45] Evidently the effective "middle substance" can be many things: the souring of depression as well as puerile sulphur (and of course it can be Mercury, which we are not discussing in this paper), as long as the experiential mode produces a vivid sense of psychic reality. Whether vinegar, sulphur, or the processes of calcining or fusion, the experiential mode is extremely *active*. Anima refinement may lead through blue moods to cool silver, but the way to that refinement seems no less rending and intense than the torments of the nigredo.

My third alchemical example of whitening refers to the Doves of Diana, also mentioned by Philalethes, but here as they were worked by Isaac Newton in his *Clavis* ("The Key").[46] For Newton, the Doves of Diana meant both the mediation between mercury and antimony (puer and senex?), and especially, it seems, an amalgam of silver with the metallic center-body (or star regulus as it was called) in the ore of antimony.[47] Newton suggests an anima possibility in this antimony, this saturnine substance of Artephius (who spoke of its vinegar). In Newton's alchemical psychology this substance amalgamates with silver. There is more to an old man's vinegar than your common sourness.

Sometimes this star regulus was called *corleoni* or lion's heart,[48] so that Diana's Doves also means a silver that has joined with the heart of the lion, a silver that has become amalgamated with the heat and light and desire of the animal king, his sulphur, his drive. A lion-hearted dove; a white-winged lion.

Philalethes' text, *Secrets Reveal'd*, which was the basis of Newton's, says: "Learn what the Doves of Diana are which do vanquish the lion by asswaging him."[49] He continues that it is especially the green lion (Ruland says a ferocious dragon) "killing all things with his Poyson" who is pacified in the embrace of the doves. In "An Open Entrance" (*HM* II; 170) the bestial enemy is a rabid dog. Jung, in commenting on this passage (*CW* 14, §185), prefers (for the word *mulcere*) "caress" for the action of the doves. Similar to Trinick's dry earth that loves the white sulphur, Newton's Doves of Diana contain a kind of love. There is a sensuous heart in the mineral body. The doves make possible "melioration," "sociability," and "mediation" of substances.[50] We should expect this venusian aspect since the dove traditionally belongs to Aphrodite (cf. *CW* 14, p. 157n). The dove tames the dragon because "like cures like."[51] These doves have the heart of a lion. One animal spirit cures another.

Newton compares work with silver with the mediating action of "Animal Spirits," a long-lasting psycho-physical idea[52] which includes our concepts of emotion, instinct, libido, and imagination. The animal spirits, or spirits of the soul to translate the term rightly, were what we might today refer to as psychosomatic functions, emotions, vegetative nervous system, or unconscious fantasy—all of which work 'between' the conscious will and the physical body. Newton's analogy between the alchemical doves and the animal spirits does lead us to "learn what the Doves of Diana are." They are the mediating activity of the anima that can present as images of fantasy what goes on in the green lion of our nature. They can tame the green lion's passion because they are also passion—though of another kind. This is a silvered passion that descends through the air, in whiteness. They are the *capacity to imagine passion* (rather than to rage it only). They are other than lions, dragons, rabid dogs, that is, images of emotions; the doves are the *emotions of images*, the animal in the air, in the mind, the mind as winged animal; and they are the excitation and tenderness released by imagining. These doves of alchemical fantasy present the mediating power of fantasy itself. They express, as they do in the traditional symbolism of the Third or Holy Ghost, Jung's transcendent function of active imagination. (*CW* 8, §167)

The transition from passive fantasy, as Jung calls it (*CW* 6, §712) to active imagination is announced by the doves—and these doves belong to Diana. As Diana (Artemis) is a Goddess of nature and the moon, the whitening here suggests a transition from reflective consciousness that is only natural and only moony, the garden of plants and animals, all things passing in somnambulist vegetative grace, to the active perception of the lunar forms, the images within nature, the presence of Artemis as an elusive White Goddess within all natural things."[33] As I see it, these Doves of Diana refer to a fundamental *re-union of nature and imagination*, where nature is seen as a vast coming-to-be and perishing of images and imagination is experienced as a natural and necessary process, not merely human, not a faculty of the psyche, not psychic at all in the usual sense of subjective, but as given and autonomous as nature. Nature becomes the display of images and images become the forms of nature. I would even hazard that this vision of imagination in the heart of nature, the imaginal white earth as nature's ground, corresponds with Isaac Newton's vision of alchemy as an essay in the middle ground or Mediation,[34] for which, as he says, silver, the middle term,"[35] is the secret.

The cliché that Newton's alchemical-religious-philosophical writings were the old-age crankiness, even tragedy, of a puer who had finished his genius at 24[56] is being dispelled as more of his manuscripts have been opened and published. Rather, it seems, he was engaged in mediating a Neoplatonic vision[57] of the universe and its world soul (anima mundi), a universe that proceeds from above downwards and whose pull is an *epistrophē* upwards—much like the pull of Corbin's white earth—with the gravitational forces of a mechanical world and its corresponding interpretation from below. His was a lifelong attempt from two sides, physics and alchemy, at a "wedding of the Hermetic tradition with the mechanical philosophy which produced modern science as an offspring."[38] My own view is that Newton was wrestling as must we all with the anima, "the secret...of the virgin Diana," in his own arcane, experimental, and seventeenth-century style—and this imaginal meditation helped keep him going into very old age. The key to Newton's "The Key" is the enigmatic figure called "Philalethes" (or two figures Eirenaeus and Eugenius) who was "one of Isaac Newton's favorite alchemical writers."[39] This "Philalethes" was perhaps the last of the great alchemical philosophers[60] of the late Renaissance whom, some have said, was none other than Thomas Vaughan,[61] the Hermetist twin brother of the English mystic, platonist and poet Henry Vaughan.

*

But what are these doves in *our* whitening? How are they *our* silver? Jung remarks in passing that "the tender pair of doves" "would be capable of an interpretation downward." (*CW* 14, §205) Here he has been brushed by their wings.⁶² Interpretation from above downward follows their descending motion that announces a new vision of things. This is the moment, in Corbin's language, of *ta'wil*, that shift in mind enabling us to experience the sensate world of perception by means of the imaginal world. And it is this move that tames the lion, depriving him of his usual power as king of the physical world. We can now see all things, not spiritually through a glass darkly or naturally through a green lens, but first through a silvered imagining, an exegesis of events that leads them out of their physical encasement.

"Interpretation from above downward" is another way of describing the gift of tongues brought by the dove. This is not some special pentecostal babbling, but rather a recognition that the dove is forever possible within our spontaneous speech, that speech is a gift and that the love of speech, its *peitho* or persuasiveness, is a tongue of fire as strong as love's desire which can at any moment ignite any thing with the whiteness of a silvered image simply by use of an inspired word. We wrote last year (pp. 44-46) of a psychology based in the visuddha chakra of the throat, psychology as an act of speech, a work of sound and listening, and we are trying to continue in that style of psychology this year. Yes, Freud was right: therapy is a talking-cure, and the doves cure the tongue of its nigredo-talk: opaque concepts, deadening ideas in dull language, densities of plodding protocols, prose—interpretations from below. The doves teach trust in the sudden word, that miraculous appearance of the silver, which interpretations from below have called complex indicators, slips of the tongue, poetic license, puns, and lunacy.

Interpretations from below are necessary when reduction in Berry's⁶³ sense is necessary. Then we need nigredo-talk, the hermeneutic of shadow: mortifying, depressive and nasty. But to carry on reduction when the dove is dawning from the lead occludes the whitening and frustrates imaginal realization. The shadow is not a panacea. The hermeneutic of shadow is misplaced especially when literalized as the nigredo, shadow as only black. For this misses the shadows in whiteness (the blues we dwelled on in the companion piece mentioned in the first note above), mistaking the albedo for primal innocence. This forces the albedo to defend itself against these injections of darkness by protesting ignorance, thereby returning the albedo to the very condition for which it is being attacked. Interpretations from below seem justified because they work as self-fulfilling prophesies. But they are based on thinking in opposites—attack white with black. Dark-field examinations of the albedo make whiteness stand out as a polarity against the shadow, forcing it into anima extremes, lofty, fuzzy or cold and hard, so that it loses its own actual shadow awareness.

The actual shadow lies concealed in the nature of whiteness itself. For as the writers on color say, and the alchemists including Jung (*CW* 14, §389) concur, all colors unite and disappear into the white. So now the sense of discrimination is absolutely crucial, else one can lose the plurality of soul in a naive and simplistic unio mentalis. The doves do not herald unity. As von Franz observes, "The dove was generally interpreted as the 'multitude of the righteous.'... as an image of plurality."[64] The idea of unity is the primary shadow of the whitening, an indication of delusional lunacy. It makes us forget that the psyche's alchemical movement is toward a red multiplicatio and a rotatio through all degrees of the compass, *i.e.,* an orientation by means of multiplicity and the precision of its tiny differences in direction. The multiplicatio already begins with the dove, as a sense of psychic plurality, those multiple perspectives emerging from the soul's myriad fantasies.

Unless the multiplicities of white are kept as its shadows—as blues, as creams, as the wan and pale feelings of grey—the whitening becomes sheer blankness. Here is a reflective consciousness that perceives without reaction, a kind of frank stare, chilled and numbed, lunar, curiously deadened within its own anima state that should have brought it life.

So, to keep whiteness from blinding itself with simplicities (instead of multiplicities), a reduction needs to be performed on the albedo, but in its own style which means turning up the heat in an anima fashion. New lunatic intensities, demanding active imaginations and fermentations that lead to ever finer discriminations (white against white), adding weight to light and rubbing the silver to more clarified reflections. This means friction, more accurate tuning of responses, and keeping to the lunatic fringe—noticing the oddity of behavior and feeling when images are first reality. We whiten the earth by earthing our whiteness. So, put the heat on anima attractions, soulful philosophizings, delicate aestheticisms, petty perceptions, global moods, lovey-dovey coziness, and the nymphic gossamer illusions that promise lions. Don't literalize the relief of the albedo into relaxation: pull the plug on Mary's bath. Silver is hard and it likes heat and truth; its telos is yellow and red, bright and loud. Get at essentials; stick to the image; greet the angel. This white earth of the imaginal is also a territory of essences, principles, *archai* (as we saw above from Corbin). The aim of reduction is not to stay stuck to the nigredo nose in the dirt but, as Berry writes, to come to "the essential, the quintessence of one's nature." To achieve this intensity of soul, whether in an hour of analysis, in a close relationship, in language, study or art, takes as much sweat as shoveling through the stable with Hercules. These essences stand out the further we can move into each image, each fantasy, each event, working at distinctions within them rather than comparisons between them. For in the albedo the very method of psychoanalysis changes from an Aristotelian observation of similarities (and its ultimate reduction downward to common denominators) to the study of singularity, each phenomenon a thing in itself, allowing and forcing the necessary angel to appear as the body in the image making its behavioral demands on the soul.

A double dove, both male and female, appears in one of Jung's own dreams, and from that dream and Robert Grinnell's[65] analysis of it, we can take a final cue as to the doves' significance, or how the silvered psyche works in our consciousness. I shan't recapitulate the dream. It is in Jung's biography. But the result of the dove's appearance, its transformation into a little girl—and do not such girls 'belong' to Diana?[66]—its speech to him and its vanishing into *blue* air, adds something more to the gift of speech and the gift of interpretation from above downwards. The result of the dove was, as Grinnell brings out, the gift of faith in images, a psychological faith, which permits belief and enjoins conviction, a fervid animal faith in the depths, a dove in the belly that gives one the sense that the psyche is the first reality and that we are always soul.

*

We have come to that place of soul described last year (pp. 45-6): "What is reflection then when there is no subject reflected, neither emotion nor external object? No fact at all? The very idea of reflection transmutes from witness of a phenomenon, a mirroring of something else, to a resonance of the phenomenon itself, a metaphor without a referent, or better said, an image."

Mental events as images do not require and cannot acquire further validation by reference to external events. The soul's life is not upheld as correct by virtue of exteriority. But neither are mental events validated by virtue of my 'having' a dream, 'thinking' an idea or 'feeling' an experience. We are beyond soul as a conglomerate of subjective functions, with imagination merely one function among others, a bureau in the department of mind. (Imagination imagines itself in this bureaucratic fashion only when it must give report of itself in the language of historical psychology that denied imagination any valid place to begin with.) Psychic events do not require my reports in the language of functions and experiences in order to be. They do not require my reports at all. Soul need no longer be captured by subjectivity, a mind owning its events and distinct from them. Neither wax tablet, cage of birds, ghost in the machine, iceberg or saddleback—functional models all, attempting to account for, give support to, a subjective base for psychic events. Let it go. We can dispel subjectivity and yet still have soul. No subject needed, neither conscious nor unconscious, neither empirical nor transcendental, neither personal ego nor impersonal self. Personal pronouns can lose their hold: whose is that cat, this music, the idea which 'I' am writing now? The event is there, shining. Have we thought it, or has it appeared, ephiphanic amid that birthing turmoil which we call work. And who are 'we' to say? Let events belong to themselves, or to the Others. "All things are full of Gods," said Euripides; it is *their* personal belongings that furnish our world. The event is there—though not in a mirror, for if the mirror vanish the event will still be there. Or better: the event is the mirror self-sustaining its own reflection. Have faith in the everlasting indestructible ground of images. They do not need us.

Do you recall the passage in Jung, who on the great Athi Plains watches the animal herds like slow rivers across the primeval scene of Africa: "Man, I, an invisible act of creation put the stamp of perfection on the world by giving it objective existence";[67] The objective world requires a human subject! *Horribile dictu*: 'I' crown the creation, those herds, by my consciousness! But what if both, all, are images? Consciousness may be necessary to the *anima mundi* in specific ways she devises, but consciousness is not confined to my mind and is not only consciousness as 'I' have defined it. The plains are, and their grazing gazelle, and these images move in the soul of the world unwitting of "Man, I" or any personal observation. Psychological faith affirms those gazelles, those images, whose appearance does not require my consent. Take joy in witness, but do not believe the world is held together thereby.

*

"Earth and moon coincide in the albedo" (*CW* 14, §154). All earthly things become whitened into lunacy; they are now apparitions, having dreamed themselves to death. All lunatic things become dense, real and slow, forms filled with earth. Lunar phantasms become ground on which to stand, because they themselves stand, faithfully. Images as things; as things in themselves; each phenomenon noumenal yet utterly here. Perhaps things appear and have *durée* simply because they enjoy their images, themselves as they are in the display of their forms. They come into the world in such good faith, exuding such confidence that we test our reality, our theories and diagnoses by means of them. Their faith gives us our certainties.

Strange to find imagination as the ground of certainty, that nothing is more certain than fantasy—it is as it is. It can be subjected to the noetic procedures of cognition but these cannot negate it. It still stands, and more firmly than the doubts with which it is assailed by noetic inquiry. When the mind rests on imaginal firmament, then thinking and imagining no longer divide against each other as they must when the mind is conceived in the categories of nous. Now *nous* can as well be *psyché*; the noetic, the psychological. Knowledge comes from and feeds the soul, the epistrophé of "data" to its first meaning "gifts." Knowledge is received by the soul as understanding, in exchange for which the soul gives to knowledge value and faith. Knowledge can again believe in itself as a virtue. Here is knowledge not opposed to soul, different from feeling or life, academic, scholarly, sheerly intellectual or merely explanatory (*erklärendes*), but knowledge as a necessity demanded by the silvered mind by means of which the soul can understand itself. In this white country where the barriers between soul and intellect do not try to keep each other out, psyche is itself a kind of knowing, a keen accounting, a wit of what is there; and nous is psychological, engaged in intelligent interlocutions among its images. The entire dialectic of philosophy becomes whitened to talk among imaginal figures. We take part in a symposium going on forever; mental life, an extraordinary banquet. Through this inquiring conversation and this display of the image by means of its rhetoric, psyche becomes knowledgeable, noetically aware of itself, though not as defined by *nous* (which limits psychological knowledge to the cognition of experience, introspection of the interiority of time, structures of transcendental subjectivity and the operations of its logic). Instead of these philosophical constrictions on psychological knowledge,

51

psyche becomes aware by means of an imaginal method: the ostentation of images, a parade of fantasies as imagination bodies forth its subtleties. *Nous* observer of *psyche*, seeing in her mirror how his mind actually proceeds. *Nous* at last psychological: all its cognitive instrumentarium become lunatic, the logic of images; psyche with logos. Here in the white earth psychology begins.[68]

IV. Terra Alba, the Whitening, and Anima

1 Cf. *CW* 14, §630.
2 These terms are given by Martin Ruland, *A Lexicon of Alchemy*, London: Watkins, 1964, entry "Materia Prima et huius Vocabula."
3 For a splendid phenomenology see Robert Graves, *The White Goddess*, London: Faber & Faber, 1948.
4 "White is a symbol of a world far above us, of silence—not a dead silence, but one full of potentialities." "It is a blank that emphasizes the beginning, as yet unborn." Will Grohmann, *Wassily Kandinsky, Life and Work*, N.Y.: Abrams, n.d., p. 88.
5 Henry Corbin, "Les Couleurs en cosmologie Shi'ite" *Eranos* 41—1972, pp. 157-68. I have deliberately denied myself any alchemical discussions of the rubedo in this paper for it would require an entire shift of perspective, rhetoric and images.
6 P. Berry, "What's the Matter with Mother," Guild of Pastoral Psychology, Lecture 1978, London, 1978.
7 Gaston Bachelard, *La terre et les reveries de la volunté*, Paris: Corti, 1978.
8 Cf. David Miller, "Red Riding Hood and Grand Mother Rhea" in *Facing the Gods*, Spring Publ., 1980, pp. 92-94, on the drum and the *magna mater* who may be both Rhea and Gè. On matter, rest and rhythm, see Bachelard, *La Terre et les reveries de la répos*, Paris: Corti, 1948, pp. 87-93.
9 Marsilio Ficino, *The Book of Life* (tr. Charles Boer), Spring Publ., 1980. *'Picatrix' das Ziel des Weisen von Pseudo-Magriti* (tr. H. Ritter, M. Plessner), London: Warburg Inst., 1962, p. 71: "Dem Mond aber gebührt der Vorrang vor den anderen Planeten in bezug auf die Regierung der unter ihm liegenden Welt des Enstehens und Vergehens. Er ist die Vermittler; denn er nimmt die Wirkungen der Planeten auf und gibt sie an die Welt des Enstehens und Vergehens weiter."
10 Dawn comes in little ways in dreams: rising, early morning, 'the alarm,' breakfast, pulling up the window shades, and in those significant dreams "just before waking" or which end with "I woke up." Dawn also appears in sexual eroticism, not only at actual dawn, but in any amorous flush that pinks the horizon. According to myths, young men (*pueri?*) are particularly subject to being Dawn's lovers, carried up and away by her. On the erotics of Dawn, see Paul Friedrich, *The Meaning of Aphrodite*, Univ. Chicago Press, 1978, pp. 36-48. From this mythological-archetypal perspective, the *Aurora Consurgens* (attributed to Thomas Aquinas by Marie-Louise von Franz) whose very title means the rising up of dawn will of course be suffused with erotic mysticism as it depicts the conversion of its author by the anima to love.
11 Bonus of Ferrara, *The New Pearl of Great Price*, London: Stuart & Watkins, 1963, p. 355 (An Epitome of Raymond Lull).
12 Aniela Jaffé, Apparitions, *An Archetypal Approach to Death Dreams and Ghosts*, Spring Publ., 1979, pp. 79ff.
13 L. Wittgenstein, *Remarks on Colour* (bilingual), G.E.M. Anscombe, ed., Univ. California Press, 1978; sections indicated following each quotation.
14 Peter Dronke, "Tradition and Innovation in Medieval Western Colour Imagery," *Eranos* 41—1972, pp. 74-76.

15 On milk and the coagulation of the white, see Bonus of Ferrara, *The New Pearl of Great Price*, London: Stuart & Watkins, 1963, pp. 277-282. The coagulated substance is "female," having received the coagulating impetus from the "male." Another name for it is the (white) earth, *Aurora Consurgens*, *op. cit.*, p. 10. The coagulant sometimes appears in dreams as cheese—mother nature turning to culture and differentiating sense awareness through fermentation and putrefaction.

16 Canon 79 in Benedictus Figulus, *A Golden and Blessed Casket*... London: Stuart & Watkins, 1963, p. 285.

17 ibid., Canon 95.

18 In Trinick, *op. cit. inf.*, p. 81.

19 Rhasis' *Book of Alums*, quoted by Wyckoff, *op. cit.*, p. 175, fn.1; cf. Norton (*HM* II:59), "the redness is concealed in the whiteness."

20 Figulus, Canon 106. Cf. Bonus of Ferrara, *op. cit.*, p. 342, referring to Arnold de Villanova on making the white elixir: "...expose it to a good fire for twenty-four hours, to a still fiercer fire for another day and night, and to a very fierce fire proper for melting, on the third day and night."

21 Bonus, *op. cit.*, p. 256-57.

22 ibid., 261.

23 Bonus, p. 262: "The sorce of the body should prevail over the force of the soul, and instead of the body being carried upward with the soul, the soul remains with the body...."

24 Wallace Stevens, "Study of Images I" *Collected Poems*, N.Y.: Knopf, 1978, p. 233.

25 M.-L. von Franz, *Aurora Consurgens*, London: Routledge, Kegan Paul, 1966, p. 233.

26 ibid., p. 234.

27 My *The Dream and the Underworld*, N.Y.: Harper & Row, 1979, p. 168-71.

28 Bonus, p. 264.

29 ibid., p. 255-56.

30 ibid., p. 262.

31 I suggest that analysis is instigator of "the ferment" because Bonus says (p. 256): "The ferment of which we speak is invisible to the eye, but capable of being apprehended by the mind." Thus what turns up the heat and/generates ferment is an intensification of the mental work, *i.e.*, deeper demands of analytical understanding.

32 The reference in Bonus has escaped my pursuit: "An Open Entrance" (*HM* II: 194) states: that the vitrified substance becomes "unsusceptible of any further change."

33 Cf.R. Lopez-Pedraza, *Hermes and His Children*, Spring. Publ., 1977, Chap. IV, for an understanding of erotic unions based on the attraction between and commingling of fantasies.

34 Cited by Arthur John Hopkins, *Alchemy, Child of Greek Philosophy*, N.Y.: AMS Press, 1967, p. 99, from Berthelot *Coll. des anciens alchimistes grecs*, III: 28,9.

35 "Gum" is a frequent reference to the 'holding stuff between', that which joins but is different from what it joins. Cf. Jung, *CW* 12: §§336, 484; Bonus, p. 279; Trinick, *op. cit. inf.*, p. 79.

36 Cf. *CW* 6, §§66, 67, 71, 77. These passages present the alchemical gum in the intellectual language of philosophy. *Esse in anima* remains a third conceptual position, a mere rational argument, unless anima has become utterly real, so sticky that one can't shake it off, staining and smearing whatever one touches. Abelard, who promulgated the philosophical position *esse in anima* (though it is already present in the Platonic metaxy) was one for whom anima was a desperately convincing experience in the person of Heloise.

37 John Trinick, *The Fire-Tried Stone*, Marazion, Cornwall: Wordens, 1967.

38 Aniela Jaffe, Letter dated 12 June 1961, in Trinick, p. 12.

39 From Ethan Allen Hitchcock, *Alchemy and the Alchemists*, Los Angeles; Philosophical Research Soc., 1976, p. 174. Original source not given.

40 Quoted from Trinick's translation (p. 19; cf. 33-41) of "An Open Entrance" (cf. *CW* 14, §§ 189-213). On the pores and puer, see my "Notes on Opportunism" in *Puer Papers*, Spring Publ., 1979, p. 152-53.

41 "For this water is a white vapour, and therefore the body is whitened with it. It behooves you therefore to whiten the body and open its infoldings," from Artephius, quoted by Trinick, p. 81.
42 Edward Kelly, *The Theatre of Terrestrial Astronomy*, published in *Alchemy* (R. Grossinger, ed.), Richmond, Calif: North Atlantic Books, 1979, p. 62.
43 Albertus Magnus, *Book of Minerals* III, ii, 5, Wyckoff, *op. cit.*, p. 198.
44 Trinick, p. 81.
45 Hitchcock, p. 80-81. "Treatment with salt and vinegar is essentially that used since antiquity for making a white pigment from lead." (The preference for vinegar is Artephius'—an old man's vision of transformation through acidity, not through 'salt' since it is he who abjured salt as deceptive and erroneous in the passage quoted above, fn 39.) *Book of Minerals*, Wyckoff, tr., p. 192n. Hitchcock, *op. cit.*, p. 80-81.
46 Betty Jo Teeter Dobbs, *The Foundation of Newton's Alchemy*, Cambridge Univ. Press, 1975, p. 252-55 (text of "The Key" from which come these passages): "... thus join the mercury, the doves of Diana mediating, with its brother, philosophical gold." "Another secret is that you need the mediation of the virgin Diana (quintessence, most pure silver); otherwise the mercury and the regulus are not united."
47 Dobbs, p. 177; cf. p. 183, 207. For an entire text on antimony, with many references to its poisonous nature and the curative powers of its vinegar, see Basilius Valentinus, *The Triumphal Chariot of Antimony*, London: Stuart & Watkins, 1962.
48 Dobbs, p. 148.
49 ibid., p. 68.
50 ibid., p. 207.
51 ibid., p. 209.
52 ibid., p. 207; cf. my *Emotion: A Comprehensive Phenomenology of Theories and their Meanings for Therapy*, London: Routledge, 1960, p. 75-6 on animal spirits.
53 We see Artemis-Diana only if we are already in her train, that is, already hunting in the vegetable matter of our symptoms and slow growth and tangly underbrush of feelings for the elusive "animal spirits." Diana's sign is not only the animal and the forest; it is also the bow and arrow. Active imagination inspired by Diana will therefore be intentional. It will aim to seize fleeing images, and it will draw our puer intensity for quest into their pursuit, even at the one-sided risk of abandoning the pleasures of the flesh for the joys of the chase.
54 Dobbs, on Newton and "middle natures," p. 204-10, 228-30. We recapitulate in Newton the theme we developed in Stevens and Cezanne (accompanying piece on "blue" in *Sulfur* I, 1, 1980): the reunion of imagination and nature which is as well the reunion of imagination and reason, since for Newton, nature is rational. This reunion requires an alchemical work, the work of an art. The great landscape painter John Constable stated it thus: "The whole object and difficulty of the art (indeed of all the fine arts) is to *unite imagination with nature*." Cited in E.H. Gombrich, *Art and Illusion*, Princeton Univ. Press (Bollingen Series), 1961, p. 386.
55 ibid., p. 183.
56 Cf. S. Sambursky, "Von Kepler bis Einstein: Das Genie in der Naturwissenschaft," *Eranos* 40—1971, Pt. II; Dobbs, Chap. 1.
57 Dobbs, p. 19, 36ff. Cf. Frances A. Yates, *The Rosicrucian Enlightenment*, London: Routledge, 1972, p. 201f.
58 Quoted by Dobbs, p. 211, from R.S. Westfall, "Newton and the Hermetic Tradition," in Allen G. Debus, *Science, Medicine and Society in the Renaissance*. In his early work on light Newton had captured Iris, the mediating rainbow (and anima mediatrix), in a prism of glass and dissected her into seven colors. Iris, the rainbow-girl, and colors themselves lost their mediating role (which Goethe tried to restore) between the phenomenal and the invisible. Colors were once the visibilities of the planetary principles; or, colors are planetary 'messages' carried from above downward by Iris—hence they must

be understood by *epistrophē*, or interpretation upward. When color becomes merely subjective (not really given with and in things), things do indeed become soulless, mechanical and dead. Even in his mature work Newton was still trying to connect changes in color to changes in particle size (Dobbs, p. 221-24), a quantitative, mechanistic reduction, searching for the source of color in the colorless, soul in reason. Newton's optics deprived the world of its multi-colored soul so that the restitution of anima ("mediation" in Newton's terms) by alchemical means became his ever-growing concern. Further on theory of color and the rainbow-girls in James Joyce, see Barbara DiBernard, *Alchemy and Finnegans Wake*, Albany: SUNY Press, 1980, p. 87-91.
59 Dobbs, p. 67.
60 Dobbs' evaluation, p. 179.
61 The controversy concerning the true identity of 'Philalethes' is discussed by Jung, *CW* 14, p. 33, n183, and more recently by Dobbs, p. 53, n25 (referring to investigations by R.S. Wilkinson).
62 Jung goes on, unfortunately, to moralize the doves, placing them into a pair of opposites with the evil rabid dog. Two does not always have to mean opposition. Two's are also co-operative as pairs, partners, mutuals, lovers—especially the last, when the two comes in the soft flutter and bicker of two turtle-doves. Two feet, two eyes, two lungs, two shoulders—must they always be seen as opposites? *In alchemical psychology we must never abstract a number from its image.* Is the image two entangled serpents, two beasts, two fish swimming away from each other? My 'two' may be opposing currents in the stream passing by and by-passing each other, whereas your 'two' may be a raging conflict of fighting beasts, or a mating *folie à deux* that cannot do without each other. The alchemical images of Lambspring (*HM* I: 271ff) depict many kinds of animal two's. The image always takes precedence over the abstraction, shapes it and adjectivizes it. This is the perspective of psyche over and against the abstract numbers and laws (of opposites) of spirit.
63 Patricia Berry, "On Reduction," *Spring 1973*, p. 67-84.
64 von Franz, *op. cit.*, p. 238. She understands the plurality here differently: for her it is tied with a problem of evil so that "pluralization" becomes "regression."
65 Robert Grinnell, "Reflections on the Archetype of Consciousness: Personality and Psychological Faith," *Spring 1970*, p. 15-39. Also my *Re-visioning Psychology*, N.Y.: Harper Colophon, 1977, p. 42-44, 50-51 on "Anima" and "Psychological Faith."
66 Cf. Karl Kerényi, "A Mythological Image of Girlhood: Artemis" in *Facing the Gods*, Spring Publ., 1980.
67 C.G. Jung and Aniela Jaffé, *Memories, Dreams, Reflections*, London: Collins and Routledge, 1963, p. 240.
68 The reader with interests in philosophy may notice that the last paragraphs of Section IV play off from and comment upon at least these more obvious references: Bergson's *durée*, Kant's *noumenon*, Socratic dialectic (as if altogether other than the *Symposium*), Dilthey's knowledge vs. understanding, Husserl's transcendental subjectivity, as well as all philosophies that place imagination in the mind (rather than the mind in imagination) and consider it a function of a subjective knower.

V. Lunacy

We began by proposing, from Hegel, that soul necessarily goes through a stage of insanity: lunacy is necessary for soul-making (*Spring, '80*, p. 21). And we suggested that this necessary stage might be what alchemical psychology speaks of as silver and the whitening of the earth. All along, however, we have been begging a question: we have used terms like "lunacy," "psychopathology," "madness," seeming never to have heard the arguments by Thomas Szasz against this medical language.

But I think these maddening terms belong first to the moon,[1] and only incidentally to medicine. They are true coinages presenting true values, minted by the lunatic mind attempting to formulate a specific lunar state of its imagining that is underworld or otherworld, shocking and abnormal, and that therefore these terms themselves become vehicles of an epistrophé, a mode of carrying us to the archetypal principle to which they refer. On the one hand, I am agreeing with Hegel and with alchemy—lunacy is necessary, as silver is a precondition of the conjunction. On the other hand, I agree with Szasz that lunacy becomes insanity when diagnosed as such by the medical model. Lunacy is a moon moment and we must be aware of what happens to the moon when assaulted by Apollonic medicine. Lunacy calls for lunar understanding.

Let us look now at two forms of lunacy in the light of the alchemical moon. The first is *delusional literalism*, the core problem in what medical psychology calls paranoid behavior, and the second is *depersonalization*.

A paranoid delusion is a factified imagination, a fantasy believed literally. The belief in this literal event, plot, or scheme cannot be shaken by appeal to feelings, by evidence of the senses, or by argument of reason. One who is held by this so-called "false belief" conforms precisely to what religions might call a "true-believer," so that the border between fundamentalism in religion and delusional literalism is subtle indeed.

What happens to an image that it becomes immutable and true? What congeals it into a delusion? Memories, dreams, reflections are usually so shadowed with uncertainty: they flicker and resonate in so many different ways. Besides, the anxious intuitions of the lunar night dispel quickly in the morning light. So what indeed happens that lunar imagination takes on solar certainty. Let us approach this psychiatric question by means of alchemical language.

Alchemy warns that only separated things can join.[2] Before any two things such as moon and sun can be conjunct or experienced as conjunct, they must be distinguished, else says alchemy a *monstrum* is born of a premature conjunction. Any union that does not differentiate its unity into distinct feeling realities is actually a monstrum. To go through the world seeing its one underlying truth in synchronistic revelations, its preestablished harmony, that God is becoming man and man becoming God, that inner and outer are one, that mother is daughter and daughter mother, puer is senex and senex puer, that nature and spirit, body and mind, are two aspects of the same invisible energy or implicate order, thereby neglects the acute distinctions joined by these conjunctions, so that our consciousness, no matter how wise and wondrous, is therefore both premature and monstrous. And by monstrous, alchemy means fruitless, barren, without issue.[3] Whenever we see sameness in two events without at the same instant recognizing their incommensurability, a sterile fusion has occurred, which means that paradox, absurdity, and overt enormity are more characteristic of a true union, than are androgynous wholeness and the harmony of the unus mundus.

The alchemical conjunction hears various disparate voices at once. The alchemical conjunction, in short, is metaphorical consciousness; or, it is metaphorical consciousness in short, more like an absurd pun than a bliss of opposites transcended. *Ananda* (bliss) in the joy of a joke: the alchemy books illustrated by grotesque cartoons, ridiculous terms, doing it in the bathtub, exact formulae laced through with metaphors—who said they did not know what they were doing. These monstrosities provide antidotes to the monstrum, the principal among which is the delusional unity of the Great Opposites, silver and gold. "The colour of the Sun does not enter into the Moon, nor that of the Moon into the Sun," says Arnold de Villanova.[4] "What is occult in gold is manifest in silver, and what is manifest in gold is occult in silver," says Rhasis.[5] Their union requires that each must be *stubbornly* different. Silver can only rightly join gold when it hides its gold, when it is not colored by the Sun, remaining manifestly silver, loyally itself, an unalloyed seed of its own planet.

We have to look carefully at our notions of conjunction. The conjunction is not a balanced mixture, a composite adding this to that; it is not a blending of substantial differences into a compromise, an arrangement; it is not a symbolic putting together of two halves or two things into a third. As a psychological event it takes place in soul, as a recognition, an insight, an astonishment. It is not the reconciliation of two differences, but the realization that *differences are each images* which do not deny each other, oppose each other, or even require each other. In fact, as differences, they have gone away. The notion of difference itself dissolves into shadings, tonalities, possiblilities, implications—the multiple relations which are in the nature of any image. Once the logical category of 'difference' gives way to the imaginal 'image' then gold and silver can be perceived in the same way, having the same imaginal nature. "From these considerations we see clearly how silver and gold are of the same nature," writes Bonus.[6]

A conjunction occurs when the problem of conjunction is no longer our focus. The problem dissolves into metaphor which is to say that the kind of consciousness that imagines in problems, the tension of opposites, the law of contradiction and paradoxes has itself dissolved into a metaphorical mode of hearing so that there is a double-speak, a polysemousness, going on everywhere. Each thing is a conjunction when consciousness is metaphorical, and there are no halves or realms to be joined. There are also no overvalued meanings that have to be held, and unified by a symbol; metaphorical consciousness does not have to refer an event to a larger realm of meanings for its significance but rather enjoys the allusions that spring from the event. Nor is there anything to be unified since what is there, as an image, is already that which it is.

Here is an example of the difference between symbolic and metaphorical perception: if I say "cross" in an association experiment, your *symbolic* reply might be: suffering, Easter, to bear, mandala, Greek, Lorraine, martyrs, cosmic compass, sunwheel, protection—or any of the meanings of the cross as world-wide symbol. The word "cross" would be deepened by reference to these larger meanings. Your *metaphoric* response might not neglect these, but it would also include: cross-patch, crossed, your fingers, my heart, the street, transgression, court, stitch, tic-tac-toe, and other spontaneous associations arising from the word as sound and image beyond its symbolic meaning. For the symbolic reply, Jung might be your guide; for the metaphoric, Joyce—and these two guides were often at cross purposes.

It is in this metaphorical way that we must read alchemy's hundreds of terms for its major symbols—Mercury, or Materia Prima, or Whitening. That is, it is precisely with a whitened mind of metaphorical understanding that alchemy proceeds, dissolving even its own favorite symbols into images—and images that shatter meaning, that are so freakish, so absurd and funny, so vexing that they refuse to stand up as symbols with universal significance. The symbolic reading of alchemy would reverse alchemy's own metaphorical method. It tries to establish definite symbolic meanings, so that in all alchemical psychology, including what I am writing here, we may lose the alchemy in the psychology. Hence the importance of the white earth which provides an imaginal ground for hermeneutics rather than a symbolic one.

We have had to expose the usual symbolic understanding of the conjunction because it bears on the lunacies we are examining. Lunacy as paranoid behavior begins already when we think symbolically: when the test of the conjunction is the synchronous appearance of an event in two realms of meaning, gold and silver worlds conjoined. Then, I feel a conjunctio has been confirmed, meanings appear in multiplication, and I believe myself to be in symbolic reality. But, these very terms: "symbol," "meaning," "two," "synchronous," "unified" are part of the delusional construct itself. What actually has happened is the concretization of metaphor. We have gone tone deaf in the amplified system of symbolic meaning; we have exchanged metaphorical illusiveness for symbolic delusion. The notion of the symbol indicates, even produces, the monstrum. Instead of saying: the monstrum is an alchemical symbol, let us now say the symbol is an alchemical monstrum.

A proper alloy does not "stutter"—this we saw last year in Section II. It takes the blows of the hammer because it is relatively malleable *(malleus* = hammer). An alchemical conjunction that is not a monstrum holds the distinct images in a loosely federated manner, precise in lines though not fixed in meaning, a malleable sort of consciousness, bending, supple, like the Chinese Tao or a Rabbinical story—it could mean this, it could mean that—but always the image remains right under your nose, and its meaning does not congeal into allegory, parable, or symbol.

So the test of the amalgamation of silver with gold is not witness of itself in the dayworld, imagination witnessed in literality, fantasies 'coming true.' The test is rather standing to the blows of the hammer as silver: that mental and imaginational realities are ungraspable elusives, quick and silver, and yet remain self-same, as they are, permanent as the white firmament in which they are lodged. So they can take every sort of pounding—query, analysis, concentration, reproduction, emotional challenge—without coming apart into two interpretive halves, a physical side and a psychic side, a good side and a bad, a female side and a male—or the image and its meaning. "A poem should not mean/but be."[7]

So pound these delusions, therapists! Hammer away at those meaningful coincidences that seem to confirm psychic reality with physical evidence. Make them stutter. Ask what stance of mind requires this sort of literal witness. Don't let the work fall back into cloudy whiteness, taking sweet comfort as 'meaning' dawns. Hit meanings with a stick until the images stand clear, by themselves, silver.

Why this urge to meaning just now in the work? Why the need to prove the psychic silver process by means of solid gold? What is this move defending against? "Poetic fright," says Bachelard in his book on the element of Air.[8]

As the volatile becomes fixed and the fixed more volatile (Mary the Jewess), imagination usurps the field—and this lunacy, this poesis is frightening. The psyche moves from prose to poetry. Bachelard calls it:

> a sort of Copernican revolution of the imagination. Indeed images can no longer be explained by their objective traits [*i.e.*, referents], but by their subjective meanings. This revolution is the equivalent of placing: dream before reality, nightmare before tragedy....in short, the imagination is sufficiently vivid...to impose its visions, its terrors, its sorrows....it is the reminiscence of a state preceding life, of a state of *dead* life....We might go one step further and put the image not only before thought, before narrative, but also before any emotion. A sort of nobility of spirit is associated with poetic fright...that forever guarantees first place to the imagination. It is the imagination itself which thinks and which suffers....The dynamic imagination is primary reality.

In this revolution we reach back for old structures, attempting to meet the lunacy, the poetic fright of the whitening, by "subjective meanings" in prosaic accounts of thought, narrative and emotion, all the fictions of our case history, desperately in search of a meaning to which we can fix the image, somewhere, anywhere outside the imagination itself. The mere being of the image, the image as a being, without recourse to meaning, psychic reality as such, is too much unless the soul be whitened. Or, shall we say, this poetic fright is one way the necessary blanching can occur. Lunacy, a necessary initiation to poesis.

This brings us again to our first form of lunacy, delusional literalism. When silver conjoins with gold before psychic reality is hardened and cooled, then it easily yields to gold in such a way that the sun dominates and covers over the moon. "The man will dissolve over the woman," as Philalethes says it (*HM* II: 265). Lunar imagining becomes solified: images reveal themselves as blazing truths, the nightworld vision and its fright converted into dayworld certainties: "It all makes sense. I see meanings everywhere." Moreover, a surging rectitude seizes the lunar world, attempting to establish its reign by means of solar energy. Fantasy speech becomes delusional declaration; lunacy becomes insanity, paranoia. The psyche can no longer hear its speaking as its own voice. Its silver resonance gilded, it hears only the overt content of its voice as literal statement, the stuttering disguised in positive and clear assertion. We can no longer see through: "Sometimes, too, the glass looks as though it were entirely covered with gold...it is a certain indication that the seed of the man is operating upon the seed of the woman, is ruling it and fixing it...," says Paracelsus.[9]

Psychology may also become one of these stuttering alloys, a gilding of silver that covers over the woman, ruling it and fixing it. Whenever we define soul, declare it to be death or image, experience, reflection or anima, perspective or metaphor, we are deluded with gold, making declarative statements, blinded by our logos brilliance, covering over psyche with an 'ology.' Psychology can take the blows of the hammer only if its glass remains backed with silver so that we can reflect as metaphor each of the psyche's 'ologies.'

"Sow gold in the white foliate earth,"[10] say the instructions. Not over the earth, covering it, but inside the silvered mind; let the sun shine in. Or, let it out: "Gold is hidden in silver and extracted from its womb," says Bonus.[11] The gold reaches the silver from within itself, life emerging from within psychic realities, charging the images with heat and beauty from within themselves. Glow, not gild.

*

The second lunatic condition psychiatry calls "depersonalization."[12] It can occur in organic psychoses, toxic states and anxiety states, in hysteria and in schizophrenic psychoses, in neurotic phobias, compulsions, and depressions, and also in normals. This symptom cannot be tied specifically to any syndrome; it can come and go or last, and it can happen at any time from puberty to old age. As one of the more universal psychic vicissitudes, it must be recognized as archetypal, therefore having a background in the poetic basis of mind and its fantasy processes to which alchemical psychology directly speaks.

During depersonalization, it is as if myself and world have become irreal and de-souled. Despite a fretful sort of introspection, there is no animation. Everything is as it is, but there is no dimension, no importance. All my functions are intact—sensing, remembering, orienting, thinking—but something primary has gone dead. Apathy, monotony, flatland, the world and my experience of it behind glass, in a vacuum or on another planet. Mechanical. Personal common life, the warmth of the sun-baked world and my responses to it, suddenly useless, frozen, formally automatic. A mirror image of the daily; underworld *eidola*; moonlit shadows of substance. Philalethes says (*HM* II: 265): "The woman has become coagulated over the man."

Let's turn to poetry rather than to medicine for understanding this condition. Wallace Stevens, in "The Blue Guitar," stanza 7, describes depersonalization in the language of sun and moon:

> It is the sun that shares our works.
> The moon shares nothing. It is a sea.
>
> When shall I come to say of the sun,
> It is a sea; it shares nothing;
>
> The sun no longer shares our works
> And the earth is alive with creeping men,
>
> Mechanical beetles never quite warm?
> And shall I then stand in the sun, as now
>
> I stand in the moon, and call it good,
> The immaculate, the merciful good,
>
> Detached from us, from things as they are?

Depersonalization reverses the condition of paranoid delusion. There, everything fits together into a deluded sense of meaningful coincidences and subjective importance: everything means me, quite literally. The silver of the soul has been coated over with gold into absolute importance and highest value. All things resonate (silver) with truth (gold); psychic images receive indestructible, ultimate, ontic status. Omnipotence.

Here, however, the warm world turns into the great cold sea, sharing nothing. The earth and its works and human bodies become merciless mechanical beetles, never quite warm. Impotence. Everything is as it is, things as they are, coagulated and present, but detached like shades departed from the sunlit world, because, as Stevens says, "I stand in the moon."[13]

In this monstrum of gold and silver, the silver dominates the gold, coagulating the day-world so that it is sicklied over with a pale cast of mooning, of introspective reflection; stale, flat and unprofitable become the uses of this world. When the moon usurps the sun's place, the solar world remains, but transfigured, as if transported to the moon, the heat gone out of it, gone the *calor inclusus* which distinguishes the living from the dead. Then we find no values such as mercy and compassion, no caring or wanting (only creeping), no good of any kind because the solar world has been silvered and resonance now means only hollowness. The very danger alchemy warned of, vitrification, has taken place. Glassiness of animation, the world a glass menagerie.

*

Back to Hegel, back to alchemy. Even should we envision these two basic conditions of lunacy in terms of gold and silver and their relation, must the soul go through these stages? Are over-gilding the imagination and over-whitening the warm workaday world not mistakes? Is lunacy necessary; could it not be otherwise? Can't insanity be prevented?

Here, I am wholly with Thomas Szasz: *insanity* can indeed be prevented by one major simple measure—call off the medics who turn lunacy into insanity by the medical model of literalizing: accounting for what happens in the soul in positivistic clinical terms. But—the pathologizing, the lunacy and its 'mistakes,' cannot be prevented because it is necessary, according to both Hegel and alchemy. The only prevention I can imagine would be an education of the psyche along the lines of an alchemical training, so as to keep the lunacy but not its clinical literalism. We would learn the metals, the seeds of the Gods in our depths, and enter a long apprenticeship to the purpose of their workings. The meaning of the word *prevention*, "to come before" would be our guide: that is, we could 'prevent' the 'mistakes' of lunacy by turning to the primordial factors that 'come before' all else and by relating what happens in lunacy to what comes before—not causally in a medical case history, but archetypally to the primordial seeds. Yet even then there is no guarantee; one may succumb to their purposes.

What then are the purposes of the metals, and what is accomplished in the soul by these 'mistakes' of silver, such as depersonalization? Perhaps *depersonalization is an activation of the seed of silvem*, asserting the impersonal over the personal, detachment over warmth, by whitening and deadening the sun of the shared world. It shows us that we are shades who can stand on the moon at any time and that what is truly real, according to the silver, is not the object and the world or even the gold as such, but the psychic imagining that the silver brings to the gold, that anima resonating factor on which the solar world actually depends for experience of its reality. We are told by this 'mistake' that we do not and cannot properly inhabit the common earth until we have sojourned alone on the moon.

Or, take the first condition, the paranoid delusion which we have placed against the background of the solification of fantasy. This too can be accepted as a purposive, necessary moment in the opus of soul-making. These literalistic delusions are attempts by the sun to seduce lunar fantasy into the world of persons and things. The intention in the seed of gold is to turn the psychological faith of the silvered dove into living conviction, giving width and connectedness to the moony reflections that by themselves remain unshared and private.

A paranoid delusion—a plot against me or a cosmic revelation or a jealousy obsession—each involves, as Freud first pointed out, an erotic component, indeed, a homo-erotic component, a moment of libidinal connectedness with sames. Here is the gold attempting its conjunction with silver, *as if it were gold*, the sun mounting upon and covering the body of the moon as if silver were the same as gold. So, an archetypal or alchemical therapy will approach paranoid delusion as a *gold*-silver monstrum, seeing there the sun's desire to unite with the moon's fantasy and bring it into the common world. And this therapy will approach depersonalization as a *silver*-gold monstrum, seeing there the moon insinuating its importance by whitening and deadening the sun.

Our approach attempts to prevent insanity by recourse to lunacy, where lunacy is understood as the first appearance of the white earth in the solar world, the first recognition of psychic, imaginal reality, yet still couched in that notion of reality given by solar definitions. Solar consciousness responds to the white earth in a solar style: the response of Apollonic medicine, so that in its clear eyes lunacy must be insanity. The medical response serves only to fix the white earth into a solar literalism, furthering the wrong conjunction and creating that monstrum called the psychiatric case.

Our task lies neither in curing what is called lunacy nor even in using the term in the old and common sense of moon-mad, passing strange, out of one's mind, deluded. Rather our task—and by *our* I mean everyone engaged in soul, not merely professional specialists—is the recognition of moon moments, of silver states, so that they can be understood as phenomena of the white earth and reverted (*epistrophē*) to it. Then we can see these conditions as inherent to, purposeful and intentional, and necessarily appropriate in the work of the soul's silvering.

The medical model is a theology, according to Szasz. It is indeed a model which represses the Gods as images and serves them as diseases. Lunacy becomes insanity, a secular diagnosis, that no longer echoes Luna. The myths have been driven out only to return as the myth of mental illness. Szasz is right to insist that the problem of mental illness and mental health, and therapy too, is myth. We need a polytheistic theology, old in the manner of Vico or new in the manner of David Miller,[14] new *logoi* to hold the *theoi* and give them articulation, each in his and her own form.

This long essay has been working at one example, a principal one, reverting lunacy to its metallic seed and planetary principle so that we can understand lunatic processes as whitening of the psychic body and silvering of soul. This example implies that there might be other planetary modes of pathologizing, such as leadenness, mercurialness, martial ironing, manic sulphurism (that we today call 'ego') and so on. A psychopathology might better be derived from the principals of the heavens and their seeds in the earth, from the elements and the myths, a psychopathology which starts in the white earth of the imagination where the mind itself begins, than deriving psychopathology from secular behavioral categories. This archetypal psychopathology returns the conditions we suffer to their authentic home in cosmic and divine events. For if we are created in divine images so too are our afflictions. Archetypal psychopathology gives credit to these events, where credit means faith in them as bearing transpersonal seeds that will out through our individual lives. What's more—and last—this mode of psychopathology which considers silver the prime ingredient and necessary origin of psychological thinking turns to those smiths of silver, the poets, as physicians, musicians of the soul.

V. Lunacy

1 Pliny speaks of silver as ."a madness of mankind" (*Nat. Hist.* Bk. 33, §31:95). The relations between the moon and 'madness' are legion; a footnote in *CW* 14, p. 156 (a page that discusses lunar madness) illumines this relation: "Not only does Luna cause moon-sickness, she herself is sick or ailing." Lunacy is inherent in the archetypal principle, an infirmity of the archetype itself, and therefore lunacy must be understood on an archetypal (alchemical) level. For a discussion of "archetypal infirmity" see my "On the Necessity of Abnormal Psychology," in *Facing the Gods*, Spring Publ., 1980.

2 *E.g.*, "The ancient philosophers have enumerated several kinds of conjunction, but to avoid a vain prolixity I will affirm, upon the testimony of Marsilius Ficinus, that conjunction is a union of separate qualities...," Edward Kelly, *The Theatre of Terrestrial Astronomy*, in *Alchemy*, Richard Grossinger, ed., Richmond, Calif.: North Atlantic Books, 1979, p. 63.
3 Ruland, *op. cit.*, p. 234: "The fruit of an unlawful and accursed copulation. They generate nothing in their turn....not produced by any honourable means but by the guile of men....These monstrosities are impotent and useless for breeding purposes....''
4 Extracts from Arnold de Villanova in Bonus, *op. cit.*, p. 332.
5 Cited from Rhasis' *Book of Alums and Salts* by Wyckoff, *Book of Minerals, op. cit.*, p. 175n.
6 Bonus, p. 260.
7 Famous last stanza of Archibald MacLeish's "Ars Poetica."
8 G. Bachelard, *L'Air et les songes*, Paris: Corti, 1943, p. 119-20; passage in translation by Colette Gaudin, *On Poetic Imagination and Reverie, Selections from the Works of Gaston Bachelard*, Indianapolis: Bobbs-Merrill, 1971, p. 14f.
9 Paracelsus, I:83.
10 Cf. von Franz, *Aurora Consurgens*, p. 384 & n.
11 Bonus, p. 260.
12 Having elaborated on anima and depersonalization in two other places, I forgo it here. Cf. *Re-Visioning Psychology*, N.Y.: Harper & Row, p. 44-46; "Anima (II)," *Spring 1974*, pp. 114-19.
13 Cf. James Baird, *The Dome and the Rock—Structure in the Poetry of Wallace Stevens*, Baltimore: Johns Hopkins, 1968, p. 145-46 on the "moon" condition. Coleridge's "Rime of the Ancient Mariner" works the same archetypal pair of sun and moon with strikingly similar images. During the reign of the Moon, the ship becalmed, the human crew drops down dead, turning into corpses, spectres, wraithes, and the narrator is left: "Alone, alone, all, all alone,/Alone on a wide wide sea!" This work demands an alchemical analysis for which this passage from Philalethes ("An Open Entrance," *HM* II: 188) offers a clue: "This is the death of the compound; the winds have ceased, and there is a great calm. This is the great simultaneous eclipse of the Sun and Moon, when the Sea also has disappeared. Our Chaos is then ready, from which, at the bidding of God, all the wonders of the world may successively emerge."
14 *The New Polytheism*, Spring Publ., 1981.

ARCHETYPAL TOPOGRAPHY
The Karma-Kargyudpa Lineage Tree

PETER BISHOP
(Magill, South Australia)

Within the main Gompa at Rumtek Monastery in Sikkim, the residence of H. H. Rangjung Rigpe Dorje, the 16th incarnation of Karmapa, is a *tanka* or icon of the Kargyudpa Lineage Tree. This picture consists of groupings of deities and historical figures in specific locations around the unifying image of a tree. The tree grows from the center of a lake. Clustered around the tree trunk are the Guardian Protectors. Generally these are wrathful figures such as Mahākāla, surrounded by flames with gruesome ornaments, dancing on corpses or other victims.[1] Above are four branches. Grouped on the front branch are the Yidams or tutelary deities, the personal 'guardians' of the meditators. On the right branch are the Buddha manifestations which can be seen as referring to potential energy aspects. On the rear branch are texts and on the left branch are the Bodhisattvas, the 'active' energy aspect. Towering above these, on the central trunk or branch, are the historical Lamas or teachers of the Kargyudpa lineage and the historical Siddhis or yogis. Dominating the center of the tree is the deity Dorje Chang (Tbt.) or Vajradhāra (Skt.) who reappears at the top of the tree.

This deliberate grouping and locating of archetypal imagery seems to qualify as a form of archetypal topography in the sense Edward S. Casey developed.[2] In exploring this Tibetan system I am hoping to achieve a double purpose: to introduce an example of imagistic topography from a living tradition of complexity and richness into the general debate, and uncover certain questions in the development of a theory of archetypal organization.

The author is Lecturer in Sociology at the Hartley College of Advanced Education, Magill Campus, and this article forms part of his ongoing attempt to re-vision sociology by means of an archetypal perspective.

Archetypal Organization

Casey asks, "What regulates the regulators? How do archetypes which impart patterns to particular imagined contents, *themselves* form an ordered pattern."[3] He calls archetypal topography the mapping of *topoi* (places and sites) such as this lineage tree; "it is a matter of determining where archetypes are to be located in relation to each other and thus of what groupings they form."[4] He seems to suggest a monotheistic fallacy that there is an *inherent* ordering between archetypes rather than seeing that they can be (consciously or unconsciously) ordered for the purpose of expressing a particular archetypal fantasy. Hence there are *many possible orderings* according to the dominant archetypal fantasy. A motto for a polytheistic psychology could be, 'a place for everything.' But this might give the impression of fixed positions. Certainly everything does not have *a* place. There are *many* places for everything but all places are not alike and are of differing significance, especially in their relation to each other. Casey also seems to ignore that the process of ordering is itself an archetypal fantasy irrespective of the particular arrangement. In this article, Casey questions the adequacy of the quarternary configuration—one appearing in the work of Jung, Bachelard and Heidegger—as a sole representative of the possible multiplicity of archetypes. For example, with Heidegger's scheme, "all the gods are lumped together under the one generic heading of 'gods.'... Are there not intrinsic differences between individual gods as well as between different groups of gods?"[5] To meet this inadequacy Casey examines two examples of multiple mapping—that of Gilbert Durand, and more important for this paper *The Art of Memory* by Frances Yates.[6]

The art of memory was a technique used from classical times through the mediaeval period and the Renaissance for retrieving and reordering the memory, the imagination, on archetypal principles. Above all it was a means, via the use of image, to move the soul.[7] By asking "where" rather than "how" or "why," the art of memory opens up space or interiority. In the early Renaissance human memory was thought of as an 'inner' treasure house or theater. Clusters or constellations of related patternings would be ordered around Gods, planets and so on.

The similitudes would be based on appearance, related functions, sounds, etc. Essential to the re-collection was distortion or the use of bizarre images. It was the capacity of the bizarre or the grotesque to reach particular locations or depths of memory or imagination which rendered them absolutely necessary for the purpose of contacting the entirety of any particular archetypal field. (Not that such an entirety is *ever* contacted in actuality!) This provides another perspective on the use of wrathful imagery in Tibetan or Vajrayāna Buddhism. Not only does the wrathful image complement the peaceful in the essential ambivalence of an archetype, nor is it simply the manifestation of the ego's fear of dissolution, but it encourages and allows the exploration of archetypal regions which would otherwise be extraordinarily difficult to reach. We are drawn to the depths through pathology.

The Lineage Tree as an Archetypal Field

The Kargyudpa Lineage Tree is of singular interest in that it combines a basic fourfold pattern with another level of multiplicity. This pattern is repeated with the four branches and central trunk of the lineage tree. The Meditation Buddhas are grouped and expanded within this overall design. Interpenetration and overlapping exist as some deities are now Protectors, now Yidams, now Bodhisattvas (*e.g.*, Mahākāla as a Protector or Yidam, Manjushrī as Yidam or Bodhisattva).

The tree is a frequent image in traditional 'psychological' systems such as alchemy. Jung develops this theme extensively in his work on the "philosophical Tree," but does not allude to its role of organizing archetypal imagery. Apart from a brief mention by Yates, the tree motif has generally been treated as a single archetypal image rather than as a system for organizing a number of archetypes. Yates refers to Lull's extensive use of diagrams in the form of trees and writes that, "The tree as he uses it, is a kind of place system.... But there are no 'striking' images.... Their branches and leaves are decorated only with abstract formulae and classifications."[8] Unlike Lull's trees, the Kargyudpa Lineage Tree has a full range of striking and bizarre images.

At the base of the tree around the lake, monks, lay people, animals and other beings congregate, a literal image of Heidegger's "gathering."[9] Such an imagining goes hand in hand with specific meditational practices as laid out in Sadhanas or texts, a complex system of oral teaching, transmission and initiations. This field of activity could be seen to constitute an *archetypal situation*.[10] As such it is somewhat misleading to isolate the iconography; we must move cautiously. The Lineage Tree is associated with one of the first meditations the student of the Kargyudpa tradition encounters in the preliminary practices or foundation work. It is a crucial display of psychic reality according to the Kargyudpa tradition, in an ordered and systematic unity.

Evoking The Image

Frances Yates comments that, according to Tullius, everyone must form his memory images for himself.[11] Casey points out that Jung's approach does not use psychodrama or guided daydreams but that a subtle process of participation or imaginative merging with the drama occurs in active imagining.[12] Hillman stresses the quality and precision of the image, even if these are fuzzy,[13] and speaks of the use of "restatement," the alchemical process of an 'iteratio' of the 'prima materia.' The Tibetan practice of visualization seems to be, with one important exception, identical. The exception is the *structured* use of *deliberate* and systematized images to trigger off imaginistic associations. The rest is there, the precision and quality of the image, the constant working over and over the same material or exercise. (A common exploration is the repetition of a meditational exercise with its associated mantra 108,000 times.) There is also no stress on the "correctness" of the image. This is a subtle matter, and the distinction between associating imaginistically on the image and wandering vaguely is fine but definite. One person's image of a particular deity will be different (or should be) from another's purpose.

The use of imagery is only connected to one path in Vajrayāna. This is generally called the Path of Form as compared with the Path of Non-Form, usually known as the Mahāmudrā.[18] This practice is concerned with letting the mind rest in its 'natural' state, without any interference in what arises. Generally both paths are used by a student so that the active invoking of images is balanced by a detached observation/participation in the rising and passing away of phenomena.

Who is Shuffling? Who Commands?

As already mentioned, memory systems can be found among such Renaissance philosophies as Giulio Camillo, with his memory theater, and among such religious disciplines as Christianity and Cabalism. It has even been referred to in connection with the Tarot.[15] Obviously the art of memory is important for access to a variety of traditions and comparison among them. Insofar as it is in vogue, my paper is intended as a kind of caution.

For example, I suggest that a perspective which sees the necessity for 'archetypal topographies' is just one among many. We must not be drawn into literalism at such a profound level. As I mention above, Casey seems to imply a single natural ordering rather than a deliberate or unconscious ordering for a particular purpose, within a specific archetypal influence. Examination of the variety of such attempts to pattern and group archetypes is itself a valuable exercise in exploring archetypal imagination. *What kind of consciousness is it that perceives in terms of organization, integration and preferred positioning of Gods?* Generally, the attempt to discover a unifying wholeness or impose a distinct pattern onto archetypal groupings is a procedure dominated by the archetype of Self.[16] Jung once wrote, "the tree is the self depicted as a process of growth."[17] Hence at the center of the Lineage Tree is the deity Vajradhāra who could easily be seen as an image of "wholeness."[18] At the heart of the Cabalistic Tree of life is the Sephiroth, 'Tiphereth,' frequently associated with Apollo. We can henceforth use the *differences* among various patternings or archetypal topographies to reveal by what commands, which God, are such shufflings and orderings taking place.[19]

Frances Yates, in her book *Giordano Bruno and the Hermetic Tradition*, documents the attempt by Christian philosophers to subsume and integrate the Cabala and the Hermetic sciences into the theology of the Church. Thus instead of providing the imagination with a variety of viewings, the multiple viewings were seen as enhancing the *one* view, that of the coming of Christ and the truth of the Christian teachings. Bruno was one of the few who sensed the danger of this move toward a religious and monotheistic hegemony. In our own era archetypal (polytheistic) psychology has highlighted this tendency towards the cooption of Jung's work and depth psychology in general into existing religious, psychological and social dogma based on a monotheistic hegemony: "Polytheistic psychology would not suspend the commandment to have 'no other Gods before me,' but would extend that commandment for each mode of consciousness...polytheistic psychology obliges consciousness to circulate among a field of powers. Each God has his due as each complex deserves its respect in its own right. In this circularity there seem no preferred positions..."[20] Of course there are positionings of many colors. Is the organization of the archetypal topography unified, loose, tight, centralized? What part is played by hierarchical arrangement as indicated by special locations—up, down, left, right, center and so on? The gathering together of apparently diverse archetypal imagery into a unified whole for the specific purpose of establishing a monotheistic truth needs to be carefully analyzed. It must be stressed that the use of alternative views—Hermetic, Cabalist, depth psychology—to expand and amplify various religious or monotheistic dogmas is not in question but their subsumption into an exclusive hegemony. Such considerations are critical for an examination of a memory system such as the Kargyudpa Lineage Tree.

The Refuge Tree is *not* a map of a generalized field of the psyche. Buddhist psychology has a definite purpose—liberation or transcendence. As such it can be described by the fantasy of growth and goal orientation. I should quickly point out that this is *not* the totality of Buddhist Mahāyāna teaching, which also includes the Prajñāpāramitā, by which such concepts as goals, liberation and so on are declared empty of substance.[21]

A similar difficulty arises when we turn to monotheism. It is not a matter of trying to ascertain the overall fantasy within which Buddhism operates if such a unifying fantasy exists, which I doubt. Neither is it a matter of reducing the Tibetan teaching to this single item of "taking Refuge." Nor is it reducing the "taking of Refuge" to the iconography associated with it. The subject of investigation is simply the iconography of the Lineage Tree. It has been said of Buddhist Tantra in its favor that it absorbs and utilizes local folk religions and cults. So the presence of old Bon-po deities as Protectors in the Lineage Tree supporting Buddha-Dharma would fit in with the monotheistic 'gathering-up' outlined above in the case of Christianity, Cabala and Hermeticism. Especially noticeable in the Tibetan case is the devaluation of other traditions through the position and use of Hindu deities, trampled underfoot and so on. Obviously a symbolic purpose is being hinted at but one cannot help wondering why Hindu Gods should be used for this purpose.

"Monotheistic psychology counters disintegration with archetypal images of order (mandalas)."[22] But this disintegration can in fact be a renewal—not as re-collecting the parts into a new structure but as an awareness of their separate distinctness. In the Tibetan approach this activity of insighting is called Mahāmudrā.[23] Without the background of Mahāmudrā or Śūnyatā we are left with a onesided approach which emphasizes the fantasies of wholeness, of growth and goal, of process and of path.

Jung repeatedly warns of the danger of identifying with the self, in this case with the image of the tree.[24] Mahāmudrā and the practice of creating and dissolving images act as protection against both identification with and reification of such constructed symbols of wholeness as the lineage tree.

Archetypal Organization and Social Reality

When we turn back to the Lineage Tree we notice along with obviously ahistorical deities historical personages, albeit mythologized, such as Lamas, teachers and Siddhis. Further, these historical figures occupy the central axis and highest positions. To my knowledge this is not a common feature of other religious memory systems or those of Camillo or Bruno. These historical personages obviously refer to the central position occupied by the Guru or living teacher in the Vajrayāna tradition, who is more important to the student than the Buddha. This axis is also referring to the central 'mystery' of transmission. Above all the figures indicate that the goal or the Buddha-quality is not abstract or in the past but an ever-present and living reality, incarnate, at the level of the Nirmāna-Kāya (the phenomenal world, as Jung puts it).

What else might such a positioning of historical figures say? I would suggest at least two things. First we can relate it to the archetype of the child, and a reinforcing of the fantasy of growth, of the natural process of health and wholeness. The growth fantasy of the archetypal child is heightened by the image of the tree. The introduction of historical figures also "provides parentage to psychic events, giving them background in race, culture, tradition... When we refuse the historical aspect in our complexes... then we create orphans."[25]

Then these historical figures raise the question of how history is viewed both within the Tibetan culture and from outside by Western students and scholars. Certainly given the social and political position of the monastic order in Old Tibet or among the refugee Tibetans, there is another if unwitting side to this. Without endorsing Berger and Luckman's phenomenological approach to the social construction of reality we can agree with one of their conclusions, that social reality is partial, fragile and in constant need of being re-created or re-produced.[26] Some experiences are so intense that the social world, or the particular associated archetypal fantasy, is strained to such an extent that it must collect, channel and 'explain' them as best it can according to the established construction of reality. Such experiences have been called 'marginal' because they occur on or beyond the limits of daily existence. Religious institutions, including mental institutions, can be seen as reality-maintenance structures, to gather up the 'energy' of such experiences and to translate them into the language of the established order. Surely this is the ultimate monotheism.

Obviously a fine line exists between religion as a stabilizing influence for a particular social order and as a vehicle for exploration. Memory systems go beyond this. They are active in evoking responses at a depth level and then *organizing* these in an archetypal fashion for a particular purpose, conscious or unconscious. It is not the evoking of archetypes which is special here, but the archetypal organizing. The social and political implications are consequently vulnerable to the indiscriminate use of this technique. For example, advertising, propaganda, political ideology and reform, could all be consciously constructed in the form of a "memory system" whereby a commitment for their message is both evoked and organized at an archetypal level. The gross *imaginal* illiteracy characteristic of much of the population would lay them open to such manipulation.

It would seem that some important Renaissance figures were aware of the social significance of memory systems for reform or the stabilizing of society. Giordano Bruno was deliberately orienting his complex system toward reform. It would also appear that Catherine de Medici had the idea of social stability in mind when she staged the elaborately ritualistic court festivals in late 16th-century France. Frances Yates continually points to connections between memory systems, theater and imperial reform.[27] Comparable work on the social and historical context of Tibetan iconography needs to be done.

There is an obvious and explicitly social dimension to archetypal topography. We can read this social dimension in at least two ways. On the one hand it can refer to social control via the penetration or drawing out and channeling of imagination and fantasies. This could open a line of research into the archetypal patterning of advertisements and other aspects of contemporary myth. The other direction is into the archetypal patterns of contemporary social ideologies (in terms of depth fantasies lived in everyday life). The systems of memory in Yates's work, especially those of Bruno, could by comparison with others reveal particularities of the social fantasies within which he worked. Comparison might reveal the array of dominant archetypal fantasies at large,[28] a way into the social dimensions of soul. And in terms of an aid to a reflexive sociology it becomes a way of soul-building.

1   Enough has been written about these deities and the psychic reality they represent to permit this brief a reference, for instance Jung's "Psychological Commentary to the Tibetan Book of the Dead" and "Commentary to the Tibetan Book of the Great Liberation" *CW*, 11, in which he writes, "The unconscious is the root of all experience of oneness (dharma-kāya), the matrix of all archetypes or structural patterns (sambhoga-kāya), and the conditio sine qua non of the phenomenal world (nirmana-kāya)....Their peaceful and wrathful aspects...symbolize the opposites." For a fuller description see J. Blofeld, *The Way of Power* (London, Allen & Unwin) 1970, pp. 110-117; G. Tucci, *The Theory & Practice of the Mandala* (New York, Weiser) 1973, pp. 67ff. Trees are frequently guarded, by rings of fire, dragons and demons, or in this case by both. Jung suggests that the growth to Self indicated by the tree is a natural process and it is dangerous to risk disturbing it. The demonic forces are guarding this process but they will also give protection to man, "provided that he summons up courage enough to climb into the tree despite its guardians" (*CW* 13, §314). Much work needs to be done on the archetypal significance of the various classes of deities. For some details of the Lineage Tree, see N. Douglas and M. White, *Karmapa, the Black Hat Lama Of Tibet* (London, Luzac) 1976.
2   Edward S. Casey, "Toward an Archetypal Imagination," *Spring 1974*, pp. 5ff. The Lineage Tree is an *aid* to meditation and the exploration of imagination; by treating it outside the context of specific practices I do it an injustice. In "Musical Therapy" (*Spring 1978*) Tom Moore describes Ficino's prescription of music, colors, images and diagrams for keeping the imagination alive. This 'massaging' and developing of the vessel of the imagination for *potential* archetypal responses is the purpose of meditating on such a device as the Lineage Tree.
3   Casey, p. 6.
4   Casey, p. 6.
5   Casey, p. 11.
6   F. Yates, *The Art of Memory* (Harmondsworth, Penguin) 1978.
7   *Re-Visioning Psychology*, pp. 91-95.
8   *The Art of Memory*, p. 187.
9   M. Heidegger, "Building, Dwelling, Thinking," in *Poetry, Language, Thought* (New York, Harper & Row) 1971. The tree growing from the lake is similar to the fountain motif in alchemy; when combined with the ring of fire within which dance the protector divinities a clear union of opposites is being expressed. "Our water is fire" (Jung, *CW* 13, §310).

10 J. Hillman, "Archetypal Theory: C.G. Jung," *Loose Ends*, Spring Publ., 1975, pp. 185-6.
11 *The Art of Memory*, p. 101.
12 Casey, p. 4.
13 J. Hillman, "Further Notes on Images," *Spring 1978*.
14 Blofeld, pp. 229ff., and more importantly Garma C. Chang, *Teaching of Tibetan Yoga* (New Jersey, Citadel Press) 1974.
15 A. Douglas, *The Tarot* (Harmondsworth, Penguin) 1974, p. 34.
16 See J. Hillman, "Psychology: Monotheistic or Polytheistic," *Spring 1971*, p. 99.
17 Jung, *CW* 13, 304/1954. The Buddha's awakening beneath the Bodhi tree has resulted in a close relation between them from the beginning. On the bas-reliefs at Sânchî, the place of Śâkyamuni is taken by various symbols. The enlightenment scene shows worshippers paying homage to the tree under which enlightenment was attained. The Tree Buddha Self equation is clear although the tree presumably represents only one aspect of the Self, i.e., that moment when individuation culminates in fulfillment.
18 Eliade points out that in shamanism it is a common belief that the world-ruler lives at the top of the tree, *Shamanism* (Princeton) 1974, p. 70.
19 Note that the Cabala with its associated Tree of Life emphasizes structure over imagery. G. Scholem points to the very masculine nature of Cabala mysticism, *Jewish Mysticism* (New York, Schocken) 1974, p. 37. The Tarot on the other hand emphasizes imagery over structure.
20 *The Art of Memory* and "Psychology: Monotheistic or Polytheistic," pp. 198, 201-204.
21 On the Prajñāpāramitā or Heart Sutra see E. Conze, *Buddhist Wisdom Books* (London, Allen & Unwin) 1975.
22 "Psychology: Monotheistic or Polytheistic," p. 200; also *The Myth of Analysis*, p. 198.
23 *The Myth of Analysis*, pp. 202-3. "Dionysus was called Lysios, the loosener." For a discussion of Mahāmudrā, see Chang, 1974.
24 Jung, *CW* 13, §332.
25 Hillman, "Abandoning the Child," *Loose Ends*, 1975, pp. 25-27, 44.
26 P. Berger & T. Luckmann, *The Social Construction of Reality* (London, Allen Lane) 1971, p. 121.
27 F. Yates, *Shakespeare's Last Plays: A New Approach* (London, Routledge & Kegan Paul) 1975. In *Theatre of the World* (London, Routledge & Kegan Paul) 1969, Yates connects the memory systems of Fludd and John Dee to Elizabethan theater design.
28 Casey, p. 15, omits this social dimension as well as ignoring the possibility of *any* specific purpose in the selection of the archetypal patterning.

STOPPING: A MODE OF ANIMATION

PATRICIA BERRY
(Dallas)

Psychological writing is a subjective confession, as Jung once noted. Let me quickly confess two fascinations, nay obsessions, behind this paper. One is an ingrained, incurable perversity—a compulsive fascination of mine with everything odd and pathological and twisted—especially the blocked, stuck, immovable regions of the psyche: the guy who can't come out of the corner, the catatonic with "wax-like flexibility," the mute child; symptoms like writer's block, stage fright, immobile depressions—as well as the blocked, stopped, stuck behaviors in all of us that don't move no matter how we try. *What is the psyche doing in these stoppings?*

Another fascination I have is myth. It has always seemed to me that myth isn't so much stories about the development of history, civilization, and consciousness as it is images of things eternal, things that repeat, or perhaps have nothing to do with time at all—rather more a "gift of life meanings," as Robert Duncan says.

To indulge these two fascinations, I'd like to circle a myth usually called the Perseus tale. This myth satisfies my craving for pathology, since it contains sufficiently contorted and gruesome imagery: blood, murder, prison, incest, and the Medusa who stops you in your tracks and turns you to stone.

Further it seems a myth about stopping, about the stopping nature of myth—that myth has to do with static, eternal realities. It is a myth about myth in the same way that certain poems are about the making of poems, novels about novels.

And so my method will look at this myth in a way that stops it. This stopping feels disruptive, since it cripples the narrative force, which

---

This paper was first presented at a Conference "Anima, Animal, Animation" (with Susan Pitt, Robert Creeley, Robert Duncan, Patricia Cox, David Miller and James Hillman) in Buffalo, N.Y., November 1980, held by the Analytical Psychology Club of Western New York.

would carry us along in a way that's more fun. Narrative arouses curiosity—what happens next, and then, and then? It feels as though something is going somewhere. Were we to read this myth as narrative we'd get a wonderfully heroic tale (more a fairy tale in fact than a myth—a distinction made by David Miller). We would get the rag-to-riches story of a young man who overcomes the circumstances of his birth (he's born in prison), defeats all obstacles, butchers the monster, redeems his mother, rescues and marries the beautiful maiden....

But I don't want to do that. What I want instead is to stop that story prepense, deliberately by staying with some of its moments—its images or complexes, and then see what mode of animation, if any, occurs.

As a first image let's take Danae, Perseus' mother. Danae is locked in a cell by her father, Akrisios, because it has been prophesied that she would give birth to a son, and that son would be her father's bane. The imprisoned Danae has been painted by many—Rembrandt, Primatticcio, Correggio, Titian—the most striking the Danae by Titian in which the fleshy maiden lounges seductively, receiving the shower of gold from Zeus into her luscious lap. Now most prefer this opulent story of Perseus' birth, this immaculate conception, golden, raining down from the heavens. Surely it's the way a hero, a redeemer ought be conceived.

But there is another version. In this version Danae is seduced and impregnated by her uncle, her father's brother. We need to gather some background about this uncle. In fact we need to go back before the uncle because the entire ancestry gives a certain basis to the pathology in the myth as a whole.

The primal ancestors of the Danaoi are twin brothers who hate each other. One brother sires fifty sons, the other brother fifty daughters. The daughters are strong Amazonic types, ferociously loyal to their father who is called "the wolf." When finally the daughters must marry the fifty sons (a massive group incest), forty-nine kill their young grooms on the wedding night. The fiftieth inadvertently betrays her father and sisters by falling in love with her victim. Although she is locked up and punished, her accident has the effect that the family line, and the myth, the mythic, is perpetuated. Myth depends on such accidents of fertility, accidents that stop myth's natural self-absorption, self-consumption, by a just as mythic collapse into unexpected generativity.

The next complication of this myth involves Danae's father, Akrisios, and her uncle, Proitos—again twin brothers who hate each other so fundamentally that they try to kill each other while still in the fundament of their mother's womb. So within the familial womb itself there is bloody conflict. They are brothers in hatred; hatred is the family fraternity.

As adults the brothers wage battle over the kingship of Argos. During the course of this battle a round shield is invented—the first shield of circular shape—as though inclusive of the warring opposites, a shield that protects by including all aspects of the family antipathy in an unbroken line.

But of course these wholeness constructions never quite work. Diagrammatic schemata and symbolic conceptions fail to wrap up the nature of myth, which no more than nature indulges in perfect circles. Symbolics can hardly shield us from the internal ancestral format, the deep pathologies in myth and the eruptions, interruptions into the myth's attempts at its own solutions.

For example, this uncle then has three daughters and a son (four: again a symbolic number of wholeness). Symbolically, one would expect these four to round things off and settle the family pattern, but instead all four in different ways get driven mad and torn to bits.

But back to Danae. She and her uncle (whom the father hates) commit incest. I'm rather attracted to this incestuous version of Perseus' paternity, since incest is in keeping with the tangled emotionality of the family background: passion, hatred, murder, nature turned against itself, raging in the womb, dismemberment.

Incest works here, because it brings a self-fertilization within the family of the family mess; the perverse circularity of incest makes for compounding, compacting the family horror. Within all this passionate hatred there is as well an incestuous self-fertilization, thickening the myth by turning it back into itself. It becomes ingrown. And how fertile this myth of myths—as Fontenrose has shown in his book *Python* there are all but five of forty-three possible mythemes in the Perseus tale, none of which can claim priority as *ur*, the rest derivative or secondary. This myth keeps generating new varieties of itself. It is a shower of gold, a fertile incest.

Another incestuous myth—Persephone captured by her father's brother Hades—is equally mysterious and equally fertile. And both Perseus and Persephone bear that prefix *perthou* (destroyer, ravager). Again a violent sort of pathology seems essential to the deepest sustaining mysteries that give meaning to human life. In the Persephone image it is Gaia, the very bowels of the earth who abets Hades' rape, and therefore insists on incest. As Freud and Jung saw, incest must be a universal complex; Gaia and Hades ordain it.

And if we carry this a step further, then incest appears in myths not just to make myths myths, make them superhuman, but to make the myths themselves. Myths demand the incest motif within them to show their own incestuous generation. Mythical consciousness is an incestuous consciousness, and so it is allowed to mythical beings (like Pharaohs) and essential to *initiation into mythical thinking* as at Eleusis or in the alchemical model of individuation.

Incest, too, is an image of stopping, for it stops the normal exogamous course of events by inverting, fertilizing something back into itself. As the family blood, the complex, in a myth thickens and gathers weight, myth becomes mythic. Myth *is* incest. It's like poetry (*dichtung, dicht* = thick, dense). It's dirty—the tales are terrible! One always wants to apologize for myth. It's not logos. It's not moral. It's not even Eros! So difficult to explicate, articulate, to draw out exogamously into the world, or in a paper like this. The incest in it, the complex in it, resists, keeps it bound in a tight internal knot, inside its own family, its own thickness.

But incest is also like prison—the prison of shame, of secrecy. How often incest images show the pair in castles, islands, walled gardens, secret rooms. So too Danae is imprisoned by her father in a subterranean tomb under the palace.

The father, Akrisios, had wanted a son to carry on the family line. He had wanted to *extend* the family. We have already seen how this family myth and complex (the nature of myth and complex) is not to extend normally, exogamously outward, but to circle back into its own blood, as this discussion circles.

The oracle at Delphi tells Akrisios that no, he will not have a son. Normal movement into the world is not possible and worse, his daughter will have a son who will defeat him. Faced with this prospect, the old man locks up his life, his anima—rigidifies, establishes, fixes his dark cellars of imagination into a dungeon of repression, and puts the soul down there. And when the daughter is locked in fixed constructs, the mythic potential of the psyche is locked and fixed as well. (Then indeed we get formulas, fixed symbolic meanings, allegories.)

*

So the daughter is locked in a tomb under the palace, and no seed, nothing fertile can get to her. Again the image is incestuous. Since the chamber is beneath the father's palace, it's like trying to keep the threatening thing, the anima under oneself. It's keeping imperiously on top of it, above what's threatening. This is incest in a neurotic, superficial sense. Rather than connecting with *mythic* depths, this defensive binding keeps one on top of one's daughter—so that thought or work or emotions stay up, on the surface, superficial and/or are imprisoned underneath. (It's like living in a duplex or split-level—you're walking around up on top while your daughter lies locked below.)

In the tale despite (or perhaps because) of all this suppression, fertilization occurs. It's like the return of the repressed, or the fertility in the repressed. This *is* like gold. There's a shower of gold in the woman's lap, which lap grows in potentiality. She is now in confinement, as we used to call it. So again we have an image of stopping. Her pregnancy is her confinement; her confinement is her pregnancy. Within the prison of this cell something germinates.

Imprisoning is crucial to a certain kind of new movement—again what we might call mythic movement. It is not your ordinary imprisonment, low country imprisonment—just being bottled up, walled in, guarded and oppressed. These conditions need to be imagined mythically, experienced incestuously, as if when one is in this low dungeon, there is something secret going on in the belly, that fantasies are confining me—not my enemies, my parents, my husband, or my fate—but that I am being held here by mythic events; then this incestuous sense of generation going on within the confinement, the imprisoning, becomes a mode of self-fertilizing. So we do need the no-no's of rigidities, the impossible stone walls we cannot escape from, or even see out of, in order to become aware that we are germinating mythic realities within ourselves.

Within this seclusion Perseus is born. As a child he sits playing happily with a golden ball. He can play with the mythic world as a golden ball because he is a child of incest, a child of the imagination. For him prison is like a little paradise. He's having a ball and, you know, for Jung the ball is a symbol of the Self—particularly a golden ball. So Perseus is playing with himself. He's playing with himself until the ball rolls out of reach and he loses himself. He cries out.

In this narcissistic image, paradisical and self-enclosed, everything is fine—and silly and useless—until one's play with oneself rolls out of bounds—beyond one's own reach. Then like Narcissus, there's no way not to tumble down into the depths—or, as with Perseus, one suddenly finds the self extending out beyond one's self. It's like the world gets important because the self is out there too, and then you get frightened, and scream out. It's like the complex cures itself. You lose yourself and then scream out, call out into the world—and then indeed you're out.

Akrisios hears this cry—it was probably meant for him—and throws them out of their containment, expels them from prison. So you see, the symptom "crying out," the unintended slip, makes the thing occur. Crying out takes them out.

The mother and child now appear in a box, a closed chest cast out to sea. Again we have an image of imprisonment: this time imprisoned in being adrift. Even though the prison under the palace, being imprisoned by the old king, was constricting and uncomfortable, nonetheless it *was* a sort of containment. You knew where you were. The walls were there, the boundaries fixed. But now those supports have all disappeared and one is adrift.

Drifting is a terrible kind of imprisonment, like an Antonioni movie. One is out in the world but without ground; exposed to the elements but in a box, not opened up. Adrift and yet isolated, cut off.

There are a number of ways for this floating imprisonment to end. You may get washed up on the shore of some solid reality, or smashed on a rock and opened, or maybe swallowed by a fish and carried east in the belly of some vague, oceanic intention—or again, one may be stopped more gently, in the bullrushes, caught up in the arms of a maiden.

But here, in this myth, the drifting ends in a net. A fisherman, Dictys (whose name means "net man") sees the floating box, and being an imaginative fisherman, construes it as something wondrous—a magnificent sea monster or a god—so he nets and hauls it to shore. He's a fisherman with imaginative sight (mythic sight). He sees monsters and gods.

Just as Perseus floating with his mother in a little box on the wide sea appears in the same image as Dictys the fisherman, so too do floating and fishing occur in the same experience. When introspections are all boxed in, horizons limited by low ceiling and walls of woodenness, then we are also fishing. How did this happen, what's going on, why am I so trapped—one is narrowed into oneself, at the same time casting around for reasons, explanations, causes.

In this case, only a big net works. Only a vision that sees wondrously—gods and monsters—can rescue the smallness of mind that goes with introspection. Drifting does not have to be met with rational, "sensible perceptions of reality," as it or they are called. Drifting is better arrested and landed by over-perceiving, perceiving the fantastical. When we let our fisherman pay out his mythical, animated imagination, then we are at once free of the box. When we can be imaginatively perceived, we can be landed. There are some good images for this art of perception in the myth, one of which occurs in the scene with the Graiai.

These are three sisters—daughters of Phorkys, the old man of the sea. The name *Phorkys* is the masculine form of Phorcis, that early mother sow goddess. So Phorkys roots down into those deepest, earliest mysteries of the earth. The Graiai, daughters of a pig-man, are pig-women. They have the pig in their background.

But the three sisters don't seem to show it. They are described as fair-faced and swan-like (that graceful bird of death). They have been gray-haired since birth and their names (Enyo, Penphredo, and Dirno) mean warlike, wasp, and terrible. There is something fair about them (attractive), yet at the same time terrible and death-dealing in that very attractiveness. Perhaps this *terrible beauty* is one way of stating the deepest mysteries of the earth, reminding of their father Phorkys and the Sow goddess who devours corpses, and who also is associated with Hades (one of whose names is Orcus—again like hog).

So in this image of the Graiai we've got Hades, hog, the devouring of corpses, and a certain deathy, swan-like beauty, young and old together, forever gray-haired. Mythologically, psychologically they are very archaic, very basic, deep goddesses (much older, for example, than the Olympians). They exist where death has beauty and beauty death; where pigs and swans concur. Their territory is a borderland between east and west, a place of darkness where the light sets and from which it has its beginning—a nowhere zone at the edge—the border of forests and rocks. The place is called the "land of rock-roses"—where the ephemeral delicacy of a rose is a rock and a rock promises this ephemeral delicacy. The animate and the inanimate are in this realm one and the same. Rock is rose and rose is rock. The most delicate, the most substantial.

Now these sisters have a single eye they pass around and share. According to one story, this is a magical eye that enables them to comprehend the tree alphabet in the forest that borders here. And their one tooth (which in some stories they also pass) is a divinatory tooth, allowing them to cut alphabetic twigs from the grove. An extraordinary detail!

Words that grow on trees. Letters, language, words hidden in wood, basic to the wood itself, matter's own words, words that matter—the words in nature and the nature in words. So, indeed, this eye that can read trees is something to get hold of. It's like the origin of mythical vision and speech, cut from nature itself.

Perseus gets the eye by lying in wait, staying very still, so still as to be invisible (he was wearing the cap of Hades). Here the image of stopping is to wait quietly, until one is not, until even one's form and very self lapses nonexistent, invisible. An utter stillness where, as Eliot says: "all in the waiting"—a kind of perfect attentiveness.

Then at a certain moment, between the movement of events out there, between the passing of the eye, one has it. For a moment one has the vision of the Graiai—that dark/light, old/young, ugly/beautiful, the rock as rose/rose as rock, animate/inanimate. For a moment one has captured a perception that opens the way to the Medusa's cave.

In the next image Perseus passes "boar-like into the cave." Now this is a very strange image. How is it that Perseus becomes like a boar? More specifically, how is it that this single eye of the Graiai, terrible beautiful stasis, makes the way become boar-like—fleshy, rutting, hurtling into the cave? From quiet stasis and a moment of perception, we get now compulsion, a one-eyed thrust into darkness.

Surely the single eye is unpsychological, cycloptic. There's no "second sight" to give perspective, distance, reflection, to "balance" vision. With a single eye one *is* the eye—narrow, urgent, and animal-like. So it seems, but the pig leads into the underworld, which is another word for the Medusa's cave. Also we remember Eubuleus' pigs who plunged through the earth to the underworld at the same moment as Persephone. So one way of entering this insubstantial realm of underworld is with all the concrete, fleshy drive of a charging boar. One enters through immediacy.

Evidently, the Graiai's eye and divinatory tooth—that single straight perception—release an animal energy, an instinctual certainty where acting and perceiving are one thrust, like a boar. But it is a dark, underworld perception—a psychic surety—a thrust not into world, but into darkness.

In the Medusa's underworld you can't look at things straight on. If you look at the Medusa, if you let your eyes perceive her, you turn to stone. There are only two things you can do. One, the most well known, is to regard her indirectly—look at the Medusa as a reflection by means of Athena's shield. Now this way of looking is guarded and self-protective, Athena as defense.

We in archetypal psychology have put this defense to good use. We have insisted upon reflection. It is crucial, we say, not to take things straight on literally—events, dreams, emotions, urges—but to reflect them as images. But there are many modes of reflection, none of which is always appropriate. For example, should I reflect with two eyes using Athena's shield while moving like a one-eyed boar, I would be undoing the very image I am in—an image whose instinctual power depends upon a one-eyed thrust, a movement straight into the thing, a master stroke. To hold up Athena's shield of reflection at a time like that would divide me from the pig who is my carrier and whose instinctual consciousness is the way.

Another problem with using Athena's shield to approach the gorgon is that Athena doesn't like gorgons. She gives them place because she's politic and wise, but that doesn't mean she likes them. In fact there are tales that it was she who made the Medusa ugly in the first place. According to one story the Medusa was a pretty girl who happened to be on the wrong side in a battle, and so Athena cursed her. According to another, the Medusa was so beautiful that she rivaled Athena and so was cursed. In yet another the Medusa was once a horse who made love with Poseidon in Athena's temple, and for this sacrilege was cursed.

Athena's origin is also radically different from that of the earth deities; she's a father's daughter who came out of a head, not a womb or the earth. Altogether she has wonderful virtues and powers—a clear-eyed sense of balance, persuasion, politic inclusiveness—and I wouldn't wish to offend her. Still, I'd like to move another way: there's a second story, a variation of the myth in which Perseus uses no shield but averts his face and, letting fortune guide his hand, feels for the head of the Medusa.

Feeling—you *feel* the Medusa. You touch, sense her quality as mistress (her name means "the mistress"). Rather than reflection through distance, the image here is intimate, reflective sensitivity, Athena in the touch—that other Athena, Athena of the crafts, Athena in the hand.

But it's not easy, for the Medusa has long been regarded as an image of horror. The Greeks saw her as terrifying. As we approach the heroic, we experience her as a stopping, static threat. Progress dreads stasis, regards it even as evil. Movement, development, activity appear all for the good, whereas to be stopped is to be afflicted. As of course we all are, and so we dread the Medusa's nature, push it away, dare not touch.

Now Perseus is warned against looking directly at the Medusa, and we learn in the tale of his wily way of indirection. But let us stop and focus on her: why doesn't she want to be looked at directly? Could it be that to look *at* creates a distance that offends her, makes her an object, whereas I become removed, a spectator. To view her as an object creates this chasm between us, she and me, separating me from the depths of my own nature. As she becomes objectified, I become "unnatural" or denatured—that heroic posture we have come to call ego consciousness.

We all know what happens to spectators in myths: Psyche looks into that box and falls down dead, Orpheus loses his bride, Actaeon gets torn to pieces, Pentheus ends up a basket case in his mad mother's lap. And when I look at the mysteries of my nature, objectify them, perceive them as though they were things, concepts: my sexuality, my body, my appetites, my feelings—the moment they become "things" to be worked upon, adjusted, fixed, explained—I've lost them. That's the Medusa's revenge on those who approach her directly. Wham! My sexuality *becomes* a thing, my feelings conceptual, literal—"I'm feeling aggression. I'm getting anxious." My natural appetites and pains become objectified so that I must take care of myself with objects—pills, vitamins, minerals, quantitative exercises, set rules—my nature becomes numbered and inanimate. That is how the Medusa stops us dead. No wonder the Perseus myth is so recurrently valid. He is indeed the culture hero who saves us from this petrified objectivity.

The Medusa can get any of us when we see nature (her nature, my nature) as an objective fact detached from, out of touch with, the inner sensate touch of life. But Perseus finds a way, in that version of the tale I have preferred, through touch. By touching the Medusa's body he traces its stasis, the outlines of its fixity, without distancing himself from it. He acknowledges that nature is as she is, simply there, but he keeps his hands on her and knows her body through his fingertips. He is intimate, concrete, near, abandoning the eye's direct perception of looking at, which makes for distance.

Through touch Perseus gets the Medusa's head, her very essence, and straps it to his back, backs himself with her immobility, her eternal deathlike vision. Thus backed, he is protected from the gorgons. He's protected because he is backed by a vision which sees the immobility, the stasis, the rock in all things. If one can experience the stasis, can back oneself with that vision, then movement is possible, because movement is her nature too, is part of her very image, her eternally writhing hair.

Entering the Medusa's cave is like going into the blocked place, frozen mood, the complex in which nothing moves, the incestuous bind, and then feeling it, feeling it in detail in one's fingers, touching; and in touching, discriminating, getting its head, its essence. Thus backed, movement is there and things animate.

Now Pegasus emerges from the headless body of Medusa: the great winged horse soars out. We have come to our final image—an image of most powerful animation. We mentioned earlier how the Medusa was once herself a horse and in that horse form made love with Poseidon in Athena's temple—for which transgression Athena turned Medusa ugly. Pegasus is the offspring of that temple copulation, so evidently not only was Medusa cursed with ugliness but also Pegasus was caught, imprisoned inside her, locked within her like spirit trapped in matter.

In this case the spirit is an animal, a horse, that energetic beast of civilization, horse power. Could it be that our Athena consciousness, with all its bridling of animals (she invented the bridle) has lost touch with the animal itself? (Her animal, the owl, is seer par excellence, the very organ—eyes—not fit for the Medusa problem.)

In cursing the Medusa for her beastly sexuality, horse-like in the temple, could it be that lower material things, the oldest goddesses (sow, phallic mother, Graiai, the Medusa)—those basest, most basic creatures of the mythic—those who hold and are the secret of stasis and animation—that they likewise have been cursed, lost, frozen, to our perception?

Wings: there are wings on Pegasus. He is wings with the body of a horse. Within the immovable stoniness of Medusa, moving in her depths, we find the power of air, a magnificent horse that carries one with the speed of thought. Here is mind and imagination that is also sinew, flank, muscle and mane. A phallic stallion, a foaling mare rearing into the air. There are wings here beyond the bees and butterflies and little cherubic angels—wings that stomp and snort, that buck and gallop. So within nature's depths, its matter, we find a body of air; within stasis we find movement; in that awe-full image of stopping there is a rush of wings, an animal power in the insubstantial air.

SOUNDINGS
An Interdisciplinary Journal

Winter 1980

M. C. Dillon	Toward a Phenomenology of Love and Sexuality: An Inquiry Into the Limits of the Human Situation As They Condition Loving
C. Eric Lincoln	Beyond *Bakke, Weber* and *Fullilove:* Peace from our Sins. A Commentary on Affirmative Action
Catherine L. Albanese	The Poetics of Healing: Root Metaphors and Rituals in Nineteenth-Century America
Sandra S. Sizer	New Spirit, New Flesh: The Poetics of Nineteenth-Century Mind-Cures
Mitchell Aboulafia	On Lying to the Dying
Paul Sorrentino	God's Cosmic Drama: Christian Tragedy in the Puritan Vision of Life

---

_____Enclosed is $4.00 for the Winter 1980 issue

_____Enclosed is $12.00 for a one-year subscription to begin with above issue

NAME _____

ADDRESS_____

CITY_____STATE_____ZIP_____

Please mail with check or purchase order to **Soundings**, Vanderbilt University, P.O. Box 6309, Station B, Nashville, Tennessee 37235.

THE ACADEMY OF THE DEAD:
On Boredom, Writer's Block, Footnotes and Deadlines

STEPHEN SIMMER
(Syracuse)

The academy is dying. Universities are slashing budgets and cutting back faculty until only a skeleton remains. On graduation Ph.D.s find no teaching jobs and must realistically contemplate an end to their academic lives. They are forced into the underworld of the career ladder, driving taxicabs or taking dictation.

Doomsayers are always right. But the crisis in education may not be destroying scholarship. It may be sending the scholar back to where he came from, reminding him of the origin of his labors. Socrates remarked in the *Phaedo* that the lover of wisdom must willingly learn to die.[1]

Scholarship is always drawn to death. It takes morbid delight in unearthing the rotting fragments of culture. It sets up shop where culture is drained of vitality, broken and forgotten, and practises its necromancy there. Scholarship always makes its stand with one foot in the grave. This is the location of its true tenure—one that promises not security and economic stability, but always teeters dizzily on the verge of darkness.

Boredom

It is popular among educational theorists to view learning as something exciting—a surprise, a peak experience, a creative moment punctuated by an aha! After all, *student* comes from L. *studium*, "zeal," "eagerness." The bobbing of heads in a class does not, however, always indicate that the students are enthusiastically agreeing with what the instructor says. More often it is a sign of a private battle between student and sleep. Class becomes nothing more than a way of killing time.

A void exists in our theories of education, a void that shows itself in students' jokes outside of class. I want to follow this laughter behind the

---

The author is a graduate of the Doctoral Program in Religious Studies at Syracuse University, New York. A companion piece, "The Net of Artemis: Text, Complex," appears in *Dragonflies* 11/2, 1980.

back of scholarship, a laughter which sees scholarship as Freud saw dreams—as a way of protecting sleep.

One of the aims of scholarship is to preserve our cultural inheritance by aiding memory. The student is supposed to experience the joy of remembering the past, but this is rarely the case. More frequently the student learns the joy of blanking out—a state of soul starkly visible in those stares which so much resemble the gaze of the dead before the eyes are closed. Just as the breath-soul cannot be caught at the moment of death, the yawns in the classroom cannot be stifled with the hand.

Does this not imply that the psyche escapes the body not only in death and in dreams but also in study? Socrates, whom we regard as the patriarch of western education, left his audience asleep in the *Symposium*, as if the *telos* of education were sleep.[2] Socrates had a narcotic effect upon his hearers. When the Athenians condemned him to death for corrupting the youth, they may have seen him as a philosophical drug dealer, peddling boredom to the young.

Many are the defenses of Socrates' behavior. Infuriated that their admired teacher should be attacked, Plato and Xenophon sought to clear him of the charge that he corrupted the young. I propose another defense, in which Socrates would face his accusers and declare:

> Yes, I admit my guilt to this charge. But this is what education always aims to do—to corrupt, bore and destroy youth. The education I am speaking of is the care of the soul, not the ego. It serves death, and helps one take his place not in Athens but in the City of Death.[3]

These deadening, boring and morbid elements in education are not accidental, not things that occur only in bad teaching and scholarship. A long and much-neglected tradition connects scholarship to morbidity. Aristotle knew that the greatest of thinkers were melancholic.[4] It is said that Philetas of Cos, one of the early scholars of Alexandria, wore shoes of lead to hold him to the earth,[5] as if scholarship were a leaden ballast weighing down flights of fancy. The symptoms of melancholy may be seen in the various names given to the academies of the Renaissance: they were called the *Idlers*, the *Insipid*, the *Shy*, the *Disheartened*, and the *Stunned*.[6]

Boredom is generally regarded as the great enemy of education. Students are supposed to stay awake, and to keep them awake Latin,

Shakespeare and higher mathematics are banished from the curriculum because they are too dull. In this attempt to make learning fun something is missing.

The Buddhist sees boredom differently. When the student first practices meditation, he expects to achieve something. But he is told to sit and watch his breath until he is bored stiff. The Tibetan master Chögyam Trungpa remarks:

> Boredom is important in meditation practice: it increases the psychological sophistication of the practitioners. They begin to appreciate boredom and they develop their sophistication until the boredom begins to become cool boredom, like a mountain river. It flows and flows, methodically and repetitiously, but it is very cooling, very refreshing.[7]

In watching the breath the attention turns to the flowing of *psyche*, another name for breath, and boredom necessarily accompanies this watching. Though boredom may seem a dismal waste of time to the ego, the soul thirsts for this cool flowing. Boredom sophisticates the psyche, and is therefore an essential educator of the soul.

Etymologically *boredom* has been related to O.E. *bor*, "auger," to L. *foro*, "to bore, pierce," and to Gr. *faraō*, "to plow."[8] The linguistic imagination links boredom to digging, plowing, and burrowing. Scholars may pierce with their insight, sift through data, dig up new material, and break new ground. But they are at the same time bored and boring: moles, bookworms, drudges holed up with books, in a rut, and plowed under with work.

Boredom moves toward depth, a digging like that required in ancient sacrifices to the gods of the underworld.[9] Turning away from nightmarish morbidity back to daydreams and doodling we flee the cold rape of the underworld. With the horror, however, goes a fatal attraction, some mysterious necrophilia which makes us return to what bores us stiff, to what bores us to death. Scholarship is just that instinct which requires us to face the boredom, enter it and be transformed.

The Deadline in Scholarship

Deadlines scare everyone but they scare the scholar most of all. Classes, readings, lectures and gradings are all imposed by the calendar without much room for improvisation. Though deadlines are generally regarded as important because they challenge the ego, they may serve another God than Efficiency.

The deadline does more than just get things done. Each deadline parallels the great Deadline. Deadlines mirror our deadliness, so that the writing of every paper is analogous to the Buddhist practice of meditating in graveyards. In the school term we feel our own termination. As the days pass, Death relentlessly approaches and every instant of experience displays a deadline of its own. Transforming the calendar from a series of homogeneous days into a spiraling descent, the deadline sends us winding on a *nekyia* through the underworld of weeks.

Our own ghost faces us in the deadline. We hear the clank of chains which hinder our writing. The deadline begins to assume stern features, and we are dragged, naked and whining, before the penetrating eyes of the judge. We feel dry, empty, incorrigibly obscure, secretly corrupt. Our foibles take on the deadly weight of necessity and seem inescapable torments. Again and again we come to a dead end. The deadline turns scholarship into an underworld agony, like the mythical punishments in Tartarus: like the Danaids, condemned to carry water in leaky pots, we may read volumes but retain little, or try to contain reality in concepts, but discover that the concepts leak and our work must remain unfulfilled.

Tantalus stands in water to his neck, but when he bends to drink, it disappears. Luscious fruit hovers above him, but he cannot reach it. Like him, the scholar sometimes feels afloat in a sea of information, yet dry within. He sits at a banquet, surrounded with facts and ideas, but cannot take them in and digest them. He becomes drawn to the work of others, tantalized by their seminal insights while his own work remains fruitless.

Ixion saw a cloud which he mistook for the Goddess Hera and tried to assault it. He was punished by being bound to an ever-revolving wheel. Like him we may fall in love with the cloud-forms of ideas but discover unhappily that our syllogisms lack substance. We become bound to reasoning that is circular and which moves us nowhere.

The giant Tityus, a son of the Earth, tried to rape Leto, but her children Apollo and Artemis came to her aid and killed him. As punishment he was pegged down over nine acres and lay helpless while two vultures tore at his liver and heart. The scholar may have passions and gut feelings that are somehow always bound to earth, and every attempt at careful reasoning may seem a violation. He is open, vulnerable, and in touch with his earthiness, but can do nothing with the feelings that devour him. He can't read the significance of his own entrails or translate the gigantic passions into ideas with an Apollonian clarity and detachment.

Sisyphus bound Death's hands so that nothing could die. For this and other crimes he was condemned to push a rock up a hill, but before he could reach the top the rock always slipped and rolled down again. Like him we place high demands on ourselves, and push heroically against our inclinations to get top grades and high recognition. But like the rock we can't stay on top of things and are always falling behind. Our world fills with half-finished projects we can't push to conclusion.

Sometimes the scholar might feel like Pirithous, who was stuck to a rock in the underworld after a futile attempt to rescue Persephone. He may feel fused with his work, unable to distinguish his personal cares from the problems in his scholarship. His subject matter then seems dead weight which he can't bring to life. To change his syntax he must first transform himself, but all his heroic strugglings cannot affect the indifferent obstinacy of his soul.

These are stories of great criminals, those who have overstepped the line. In these cases we can read a background to our horror of overstepping. The deadline poses an underworld of terrors, causing us to trace our mythical lineage to the dead.

We often think of the deadline as a brazen intruder into creativity. There are mysterious rhythms to creation, we say, that shouldn't be violated. But the deadline fulfills a need of the soul—a need not simply for efficiency, but for deepening. If the deadline seems to intrude it is because death always appears this way to the evasive soul. The deadline serves not only to finish a work of scholarship. It puts it into its misery, filling it with a sense of finality.

Writer's Block

We often think of writer's block as an irritating impediment we would like to remove. But perhaps writing needs a block like Sisyphus needs a stone. When Zeus had an affair with Aegina, Sisyphus tattled to her father Asopus. Zeus escaped by changing himself into a large stone, like the one Sisyphus pushes in the underworld. Perhaps a God or Goddess hides in the block and touches our actual words, *mythos* touching *logos*. Perhaps pushing against the block is one of the archetypal labors of the scholarly underworld.

Something bitchy in writing puts its foot down, stamps on the floor and screams No! Eucrates, one of the characters in Lucian's "Lover of Lies," tells of an encounter with the Goddess Hecate. Dogs barked, the earth shook, and a huge woman appeared carrying a torch and a long sword. She had snake feet and snake hair, and resembled a Gorgon.

> Well, at the sight of her I stopped, at the same time turning the gem that the Arab gave me to the inside of my finger, and Hecate, stamping on the ground with her serpent foot, made a tremendous chasm, as deep as Tartarus; then after a little she leaped into it and was gone. I plucked up courage and looked over, taking hold of a tree that grew close by, in order that I might not get a dizzy turn and fall into it headlong. Then I saw everything in Hades, the River of Blazing Fire, and the Lake, and Cerberus, and the dead, well enough to recognize some of them. My father, for instance, I saw distinctly, still wearing the same clothes in which we buried him.[10]

Eucrates stopped when he saw the Goddess: Hecate appears in our stopping. Like a Gorgon she causes a stone-like paralysis. This stopping occurs again in the *Homeric Hymn to Demeter.* When Persephone was abducted by Hades, Hecate and Demeter stopped the horses of Helios to ask him what he had seen.[11] Hecate's image was traditionally placed at crossroads, and she was called *Enodia,* "in the way." She represents the double binds, those points of impossible decision that cause stoppage, always in the way. Her image was also placed beside doorways, and she was often called a keyholder. Facing Hecate is facing a closed door.

Paradoxically Hecate also has something to do with psychic movement. Porphyry calls her the soul of the world responsible for animating all things.[12] Her appearance in a dream symbolizes movement according to Artemidorus.[13] Her madness moves, too: she causes a pathology called *phoitais,* literally "walking."[14] One stricken with this madness often jumps from bed and runs outdoors.[15] She herself was called "night-wandering,"[16] and "changing."[17]

Hecate has many heads on her statues, but how can she mean both stoppage and movement? Perhaps there is action only when there is stoppage. When the writing is not blocked nothing is really moving. There is only the caricature of movement, "busy work." Writing of this kind really evades writing, because the work is without the weight of dilemmas. The block causes profound movement in writing, agitating its depths like Hecate's earthquake.

Socrates said that when his daimon spoke to him it was always a denial.[18] Hecate is called *antais theou,* "antagonistic goddess."[19] She impinges on writing as a daimonic No, ripping it apart with her scream. This No is the cutting edge of writing—Hecate's sword in Eucrates' vision—where the deepening of insight is demanded.

She stomps open the underworld, exposing the dead. This underworld explicates and annotates her great No, revealing a chorus of inhibiting spirits. The block forces a new relation to the limits of will, where will is in relation to daimones, the principles of inhibition. By writing we actually forge ourselves into a new daimonic existence.

Bodhidharma, the first patriarch of Zen Buddhism, taught a meditation called "wall-gazing." It is said he sat before a wall nine years without interruption.[20] The writer needs to practice this kind of vigilance before his block. The block is like the Zen koan that one scrutinizes with all his bones and pores, "making your whole body one great inquiry," as Mumon says.[21]

One of the most important koans is known as Joshu's Mu. The question was posed to Joshu: Does a dog have Buddha nature? He barked, "Mu!" which means No. The riddle is similar to that posed by Hecate, for the baying of dogs always signals her presence.

This dog that barks No is important to writing. It bares its teeth menacingly at all who approach. It protects the individuality and integrity of writing, judging all ideas by scent. It bristles at dishonesty even in impressive garb, but like Odysseus' dog Argus it can recognize the master even when disguised in rags.

Dogs strain at the leash, yanking their masters along. Like Hecate they are *admētē*, "untamed."[22] The No rejects the expected directions and urges the writing toward wildness. Nose to the ground, it leads the hunt of our writing, furiously hounding the trail of blood, driving the quarry to cling terrified to a tree, the dogs baying beneath.

Studying a koan is like hanging over a vast abyss, according to Hakuin. But while Eucrates held tight to a tree over the raging underworld, the barrier of the koan is broken only when the hands are suddenly released and we plunge feet-first into the No, following Hecate. Those who have not passed the barrier of the Mu koan are phantoms haunting trees, according to Mumon.[23] When we leave the detachment and woodenness of the ego and jump into the No, writing becomes a dogfight with the daimones. But it has bite and blood and fury, and movement begins again.

STEPHEN SIMMER

An Imaginal Sociology of Education

In one of his many satires set in the underworld Lucian tells of a great battle between the blessed and the damned. Socrates, who usually found a safe hiding place during these disturbances, fought bravely. As a reward the blessed gave him a park in the underworld where he founded *Nekrade mia*, the Academy of the Dead.[24] This academy had apparently been projected for several centuries, no doubt with planning commissions and fund-raising drives. In Plato's *Apology* Socrates had mused:

> What would not a man give if he might converse with Orpheus and Musaeus and Hesiod and Homer? Nay, if this be true, let me die again and again.[25]

We usually regard the social milieu of education as literalist and humanist—with teachers, students, seminars, and faculty meetings. The newly developed field of the sociology of knowledge begins with this common-sense view. It assumes that all knowledge is the result of human social interaction.[26] This view misses much of the sociological and psychological richness of education. Especially it misses the pathology. We need to turn attention to Socrates' park in the underworld, the academy where the ghosts argue. This academy presents an imaginal sociology of education. It has a long tradition. Socrates spoke of a daimon which inhibited him at times,[27] and this notion was developed by Plato and others into the idea of a personal spirit with an educational function.[28] The Latin notion of the *genius,* originally the generating spirit for each family, was amalgamated with the Greek idea of the *daimon* by the second century.[29] Ammianus Marcellinus suggested that the great man received instruction from the genius.[30] Augustine spoke of Christ as the guardian truth within the mind which is the real teacher, and which aids us in judging the truth of the words spoken by the merely human teachers.[31] Petrarch also spoke of the "silent master within" who was the teacher of the great man, and suggested that this master was Christ.[32] Nietzsche too regarded his major teachers as imaginal beings, and listed them as Epicurus, Montaigne, Goethe, Spinoza, Plato, Rousseau, Pascal, and Schopenhauer.[33] Even Freud's notion of the superego may be regarded as an internalization of the figure of the educator,[34] an exacting "teacher within" which judges and punishes.

Books prey on our minds. Most that we read we easily forget. But some refuse to be buried. We can't put them down, even when we are done reading. They pop into our minds at night and stay too long, like guests. They pursue us into the marketplace of our lives and pester us there. They shout, "Remember me!"[35] like the ghost of Hamlet's father.

To gain some peace we soon turn and argue with them. Strangely we hear arguments in return, patiently developed with admirable pedagogy. We imagine we are talking to the authors—Freud, Plato, Emerson—and one day we meet an author with whom (in imagination) we have been speaking for years. Dismayed we think: "*This* cannot be the author—this old fool, this pedant, this fuzzy-headed drunk!" We conclude that this person who claims to be the author is an imposter, and return to our imaginal dialogue with the *real* author.

We experience the ideas that grip us as fictional characters in dialogue. They are not faculty in a university, they are faculties of the soul. As readers we were right. The author of the book is not this meek person. For his book, too, was written through his own internal dialogue, his own imaginal faculty meeting. Any author writes fiction when he places his name on the cover. The real authors are under cover—the invisible daimones refuse to be forgotten.

In the Homeric view of the psyche, experience was viewed as permeable, subject to possession at any moment by a daimon.[36] Any violent emotion—fear, anger, love, envy—was seen as daimonic possession. All sorts of characters wait in the darkened wings of the soul and may enter the stage of experience at any moment. The soul is fundamentally sociological—not an individual self, but a dialogue of daimones.

At the same time, social relationships are imaginal. They are not just encounters between egos. They provide occasions for dramatic struggles between daimones. Jung and Freud, Socrates and Plato and Aristotle continue to enact their conflicts through our interactions with other persons.

Let's suppose Dr. Orin Underwood is answering questions from the floor in a review session on Socrates. In teaching effectively he is no longer simply Dr. Underwood. He becomes a spokesman for a tradition. In answering a question he cannot simply search through his memory for the answer Socrates gave. That would lead merely to "right opinion," as Socrates would say. To keep Socrates from slipping away he must give a "Socratic answer." This requires dramatic skill. If he plays the role well he disappears and Socrates comes alive in the classroom speaking to (the imagined) Phaedruses and Menos. Socrates is the real teacher. Not the literal Socrates; the famous syllogism concludes that Socrates the man is mortal. But as he argued vehemently in the *Phaedo* and *Apology*, Socrates the soul continues to live. "Think of the truth, not of Socrates."[37] We can find his immortality in the restless search for knowledge, in the daimon which inhibited him and goaded him to truth. This search for truth existed before and after the life of Socrates the man. "Socrates" is a fiction, as for Plato and Lucian. We use his name to designate a sly, contentious spirit that still haunts our streets.

We often think of culture as the object of scholarship—a passive body of data on which we operate. But culture plays a more active and intimate role in scholarship. In antiquity when the sacrifice for Hecate and the ghosts had been prepared, one walked away without looking back.[38] The daimones sneak up behind experience. They are not static data, but rather *a priori* forces which pursue us to study. In an oracle Hecate asserts, "I dwell behind the Father's thoughts, I, the Soul, who with heat, do ensoul all things."[39] To imagine Hecate and her company of ghosts we must reflect psychologically on what dwells behind the thinking. Culture possesses the scholar, so that his work on culture is really culture's work on itself. The scholar is the occasion for a dialogue of culture with itself, daimon with daimon.

Hecate and the Footnote

> As the dead prey upon us
> they are the dead in ourselves,
> awake, my sleeping ones, I cry out to you,
> disentangle the nets of being!
> Charles Olson

Why do scholars footnote with such ritual precision? We devote scrupulous attention to that demanding mistress Kate Turabian, whose *Manual for Writers* is in its fourth edition. But like the sacrificers to Hecate—that other Kate—we walk away without looking back. What daimon lies behind this compulsion?

When we footnote we imagine in a unique dialect. Like linguists we need first to locate this dialect in its mythic landscape. On the page footnotes sometimes hover just below the line, as if the page portrayed a cosmos divided into upper and lower worlds. Sometimes they gather after the end of the text, part of the eschatological fantasy of what comes after endings. In either case they are dominated by principles different from the prose text. What are these underworld, eschatological principles of the footnote?

The text in any essay unfolds in a linear progression, characterized by what Northrop Frye calls the "rhythm of continuity" of prose.[40] Like the ego the essay has a coherent identity and follows a continuous path with a beginning, middle, and end. Footnotes can't be read continuously. They seem to be a heap of comments and references without direction or coherence. Piled vertically, the footnotes are outside linear, horizontal time. They suggest the dimension of depth.

Prosaic thinking does not proceed straightforwardly despite one's intentions. It runs into crossroads, alternate directions in thinking, crosses the path of another, crosses one's own path. We place footnotes at these crossroads: the content footnote, the reference footnote, and the cross-reference footnote.[41] We even use a pictography of crossing to designate a footnote, the asterisk and the dagger.

The Content Footnote—We use the content footnote when we can't contain our thinking in the prose line. One path just won't do. The content footnotes make reading a journey through a labyrinth, where "time forks perpetually toward innumerable futures,"[42] as Borges writes in his story "The Garden of Forking Paths." This story tells of a man who had written a book and built a labyrinth. "Everyone imagined two works; to no one did it occur that the book and the maze were one and the same thing."[43]

In ancient Greece and Rome the Goddess of the crossroads was Hecate, having the epiphets of *Trioditis* and *Trivia*, "at the meeting of three roads." As we have seen she led the restless ghosts that haunted the crossroads. To propitiate Hecate and her entourage, meals were left at the crossroads at the end of each month in an offering called *deipna Hecatès*, "Hecate's suppers."[44] Left at the crossroads were *kaktharmata*, literally "garbage," the leftovers from the sacrifices performed inside the house.[45] In the content footnote we find a dump site for our intellectual garbage—the trivia and leftovers the essay can't digest.

Hecate, according to the mythographer Fulgentius, is derived from the Greek *hekaton*, "hundred,"[46] also used loosely to mean simply "many." Whereas the prose essay is single-minded in its direction, content footnotes go many ways. Hecate was often portrayed in statues with three or four heads looking different directions. So important was this multiple character of Hecate that Artemidorus called it bad luck to dream of her with only one head.[47] She was described as *triglēna*[48] and *polyglēna*[49], "three-eyed" and "many-eyed." Footnotes present a many-sided vision, an irreducible congregation of ideas and references: "*Ō Katē plētheus*": "O Hecate! what a crowd!"[50]

Like Hecate footnotes are often obscure.[51] When they qualify the argument in the essay they are, like Hecate, *antaia*,[52] "opposed, hostile," representing hateful complications to the flow of the prose. They shed light on the essay, but the light is often, like Hecate, *hypolampteira*,[53] "shining under," a glimmer from below as if caused by the many torches Hecate carries. The illuminations magnify the many shadows of the argument, casting it in a more uncertain light.

The Reference Footnote—On first glance, the reference footnote seems simply to give credit to the originator of an idea. But ideas are not like veins of ore that wait passively to be discovered. Ideas are active, powerful, and autonomous. They, not the writers, create the work. The ideas may achieve momentary expression in the scholar's work, but they lived before and continue to live after the date of publication. To attach a name, date, and publisher to an idea seems arbitrary and presumptuous, because ideas are daimones that we serve.

So why footnote? Perhaps we are mistaken if we understand them as referring to a particular work by a historical person. The daimones of the great ideas haunt the page, drawn to the discourse as the dead were drawn to Odysseus' basin of blood. These dead are *eidola*, "images," and the names we give them—"Plato," "Montaigne," "Nietzsche"—should be regarded as images as well. Footnoting is an imaginal naming of the daimones. But what is the character of this imagery?

In the Homeric Hymn to Demeter no one would tell Demeter what had happened to her daughter. Finally Hecate came with accurate news *(angeleousa)*.[54] Bearing news was part of Hecate's nature. She was called *Angelos*,[55] a name also applied to Hermes. But while Hermes was often called "luck-bringing messenger,"[56] the *Hymn* tells us that the message delivered by Hecate concerns what "grieves the heart," *(ekakhe thymos)*[57a]. This very un-Hermetic type of message is typical of Hecate, for she is frequently associated with suffering and terrors. For Hecate pain is a message, full of meaning. When Hecate asks Demeter who stole

Persephone and grieves her heart, she asks Demeter to reflect on the image the agony bears. By asking the question "who?" Hecate is asking Demeter to personify her emptiness and loss, to imagine the daimon which is active in the heart's grief. Personifying what grieves the heart allows one to gain distance from it, and immediately after asking her question Hecate rushes with Demeter to Helios, the sun, who is called *skopon,* "spectator" of gods and men.[57b] Hecate's question provokes a reflective observing, so that the grief and emptiness may be observed mythically as personified image. This distancing that she enables is reflected in the most common etymology given for her name—from *hekatos,* "the distant one."

Like Hecate, the reference footnote poses the question "who?" and may be seen as a reflection on the guilt, inferiorities, and anxieties of the heart, a personifying of the daimones that haunt thinking and writing. Footnotes offer an imaginal language for the differentiation of the daimones which plague us and stand in our way. They "disentangle the nets of being," as Charles Olson says in the passage above.

Hecate rules the underworld.[58] This may be understood not just in the ancient sense of "Hades," but in terms of our own common use of the term "underworld" as well—the world of thieves, murderers, and derelicts. Hecate herself was a thief, having stolen from Hera.[59] Heckenbach connects her with crime when he suggests that the fear of highwaymen was the impulse behind her epithet of *Enodia,*[60] "of the path." Plato suggested that murderers be slain at places where three roads meet, sacred to Hecate.[61] And criminals were punished on a beam called *hekatè.*[62] Furthermore, although it was considered a sacrilege to touch the sacrifices left at the crossroads for Hecate, thieves and the poor often did.[63] The criminal sacrilege must have eventually become an expected part of the ceremony.[64] Crime seems sacred to Hecate: she was called *paranomos,* "contrary to law."[65]

Reference footnotes are a criminal record. In them we confess our guilt to crimes of theft, fraud, extortion and murder. We admit the poverty and dishonesty of our own insight; little or nothing of what we say really belongs to us. In footnotes we are revealed like a criminal in the stocks, with our crimes displayed below for all to see. "I have pillaged the grave of Plato, I have stolen from Emerson, I have maimed and slaughtered Freud, and you can see for yourself how wretchedly I have wronged them." Hecate was a goddess of revenge,[66] and the reference footnote signals that this vengeance has been exacted. The author cries out with Robert Burton, "that which I have I have stolen from others...[next, quoting Martial] My page cries out to me, You are a thief."[67]

The term "bitch" might be applied to Hecate in every sense of that term. As we have seen, dogs were sacred to her, and appeared in dog form. There is something doglike in scholarship, as if *school* had to do with *skylax*, "dog." Dogs are always digging up bones and corpses, just as scholars are always digging up the past, unearthing facts, preoccupied with the rotting corpse of culture.

William Empson says that the word *dog* "reaches across to something deep, personal to you, and despised."[68] This describes the "bitchiness" of Hecate—her spiteful, vengeful character. She was called *ekhthrè*, "hostile,"[69] and one of her ceremonies was named *oxythumia*, "sudden anger."[70] The school of philosophy named after dogs, the Cynics (from Gr. *kyòn*, "dog"), assailed its culture for foolishness and self-indulgence. When it is cynical, biting, critical, and pedantic—when it "has a bone to pick"—scholarship serves Hecate.

Hecate is "bitch" not just because she is doglike and spiteful, but because she is whorish. Unlike Persephone, with whom she is closely related, Hecate is never virginal. On the contrary, Posidonius lists her as an orgiastic deity,[71] and in Thera she was worshipped with Priapus, whose penis was always erect.[72] Kerényi calls her crassly sexual and associates her with the ithyphallic Hermes.[73] Sappho referred to her as "Aphrodite's golden-shining handmaid,"[74] and in Zerynthia she was identified with Aphrodite.[75] She had magic which attracted lovers.[76] She was even identified with Baubo, who made the grieving Demeter laugh by raising her skirts and exposing her vulva in an obscene dance.[77]

Meister Eckhart offers a psychological interpretation of virginity as the condition of being void of alien and vile images.[78] In contrast Hecate's nature may be characterized as a fullness of alien, crass imagery, a perpetual contamination with the seeds of the underworld. Scholarship is never virginal, its territory is never pristine. It has "been the rounds," has been tramped over and over. When it footnotes scholarship exposes its whorish fecundity like Baubo, its contamination with all sorts of extraneous ideas, its susceptibility to a promiscuous passion for the underworldly—always open to penetration from below.

When Hecate appeared to Jason in Apollonius' *Argonautica* the sound of footsteps was heard and the earth shook.[79] In the passage from the "Lover of Lies" quoted above, Lucian says that Hecate stamped open the underworld. Elsewhere Hecate is called *phoinikopeza parthenos*,[80] "maid with red feet," because her feet were covered with the blood of corpses.[81]

In footnoting we notice by the feet. We are always stepping on graves, opening the horrors of the underworld like Hecate. Scholarship always has one foot in the grave, covered with the gore of corpses, tyrannized by what Harold Bloom calls the "anxiety of influence."[82] The great works of tradition "engross, prejudice, and intimidate,"[83] as Edward Young says. And the situation is dramatized in Lucian's dialogue "The Dead Come to Life," where the protagonist is pursued by the ghosts of the philosophers—Plato, Socrates, Aristotle, Epicurus, and Diogenes—for abusing their teachings.[84]

We are told that Hecate's mysteries at Aegina were founded by the poet Orpheus.[85] The mysteries of the footnote are poetic mysteries. The reference footnotes poetically name the imaginal characters who speak, listen, argue, and evaluate in the dialogue which lies behind the essay. We can read reference footnotes as a playbill and stage directions for the drama of scholarship. Enter Plato, with trumpets.

Seen through the footnotes the essay is a dialogue of the dead. The thought appropriated as the author's own in the text above the line may be re-imagined from below as a collaboration of ghost-writers, each placing his own demand on the work. Scholarship is *daimonic* in its original meaning of "divided."[86] This multiple authorship is what legitimates the grammatical use of the fimst person plural in scholarly writing; it is *we* not *I* who speak.

The work consumes the writer in its own daimonic process of creation. This process may be regarded as a *Deipnosophistai*, a "Learned Banquet" or "Doctors at Dinner"—the title of a symposium by Athenaeus where the learned converse at length over a meal.

A *skolion* was an ancient kind of drinking song sung at banquets. One guest would sing a line, then pass the laurel bough to another, who was required to continue. The song got its name, according to some sources,[87] because of the crooked (*skolios*) course of the branch as it was passed through the group. Scholarship is a *skolion*, a drunken, crooked song sung by many guests. It is a symposium (literally a "drinking party") like Agathon's feast in Plato's *Symposium*. The experience of the individual scholar becomes transformed in the symposium of his work. His personal bitterness and plaintiveness is turned to wine, which draws the dead to drink and sing.

> Among the beams of the dark belfries let
> yourself ring out. What feeds on you
>
> will grow strong upon this nourishment.
> Be conversant with transformation.
> From what experience have you suffered most?
> Is drinking bitter to you, turn to wine.
>
> Be, in this immeasurable night,
> magic power at your senses' crossroad,
> be the meaning of their strange encounter.[88]

1. Plato, *Phaedo*, 64a.
2. *Symposium*, 223 b-d.
3. This imagined defense is not really so far-fetched. It is a paraphrase of Socrates' arguments in the *Phaedo*, Plato's second, more esoteric defense which must be placed alongside the public arguments of the *Apology*.
4. Aristotle, *Problemata* 30. 953a.
5. John Edwin Sandys, *A History of Classical Scholarship* (3rd ed., Cambridge, 1921), I, p. 118.
6. John Sandys, *Harvard Lectures on the Revival of Learning* (Cambridge, 1905), p. 86.
7. Chogyam Trungpa, *The Myth of Freedom*, ed. by John Baker and Marvin Casper (Berkeley and London: Shambala, 1976), p. 54.
8. Eric Partridge, "bore," *Origins*, 4th ed., 1977, p. 54.
9. Jane Ellen Harrison, *Prolegomena to the Study of Greek Religion* (2nd ed., Cambridge, 1908), pp. 8-12, 55-65; Erwin Rohde, *Psyche: The Cult of Souls and Belief in Immortality Among the Greeks*, trans. W.B. Hillis (London: Routledge, Kegan Paul, 1950), p. 116.
10. Lucian, *Philops.* 22—24. Trans. A.M. Harmon, *Lucian* III, Loeb Classical Library (London, 1921), pp. 355-357.
11. *Homeric Hymn to Demeter*, 59ff. The two goddesses may be regarded as almost identical at this point in the story. Cf. C. Kerényi, "Kore," in *Essays on a Science of Mythology* (with C.G. Jung) (Princeton, 1969), p. 110.
12. Augustine, *Sermons* 241. 7.
13. Artemidorus, *Oneirocriticon* 2. 37.
14. Euripides, *Hip.* 141.
15. Hippocrates, *Morb. sac.* 4. 30.
16. Apol. Rh., 4. 829; Euripides, *Ion* 1048-1049.
17. She was called *aiolomorphos: Orph. Arg.*, 975.
18. *Apology*, 91d; *Phaedrus*, 242c.
19. Sophocles, fr. 311.
20. Heinrich Dumoulin, *A History of Zen Buddhism* (Boston: Beacon, 1969), p. 71.
21. Zenkei Shibayama, *Zen Comments on the Mumonkan*, trans. Sumiko Kudo (New York: New American Library, 1974), p. 19.

THE ACADEMY OF THE DEAD

22 Abel, *Voc. h. mag.*, 3. 3.
23 Shibayama, *Mumonkan*, p. 19.
24 Lucian, *Verae Historiae*, 2. 23.
25 *Apology*, 41a, trans. Jowett, *Dialogues of Plato* (New York: Random House, 1937), I, p. 422.
26 Peter Berger and Thomas Luckman, *The Social Construction of Reality* (Garden City: Doubleday, 1966), Robert Merton, *Social Theory and Social Structures* (Chicago: Free Press, 1957).
27 *Apology*, 91d; *Phaedrus*, 242c.
28 For Plato's idea of the daimon and its importance in education, see Paul Friedländer, *Plato: An Introduction*, trans. Hans Meyerhoff (Princeton, 1973), p. 36.
29 For the development of the Latin notion of the genius, see Jane Chance Nitzsche, *The Genius Figure in Antiquity and the Middle Ages* (Columbia University Press, 1975), pp. 7-41.
30 Ammianus Marcellinus 21. 5.
31 Augustine, *De Magistro*, 11. Cf. *Soliloquies*, 1.1.1.
32 Petrarch, *Four Dialogues for Scholars*, trans. Conrad H. Rawski (Cleveland: Western Reserve University, 1967), p. 59.
33 Nietzsche, *The Portable Nietzsche*, trans. Walter Kaufmann (New York: Viking, 1964), p. 67.
34 Sigmund Freud, *Moses and Monotheism*, trans. Katherine Jones (New York: Vintage, 1939), p. 149.
35 *Hamlet*, I. 5. 91.
36 E.R. Dodds, *The Greeks and the Irrational* (University of California Press, 1968), pp. 10-14.
37 *Phaedo*, 91c.
38 Aeschylus, *Choeph.* 98, and *Schol.*
39 Proclus, *In Tim.* 11.16.22, trans. in Hans Lewy, *Chaldaean Oracles and Theurgy* (LeCaire: Institut Francais d'Archeologie Orientale, 1956), p. 45.
40 Northrop Frye, *Anatomy of Criticism* (Princeton University Press, 1973), p. 263.
41 Since the cross-reference footnote is really a special case of the reference footnote, it will not be treated separately here.
42 Jorge Luis Borges, "The Garden of Forking Paths," *Labyrinths*, ed. Donald A. Yates and James E. Irby (New York: New Directions, 1964), p. 28.
43 *Ibid.*, p. 25.
44 Kirby Flower Smith, "Hecate's Suppers," *Encyclopedia of Religion and Ethnics*, VI, pp. 565-567.
45 Rohde, *Psyche*, p. 325, n. 104.
46 Fulgentius, *Myth.*, 10.
47 Artemidorus, *Oneirocriticon* 2. 37.
48 Athenaeus, *Deiphosophists* 325a.
49 Phot., *Lex.*, *Triglina*.
50 Callimachus, *Iamboi* 1. 99, in *Callimachus and Lychophron*, trans. A.W. Mair, Loeb Classical Library (London, 1921) p. 273. According to the reconstruction by Mair, this fragment exclaims over the many dead Charon must ferry over Acheron, p. 273.
51 Hecate is called *Skotia*, "black," "unclear," Diodorus Siculus, 1. 96; PGM 4. 2338.
52 Sophocles, fr. 335.
53 *Schol. Apollonius Rhodius*, 3. 861.
54 *Homeric Hymn to Demeter*, 40-58.
55 Sophron, in *Schol. Theocritus*, 2. 12.
56 Homer, *Odyssey* 5. 29; *Homeric Hymn to Hermes*, 3.
57a *Homeric Hymn to Demeter*, 56.
57b *Ibid.*, 62.
58 She is called *nerteron prytanis*, "ruler of the netherworld," *Schol. Theocritus*, 2. 12. In Vergil, *Aeneid* 6. 118, 564, Hecate put the Sibyl in charge of the underworld.

59. Sophron, in *Schol. Theocritus*, 2. 12.
60. Heckenbach, "Hekate," PW VII, p. 2775.
61. Plato, *Leges*, ix. 873b.
62. Hesychius, *hekate*
63. Smith, "Hecate's Suppers," p. 566-567.
64. Apologies to Kafka: "Leopards break into the temple and drink to the dregs what is in the sacrificial pitchers; this is repeated over and over again; finally it can be calculated in advance, and it becomes a part of the ceremony." *Parables and Paradoxes* (New York: Schocken, 1958), p. 93.
65. Diodorus Siculus, 4. 45. 2.
66. Steuding, "Hekate," p. 1893.
67. Burton, *Anatomy of Melancholy*, p. 22.
68. William Empson, *The Structure of Complex Words* (Norfolk, Conn.: New Directions, 1951), p. 164.
69. *PLG* 3.4.
70. Smith, "Hecate's Suppers," p. 566.
71. Strabo, 468.
72. Steuding, "Hekate," p. 1886.
73. C. Kerényi, *Hermes, Guide of Souls*, trans. Murray Stein (Spring Publications, 1976), p. 65.
74. Sappho, fr. 24.
75. Theodore Kraus, *Hekate* (Heidelberg: Carl Winter, 1960), pp. 63f.
76. Theocritus, *Idylls* 2. 10-16.
77. Rohde, *Psyche*, p. 591.
78. Franz Pfeiffer, *Meister Eckhart*, trans. C. de B. Evans (London: Watkins, 1924), p. 35.
79. Apollonius Rhodius, *Argonautica* 3. 1039, 1218.
80. Pindar, *Paean* 2. 77-78.
81. In an invocation to Hecate recorded by Hippolytus (*Refutatio omnium Haeresium*, 4. 35), Hecate is described as wading through corpses, thirsting for blood.
82. Harold Bloom, *The Anxiety of Influence* (Oxford University Press, 1973).
83. Edward Young, "Conjectures on Original Composition," in *Criticism: Twenty Major Statements*, ed. Charles Kaplan (San Francisco: Chandler), p. 215.
84. Lucian, *Nec.*
85. Pausanias, 2. 30.2.
86. The most common etymology of *daimon* is from *daio*, "to divide."
87. *Schol. Plat. Grg.*, 451e. Plutarch, *Quaest. conv.* 1. 1. 5. *Schol. Aristophanes Vesp.*, 1222. These and other sources relating to the origin of the term *skolion* are collected by J.M. Edmonds, *Lyra Graeca*, III (London and New York, 1927), pp. 548-561.
88. Rainer Maria Rilke, *Sonnets to Orpheus*, II, 29, trans. M.D. Herter Norton (New York: W.W. Norton, 1962), p. 127.

SIX APPROACHES TO THE IMAGE IN ART THERAPY

MARY M. WATKINS
(Belmont, Mass.)

To my dismay, I have painfully discovered that there is no natural kinship among psychotherapists who depend on images for their theories or therapeutic technique. No number of annual meetings, foundings of new journals, societies or departments based on the image will create such a kinship. Use of the image does *not* form family ties among such diverse orientations as behavior therapy, Jungian therapy, guided daydream therapy, psychosynthesis, psychodrama, Freudian therapy, gestalt therapy. Nor does the explicit founding of a single kind of therapy (for instance, art therapy or sand play therapy) coalesce its group of practitioners. *Within* it there will be radical differences in the approach to the imaginal.

Let us look beneath the disguise of family resemblances, and list a number of theoretical allegiances one may serve in so-called "working with the image." Though these distinctions can be used whether we work with our own images or dream and fantasy images of patients, we will choose the images in art therapy as an illustration. Each of the six approaches to the image I shall describe has its own history (Watkins, 1976). Here, however, our concern will be with how these approaches negate, limit, or nurture one's relation to the imaginal. My allegiance is clearly with ways of relating to images that allow *them* to teach both patient and therapist the depth of meanings—historical, existential, mythical and poetic—lived by the patient.

ONE. We begin with what we shall call the *diagnostic approach*. Here the image is not evoked for the purpose of the patient's insight, or from any notion that the experience of an image is beneficial in a direct way. The image is evoked by the clinician for his own understanding and is

---

This paper both condenses and expands an address given in April, 1980 to the annual meeting of the New England Association of Art Therapists in Cambridge, Mass. Mary Watkins is the author of a classic study, *Waking Dreams*. She is a practising psychotherapist in Boston.

elicited often before the beginning of treatment or when treatment has gone awry. But it is not felt to be part of treatment. The power of art to express psychodynamic issues and developmental level is so well accepted that using pictures to diagnose and form a treatment plan has been virtually coopted by the psychological tester in her Draw-a-Person tests, Kinetic Family Drawings, tree drawings, etc. When art's contribution is narrowed to diagnosis, the art therapy room is drained of much of its vitality. There is little interaction with the patient around the drawings. The paintings are confiscated by the art therapist for analysis. Though the insights derived find their way into the psychologists' diagnostic reports, the images are discarded. The rhetoric of clinical reports has largely banished the language of images, for fear of fostering that culprit of pathology: so-called primary process, mythical or primitive thought. Roy Schafer (1976, pp. 168, 175) is the border guard here, arguing that through our metaphors and images

> ...we introduce primary process modes of thought into systematic thinking, and so, as we do in the spooky theory of introjects, we contaminate the explanation with what is to be explained.
>
> A soulful language cannot help us understand all we wish to understand about "soul," "soulfulness," and, in Schreber's phrase, "soul-murder"...

As the language of image is "raised" to the level of abstract thought, the precision of the image is lost. The image of dry, wintry bleakness, of a tree without leaves in a barren landscape, and the image of a dark, rough sea with growing storm clouds of purple and gray are homogenized when "depression" is the insight digested from these startlingly different pictures.

Unfortunately Jungians too betray the image through their own brand of diagnostic reductionism. Here radically different images are subsumed under a single category—whether "anima," "negative mother," "shadow," etc. Once adopted these terms too erase the particularity of the image artistic effort has been at pains to present.

Given the richness of her medium and the sensitivity of her eye, the art therapist may understand the patient more subtly than the psychologist or the psychiatrist. But as long as diagnosis is the aim, the possibility of working therapeutically through the medium of art is minimized. Where diagnosis is the prime concern, artistic productions fall prey as utterances and interactions to a point of view which assesses weaknesses and not strengths. The image merely expresses symptoms, deficits, and madness in one guise or another. The image can only be evidence to support one theoretical construct rather than another, one characterization of development over another. The particularity of the image is not allowed to create its own phenomenology of the patient's world, or to suggest a possible development inherent in its own structure. When this is the case (and I would argue that much of the art-therapy literature deals with this diagnostic concern), art therapy has betrayed itself by letting its diagnostic efficacy be the only avenue to respectability within the psychiatric hierarchy. When one focuses on how art can be *used* in diagnosis or to evaluate developmental phase, one obscures how art itself can aid development (not just assess it), how it can create conceptualizations (not be reduced to them), can form the substance of therapy (not only pave the way for it or be adjunct to it). Too often our intellectual curiosity sharpens our diagnostic skills and diverts us from therapy, so that as the patient passes through the hospital, special school or residence she is diagnosed by everyone and treated by no one. For all its value the focus on diagnosis can create a distance between art therapist and patient that precludes direct and prolonged involvement with the disturbing images that often arise during a period of crisis. The reasons such distance may be preferred (or unwittingly encouraged) are indeed complicated. But one contributor—an essentially negative view of images and of the "unconscious"—leads us to a second basic approach to the imaginal.

TWO. This second point of view envisions the unconscious and its products as *dangerous*. Asking patients to open themselves to the imaginal level of experience is tantamount to offering a system of delusions, encouraging a schizophrenic break, aligning therapy with the worst and weakest in the patient rather than with ego strengths and defenses. The lines in this war of theories are clearly drawn. In some settings, a blatant feeling of the irrelevancy of a patient's images disguises a deeper fear surrounding the imaginal. If the images can be kept in the basement, so much the better. If medication is needed to achieve this, it is given without question. If art is included at all in places taking this attitude, it is merely occupational, like playing bridge or shop work—something to keep the patients busy, to keep their minds *off* the images which distress and disturb. Crafts or representational art may be emphasized, but not art that reaches toward fantasy. More often it is not given a place. This position is easy for us to fight. Most of us would deny any relation to it. But no sooner do we congratulate ourselves, than its close relatives arrive at our door claiming our kinship after all.

Art-therapy books are full of cautions against the use of art therapy for various kinds of people—usually those most disturbed by their imagery. In these cases, art is given credit only for evoking imagery in a person already overwhelmed with it, rather than credit for the boundedness that expression of an image through a concrete medium can give. Art demands an alertness, an activeness, an attention to materials and to aesthetic concerns.

In the second view, images are conceived as positive in most cases, but as negative when the boundaries between real and imaginary, between conscious and unconscious are considered too permeable. On that border are those clients who are often the ones struggling hardest with images. It is quite a trick to practice therapy while pretending you can steer persons away from the very images that most preoccupy. With more disturbed patients we need to recognize where our hesitations to work with images come from to gauge if we believe involvement with their most disturbing images would be "overwhelming" for *them*, or because *we* are not sure how to receive them, and help patients work with them.

"Being overwhelmed" is itself an experience which comes in different images: being raped, tidal waves, drowning, quicksand, dissolving. The one being overwhelmed, while most often painted as an innocent victim of alien malevolence, can also take many faces: denying fighter, passive limp surrenderer, bitter vitriolic victim, etc. In image-work when a person enters into the experience of "*being* overwhelmed," we want not to stop images but to find the one which gives *form* even to this experience. Whom do they feel like? Who do they imagine me as: malevolent overwhelmer? withholder of salvation? anxious mother rushing to protect? What image precisely expresses the particularity of this psychological experience? (The fact of making the image precise can make it less overwhelming.) There are practical ways to help people feel safer working with images, but these should not replace an attempt to make imaginal whatever experience tends to disrupt the work.

You can remind the patient that she can always put the image-work aside for a while, suggest media that give expression to the image so that it is both externalized and communicable (painting, writing out dialogues with characters, etc.), or limit the time spent on such work at a sitting. For some people these bounds can make the experience feel safer, while still allowing the person access to her own experience. Again, though, one needs to work with the images around "unsafeness" and "safeness." We mustn't rush to reassure when we are not at all clear about the psychic landscape that has given rise to these terms.

THREE. Here the imaginal is recognized and encouraged to come into the clinic or special school for the sake of *treatment*. Notice that the image is beckoned in order that *it* may undergo therapy. The image does not heal; we heal the image. The art therapist suggests another color to the child than the black he has used for the last four pictures. One gives less attention to pictures with disturbing imagery and prefers to concentrate on ones that express so-called 'ego-strength,' or one emphasizes what is considered to be 'positive' in the picture (the green bud, the emerging light, the centeredness, the balance of opposites, etc.). For instance, in Edith Kramer's classic book, *Art As Therapy With Children* (1971), a picture of a giant (which actually expressed more of the child's impotence and emptiness than his ego-strength) was placed rather quickly into a drawer until the child, Kenneth, could one day give the giant the strength usually expected from such beings.

Let us not turn aside from Kenneth's giant (see Picture 1).

> Kenneth: Kenneth, a six-year-old abandoned child who had knocked about in many foster homes, was much given to grandiose fantasies that consoled him in his isolation and helplessness. One day he wanted to paint a picture of a giant 'as tall as the art room'. He climbed a high closet from which he could reach the ceiling and measured out a long strip of brown wrapping paper reaching from there to the floor. While he was measuring, Kenneth declared that he wanted all the colors because the giant would be very beautiful.... He chose black crayon and at the top of the paper drew a life-sized head with faint features. Then he drew two lines reaching from the head down to the bottom of the paper, representing legs and body at once. In the middle of this configuration he placed a small rectangle—the 'penis'—above it a tiny circle—'the bellybutton.' That was all. I asked Kenneth if the giant would have arms. Kenneth did not respond. I offered him a tray full of 'all the colors'; he did not take them. There was a moment of sadness. Both Kenneth and I knew that there was nothing we could do. To urge him on would only have deepened his sense of defeat. We rolled the paper up and put it away with Kenneth's other work. Maybe a time would come when he would have the inner strength to paint it.
>
> Kramer, 1971: pp.29-30.

Kramer realizes that this giant expresses much of what Kenneth feels—a creature created to be powerful but who is unable to fulfill this role. It shows how Kenneth may experience a split between whom he is supposed or wants to be and how he feels inside.

Is there not a way in letting this story be told and showing empathy for this predicament that Kenneth can leave the art room more "developed"? How might *we* go about it? Young children are ready to give a story to almost any set of lines or formless colors. For the child the scene he paints is not a static snapshot of a single moment, but contains the past and future of its characters. To test this, one need only show interest in the child's picture; soon enough one finds oneself confidante to an amazing session of story-telling.

I would help Kenneth say something about where the giant is, how he feels, what he is thinking about and doing, how he spends his day. I am interested in Kenneth's giant and I show it. If Kenneth's conflicts are close to his awareness, I might empathize with how hard it is when *others* want you to be a giant, or when you feel you *must* be the one to take care of things, to be protected and safe. I would be careful to choose my response from feelings I know Kenneth can have and from

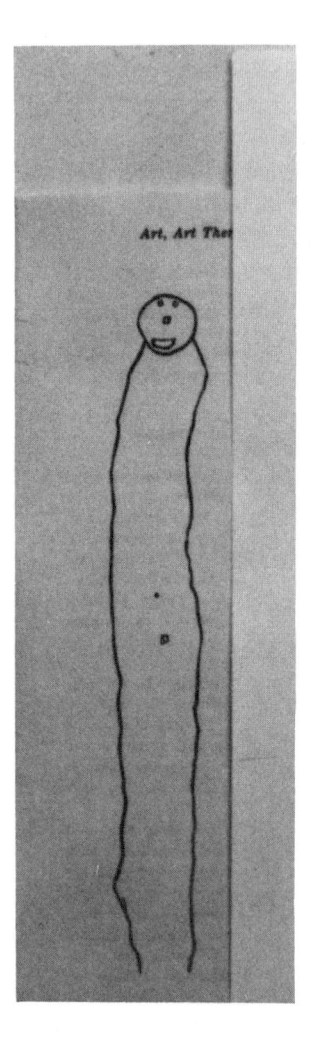

Picture 1

what the giant is sharing with us. Or if the conflict is further from awareness I would talk with him about giants' feelings when they are expected to be strong and to scare or care for everyone. *I would restrict our talk to giants,* focusing attention on the imaginal scenes and figures that preoccupy him. I want to keep the giant out of the drawer and let him have space with Kenneth and me. I might join Kenneth in speaking to the giant. When we play a game or talk about home, where is the giant? How does he feel? What does he think?

In fact, when an image like the giant is central you may encourage a series of pictures and stories about the life and times of this character. One four-year-old boy began unprompted to cut out pictures of characters he had drawn so they could interact with one another. He had me keep them during the week and at the next session would eagerly pull them out for yet another play. While such figures may arouse fear, sadness or anger, finding ways to relate to them inevitably arouses one's liveliness. Let us remember that this liveliness is not a Pollyanna gloss imposed by the therapist, with suggestions of superficial change in the image or the favoring of one over another. It evolves from a relation to the image *as it is,* as it presents itself.

In this third type of treatment attitudes toward the image, the tendency is to look for the positive in the picture, even if this means staring through what it presents. There are certain notions of what good and bad images are—light is good, dark is bad. The therapist treats the person by ridding him of the bad image and implanting or encouraging positive ones. This finds its most suspicious expression in techniques that do not allow the person to draw what comes spontaneously, but ask for a particular family of images (like mandalas). Guggenbühl-Craig labels these as efforts to "sweeten the image" (1977).

This approach includes intervention toward making images correspond to naturalistic criteria. James Hillman has called this the "naturalistic fallacy" (1979: pp. 157, 142). Edith Kramer presents an example of introducing such criteria to change the image from outside.

> Clyde: Eight-year-old Clyde, an intelligent, inhibited, and depressed child had grave doubts about the size, permanence, and intactness of his sexual organs, even though they were normally developed. Clyde was a good sculptor. One day he modeled a gorilla, standing upright with raised arms, about a foot high. He wanted to give it a penis and asked me how big he should make it. When I suggested that

he show me what *he* thought, he shyly proffered a clay sausage the size of an adult penis. I made him hold the clay penis against his sculpture and pointed out that *it* was as big as the gorilla's legs. I asked him whether he had ever seen a person with a penis as large as his leg. Clyde smiled, and shook his head. Looking down on his lap he seemed to ponder the relative size of leg and penis. Then without further hesitation he sculptured a very life-size sexual organ in a state of erection, complete with testicles. Kramer, 1971: pp. 34-5.

Kramer claims that her response was helpful insofar as it led Clyde to ponder the relative sizes of penises and "demonstrated to him the absurdity of his first idea." She claims that had she "encouraged Clyde to stick an outsized penis onto his gorilla, this would have aggravated rather than allayed his anxieties" and he would have seen his therapist as "seductress and a fool."

Is what Kramer imagines necessarily so? What if Clyde had been encouraged to give the statue the penis he felt it required and to express how this creature felt? *You can give the child information about reality without restructuring his fantasy.* You can allow that penises are relative to body size and still acknowledge that people may *feel* their penis or a gorilla's to be enormous or tiny. We want the child to understand what goes along with this feeling of having a tremendous penis. What is the gorilla up to? How would he, Clyde, feel with the gorilla? What would they do together? We should draw back from assuming what an image is about. If we do not let the gorilla and his penis remain as the image dictated, we end up with understandings of persons that mirror only our 'normalizing' preconceptions, which have not arisen freely from the dialogue between the image as it is and our theoretical framework. We too eagerly impose our notion of what development of the image would be (i.e., an average penis) and fail to follow the line of development suggested by the image.

One common mistake in dream interpretation and working with waking dreams is the tendency of the therapist and the patient to side together favoring one character over another. When the dream-ego suffers the image of some awful figure, one thinks the solution lies in ridding the dreams of that figure, by understanding it as some concrete referent in the patient's history, or by training the dreamer to act differently in the dream. But let us slow down a moment and look at the dream or waking dream less as a narrative where this causes that, and more as an image—where all the parts co-determine each other. If we do this, we will agree with Patricia Berry (in "An approach to the dream," 1974: p. 99), that

> There is no way I can say this character is a good person, this is a bad one, this figure made the wrong move, or see how unconscious he was. Characters are unconscious. Given the arrangement they all do what they have to do, and given the characters the situation has to be as it is.

Our task is not to criticize one character and praise another. Through painting more pictures and engaging in active imagination we want to understand what the viewpoints of the various characters and landscapes are, and how indeed their modes of being are co-constellated. Hillman and Berry suggest the dream ego often mirrors the ego viewpoint, whereas more unconscious viewpoints are personified in the *other* characters, who consequently are particularly important to understand.

I argue against this third approach because though such therapy employs the image, its conceptualization of the unconscious stands squarely against an imaginal psychology. Rather than expressing the spontaneous and recurring issues in a person's life, an image is used to introduce a therapist's normalizing goals or the patient's collective ego values. The direction moves away from involvement in the unconscious via the art itself, which results in a basic disrespect for the form in which images spontaneously occur. There is no appreciation of the constructive, purposive or prospective functions of the unconscious. Implicitly fearing imaginal experience, the treatment approach hastens to substitute one image for another, suggesting small or gradual changes (improvements) in an image. Persons are steered away from the images that are their actual and immediate preoccupations.

FOUR. In the psychoanalytic *interpretive* approach, the latent meaning derived from interpretation is more valued than the manifest image. The image becomes a story to be deciphered into the elements of past life, to which images are believed to refer—particularly to traumatic events and psychosexual issues. Like Freud's notion that analysis could terminate dreaming by emptying the contents of the unconscious, this approach deals with images as though intending to be rid of them. Imagination itself is placed only in relation to the inadequacies of reality and the strength of one's desires and wishes. The presumption is that were reality more adequate, or the distance between desire and actuality collapsed, imagination would cease to dream. Imagination is a way to master, to adapt to, to supplement reality. I don't debate these functions of imagining; they are obvious and important. But they do not exhaust the activity of imagining.

The fourth approach does not claim for art a privileged position among the therapeutic modalities, nor does it grant to art or expressive therapies that make use of the image what is distinctly valuable about them. For one can use behavior in a group, transference, or free association to derive the same psychoanalytic insights. The path, as I see it, proceeds from image to insight and interpretation, from image to actual event, not the other way around.

FIVE. Here the expression of the imaginal becomes curative in and of itself. It is not the interaction between patient and therapist, or the interpretation of the image that benefits the person, but simply his or her 'experience' with the image. This view does not benefit from the globality at which its explanation usually stops. What actually is curative, what actually helps is left unclear. Supposedly, one need only allow the 'conscious' to be open to the 'unconscious,' whatever these theoretical constructs point to, for healing to occur. When this is the case the art therapist has the responsibility of creating an atmosphere in which art can happen, particularly art that is expressive of fantasy life. This approach underplays the importance of her ability to understand the picture, to reflect these understandings, and help the patient work with them. Connections between the artistic product and the patient's daily life are not sought. There is virtually *no* attempt to form an insightful integration of the imaginal and the daily.

A paradoxical effect of this approach is to strengthen the alienation of imagination from 'reason,' of images from 'reality.' One is tacitly taught that images occur when one is in a special situation (an art room, at a sand tray, actively imagining, writing in a journal), and not that art is but a medium to bring forth images already active in our moment-to-moment lives.

SIX. Our critical comments thus far have hinted at a sixth approach. Here the image is not *merely* one more expression amenable to diagnostic interpretation. Here the image is respected in spite of our possible fear or doubts. There is not prejudice against certain images which leads one to suggest changes, substitutions, improvements, deletions, or to ignore/repress them, or see them as psychoanalytic disguises for latent meaning. Though the experience of actively imagining is supposed beneficial in itself, the sixth approach urges us beyond the simplicity of the fifth.

The sixth understands the particular image which arises as the best possible way of representing meanings as yet unknown or not fully grasped. We ask less "What does this image mean?" and more "What are the images intrinsic to the activities, thoughts, and feelings I am engaged in?" What images am I in when I feel exhausted, when I am shy or ambitious, when I am relating to my husband, child, or my own body? The image in its specificity lends us the imaginal background to each experience, thus raising the dayworld onto the plane of metaphorical meanings. As image and experience interpenetrate, the image is not discarded but becomes an eye through which one perceives and senses.

Working from this approach the art therapist is far from an appendage to diagnostic procedures, an arts and crafts clean-up lady, a sanitizer and straightener of images, a watchdog for impending fragmentation, or a kind, friendly presence while one paints and draws. She is someone alert not just to the literal image which is drawn, but to images in the patients' gestures, tones of voice, ways of interacting, presenting complaints and history. Through this alertness she helps the patient interact with the image being expressed in order to see more metaphorically his or her daily struggles, fears, and preoccupations. Her questions and suggestions are aimed at extending the presentation of the image *as it is,* and in helping to establish a way of reflecting on images such that they begin to move the imaginer from the figured page to an awareness of multiple moments when an image is being lived. The art therapist should attend to the structure of an image, so that its myriad details are seen not as random expressions, distortions, or disguises, but as necessary to the precise meaning of the whole image.

When, for instance, a child refuses to go to sleep at night, kicks, screams, and protests, keeping not only herself but all others awake, we want to know, and to help her know, what this "going to sleep" is really about. For suddenly or gradually the situation of going to sleep has begun to take on different meanings, until our talking to her about going to sleep is not at all what she is concerned with, though she would be hard pressed to express in words just what that latter is. An eleven-year-old with a long history of illnesses, operations, of noncompliance with medical procedures that could end in shortening her life, began having trouble retiring after four months of hospitalization in a residence for children with psychological problems which exacerbate serious physical illnesses. She would refuse to go to her room. When forced she would wake the other children and involve them in her antics. She would engage in physical struggles with the staff and create distress for all. The most she could say to me, her therapist, was that she felt at these night times as though the nurses' station was too far away and they probably would not hear her if she called. She could not say why she might want to call, what she thought about during the fall-asleep time, or why her activity escalated in a way atypical of her. One day during this period she introduced into her squiggle drawings the theme of a child lying in bed at night.

Let me tell you a bit about how I proceed with children's squiggle drawings. I follow Winnicott's suggestion, combining these drawings with mutual story-telling. One person makes a squiggle on a sheet of paper with eyes closed. The other person looks at it, imagines what it might be and completes it. Then the process is reversed, and the second person makes a squiggle. When we have four to eight squiggles, the child and I select a few of the pictures and we tell a story together about them. We may pretend that they are illustrations to a book we are writing together. Some children will dictate to you from beginning to end their own story. Others will write a story themselves only if you look away from them and keep busy writing one yourself. Usually you can alternate sections. You as therapist can use your turn to encourage the child to say more, to focus on the feelings of a story character to articulate the underlying mood, or bring the child's attention back to an element of the story she is ignoring because of its difficult nature. In sum, one tries to *deepen or extend* the child's own line of imagining rather than suggest alternatives. Children will almost always fill an empty space in a narrative. If the child says, "The grasshopper was looking for food," you can respond, "and he looked here and he looked there before..."and leave a space for the child to continue the story.

With this girl the following pictures were named and finished by her: a mushroom, a worm, a necktie, a mother bird and her baby, and a boy lying down in his bed (see Pictures 2-6). She was amenable to our using her pictures to write the story. I took the lead and began the story using her picture of a boy lying down in his bed. I wanted to help her bring forth the images around this situation of going to bed.

SIX APPROACHES TO THE IMAGE IN ART THERAPY

Picture 2

Picture 3

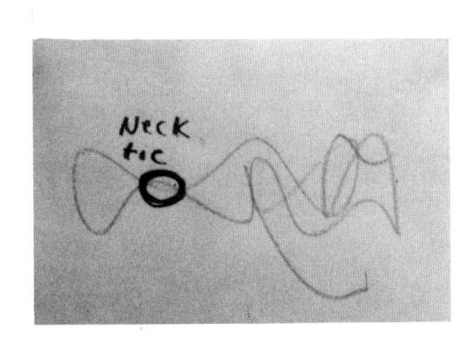

Picture 4

Picture 5

119

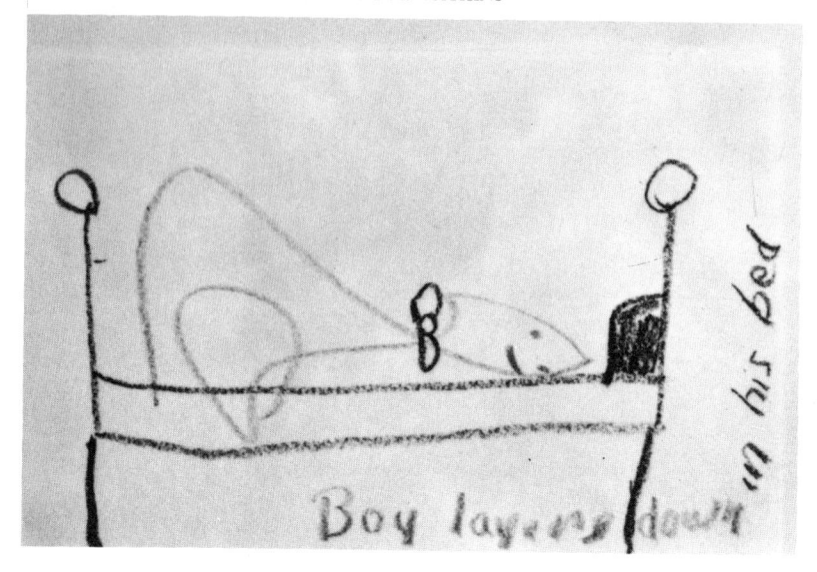

Picture 6

Therapist: Once upon a time there was a boy lying down in his bed.
Child: And the mother bird was singing to her baby bird.
Therapist: And the boy heard this and it made him feel...
Child: Lonely. And then he saw a necktie on the floor and he picked it up and wore it. It was his Dad's.
Therapist: This necktie reminded him of his Dad, and when he thought about his Dad, he felt...
Child: A little better. And then he found a worm and picked it up and gave it to the birds and they were singing and they were happy that the boy gave them a worm because they were hungry.
Therapist: But the mother bird and her baby were thankful to the boy and wanted to do something to make him feel better. And so, they asked what they could do for him.
Child: He said, "Do you know where my father is?" And they like tweeted. And he said, "Could you try and find my father because I don't know where he is?"
Therapist: At this point, the boy felt very sad, and he began to cry, because he missed his father and didn't know where he was.
Child: And then the birds went to go and look and found him. Then the boy whispered in his ear and said, "Let's do something to help the birds."
Therapist: The mother bird wondered if the father knew how much the boy had missed him, as he had lain awake in bed that night.
Child: And then the boy found a mushroom and gave it to his father.

Therapist: He wondered if his Dad would go away again and the mother bird knew that this was what he was worried about.
Child: And he knew his father wasn't going to go away again and so he lived happily ever after.

There is much one could say about these pictures and this story. Her mood changed as we completed the story. She appeared relieved, playful, closer to me. Indeed, as in the fifth approach to the image, the experience of the image emerging and developing already produced a positive change in her mood. This was so in spite of her involvement in a painfully disturbing issue—not knowing where father is. Her knowledge that she was opening to what the problem around going to bed was—not just with me, but with herself as well—brought relief. She seemed proud of herself, as she did on occasions in the past when she allowed some psychological work to occur. She wanted to make photocopies of the pictures and story for me. She took the originals into the hall where she lived, reading the story with great animation and pride to the staff and a best friend.

If we try to learn from the story and its pictures what image she was in at bedtime, we can say that going to bed was a time of being a virtual audience to other small creatures being mothered, though left out herself. She felt lonely. If we follow the story along, however, we find a number of transformations which occur in this initial situation. It is important to emphasize that these transformations are not gained by alterations in 'reality'—in her relations with her actual family or the milieu staff. They occur spontaneously through her involvement with the images.

For the boy lying down in bed is a time of mother bird singing to baby. It is not *his* mother singing to him, but rather he is a *lonely* spectator to this mothering of which he is not the object. From this lonely feeling he is able to find a father-thing and to bring this near to himself. While baby bird is sung to by its mother he puts on Dad's tie, becomes as Dad, and feels "a little better." Once as Dad, or when in Dad-likeness, he is able to perceive the others' hunger—yes, hunger in even those that have mother's singing. He is able to find a worm, some food, and give it to them. And in his doing so, mother becomes not the only one to sing; the baby sings as well. In the boy's being like Dad, the characterization of the baby bird has deepened from a passive and presumably gratified recipient of mother's melodies to being also hungry. Hungriness, loneliness, is no longer perceived in just the boy. The boy is not only able to perceive this hunger in others but to act on it as "giver"—indeed, he is able to give even to mother. When he gives to the birds he can address his not knowing where his father is, and he can ask for help in finding him. The father is found by the bird friends, and the child once again wants to give gifts—first to the birds and then to father. Being like Dad and finding Dad bring out feelings of his own abundance, which stands in genuine contrast to his initial loneliness and deprivation. This dramatic sequence not only helped to lift the going to bed difficulties onto a more imaginal level, but enabled the child to *move* on this level.

Problems with the literal father and with the staff's understanding of the dynamics of the child's bedtime struggle needed to be addressed, as her spontaneous conversations afterward showed. But in the dramatic sequence—before any correction of reality with the real father or staff had occurred—we find the *image working out its own solutions.* Though the explicit focus of the story is the lost father, the boy is involved in much more than this lostness. He has already found ways to be like the father. In the father's absence and in his presence, he wears the tie, he feeds the birds. He also allows himself to ask the birds about the father and try to enlist their help. Given this child's real-life situation, of being removed from her home and placed in the care of others, the step of engaging with the birds as helpers was important. She can communicate with the birds. This move in fantasy was not expressive of her usual indirection in dealing with her needs.

Father-things and the birds enable the child to shift from a position of initial loneliness in the face of others receiving to a more differentiated and articulated self. As the characterization of the imaginal other deepens, so reciprocally does the self's. As baby bird moves from gratified baby to hungry bird to helping and being helped, so does the boy become not only lonely, but perceptive, giving, asking, and grateful.

Is the father's staying only a matter of wish-fulfillment? Or has some shift occurred for her with regard to the feeling of the presence of the father, regardless of static objective circumstances? Was I as therapist wrong to suggest the boy was worried about the father's going again? Indeed, as I look back on the end of the sequence, the child's concern was with the giving of gifts to the helpers. My intervention perhaps forced her to retreat back to the father, to give *him* the gift. Perhaps I reinforced her preoccupation with the father when she might have been healthily ready to let it be for then. The sad thing is that I won't know. My own preoccupation interrupted the stream of her fantasy at this point. I can only try to get more out of the way next time.

It is true that the child had serious concerns with her actual father. After this story-telling she became increasingly able to acknowledge her fearfulness that she would never see him again. In his depression, he had confused leaving his wife with losing his daughter, and had not been able to reassure either himself or her of the continuance of the relationship independent of his marriage. Her father needed to be reminded of the importance of his tie to his daughter, and that he could establish a relationship with her independent of the destiny of his marriage. The child needed to hear that her father's leaving her mother was dependent on *his* relationship to the mother, and not on her—as the fantasy of gifts to the father in the story suggested. Listening to the dramatic sequence helped the bedsettling staff to see more clearly that the annoying and infuriating behavior which at times seemed directed at them could be understood as the child's struggling with feelings of loneliness, of motherlessness, of uncertainty as to where the fathering was. Once they could respond to *this* situation, by taking time to read to her or talk to her about her day as she snuggled into bed, or enlisting her help with the younger children, the need for punishment ceased.

These attempts to aid the child in her concrete relations are crucial. Unfortunately, as clinicians our focus on them often diminishes our appreciation of what has *already* been accomplished and experienced through participation with the image.

Aristotle claimed that the best interpreter of dreams was one who could grasp similarities. When we work with images we want to be alert with our patient for similarities and analogies. With the bedtime girl I used the story to focus on bedtime per se, but if we approach any image through analogy we realize that there are many moments when a child is acting as though in that image. For instance, we would want to be alert to when she "puts Dad's tie on," when she feels all the mother-singing is for others, etc. With adults, you can ask *when* they feel like or inside a particular image they have presented. They can keep the image close to awareness as they move through the week and find instances of when the world that surrounds them is "as-if" the one in the image. I am arguing against a one-to-one correspondence between image and event. I am arguing for how the image precisely describes different ways of being in the world (and different worlds to be in).

For instance, Boss (1958: p. 116) writes of a man whose dreams were filled with all varieties of magical mothers. Boss claims that the man had surrendered his existence to being a child and thus he called out in both waking and dreaming life for his world to be peopled with mothers. Similarly, an emotionally detached engineer whom Boss treated dreamed only of inanimate objects and lower forms of life for months. There were no people in his images, as his life was not attuned to them (*ibid:* p. 113). In this way the image is not discontinuous with everyday existence, but describes in its own way the world of the imaginer.

And what, you might ask, is its "own way?" My answer to this has been to learn from dreams the structure of an image. Note that dreams are essentially dramatic. Though characters may be depicted in a present moment, there are allusions to their past and future. The dream releases us from the confines of daily time and space. One can dream of being in any era, country, time of year or day, type of landscape. The dream can also release us from our habitual identity, attitudes and actions; a woman can be a man; a man a child; a sad person angry. Also when we are dreaming, the dream is not experienced as occurring in our heads, but rather we are surrounded by its world.

An image has a totality to it, such that one part calls out another. A certain character could only have one kind of room to live in, or tone of voice with which he speaks. In a drawing when one part of an image emerges, often a question allows the rest to unfold: Where does this take place? What time of day is it? What does the air feel like? What is the atmosphere of this place? Who is present? What happens here? What just happened? Where are you in relation to this scene? If the picture is of a person, one might ask what he/she is thinking about, where he/she is, where one is in relation to the figure. One might ask what seems familiar about the person or the mood around the person. One can suggest that the painter step inside the picture, into the place or into a relation with the figure depicted. But always the focus is on the image.

Jung said, "Only what is oneself has the power to heal." From this point of view all the good intentions that attempt to transpose images, to disinfect horrifying ones, close the door to exploring images, introduce positive images—all these seemingly benevolent efforts—sidetrack a person from what has the power to heal. But given the fears and prejudices of much of our discipline concerning the unconscious, how can we be trusting enough to convey to another an openness to images which arise spontaneously and which stand in an autonomous relation to the conscious personality? Perhaps the only way to develop this faithfulness is through one's own experience with the imaginal. Just as analysts are required to experience the entire process of analysis in order to be in a position to help create a narrative from the patient's streams of association, we who work with images must stay close to the images that form the structure of our own psychological experience. We must write out our dreams, illustrate them, speak to their characters, paint spontaneously, seek for the images that determine our responses to others, to ourselves, our patients and our life. It is in this process that we will gain a trust in images. Gradually the small ways we reveal our theoretical alliance to this viewpoint will become more apparent to our colleagues. Gradually too we will betray the people and the images we work with less.

P. Berry, "On reduction." *Spring 1973*.
M. Boss, *The Analysis of Dreams* (New York: Philosophical Library, 1958).
H. Corbin, *Creative Imagination in the Sufism of Ibn' Arabi* (Princeton: Princeton University Press, 1969).
A. Guggenbühl-Craig, "Summary of a contribution to the Dallas meeting." Collection of papers for a seminar on archetypal psychology held at the University of Dallas, January 1977.
J. Hillman, *The Dream and the Underworld* (New York: Harper & Row, 1979).
C.G. Jung, "The transcendent function," *The Structure and Dynamics of the Psyche (CW 8)*.
E. Kramer, *Art as Therapy With Children* (New York: Schocken, 1971).
R. Schafer, *A New Language for Psychoanalysis* (New Haven: Yale University Press, 1976).
M. Watkins, *Waking Dreams* (New York: Harper & Row, 1976).
D.W. Winnicott, *Therapeutic Consultations in Child Psychiatry* (New York: Basic Books, 1971).

Ancient Mayan myths penetrate our skin with the warm sun of the Yucatan. The cool stillness of the Black Forest enchants us into fairy-tale realms of the Brothers Grimm. Music of Tir-na-nOg, the Celtic Other World, drifts to misty shores on Ireland's Connemara coast. Pinon logs burn fragrantly in New Mexico's crisp night air, aromatic with secrets from ancient Hopi & Zuni teachings.

Our inward journeys into story, myth & dreams find completion in outward Travel, Pilgrimage & Quest. We fulfill our quests in journeying to sacred places, far & near.

StoryFest Travel's unique & unforgettable seminars celebrate our Inward/Outward Journeys through myth & storytelling. Each is limited to 18 people seeking good company and memorable experience. Carefully chosen accommodations enhance dramatic scenic settings with pleasurable meals & comfortable lodgings. (Besides exotic destinations, weekend seminars closer to home provide relaxation conveniently nearby.)

Dr. Robert Bela Wilhelm, director of Mythos Institute for research in mythology & storytelling, leads many of these seminars. He is a master storyteller, steeped in lore & legends of sacred lands, and skilled in the creative process of ritualizing and celebrating myths.

1981: **New Mexico, Creation & Re-Creation.** At the Ghost Ranch in Abiquiu, near Taos & Santa Fe. Native American myths, Trickster tales, Southwestern legends. Nearby pueblo sacred dances. (November 15–21)

1981: **Telling Your Story**. A relaxed, festive weekend retreat in the Pocono mountains, Pennsylvania. Jungian/Gestalt approaches to myth making in our personal quests. (November 6–8)

1982: January, **Mexico**/ February, **Louisiana Mardi Gras**/ Brochures: March, **Ireland**

STORYFEST TRAVEL
4912-T California Street
San Francisco, CA 94118

ART EDUCATION AND ARCHETYPAL PSYCHOLOGY

HOWARD McCONEGHEY
(Albuquerque)

Introduction

As we move into the decade of the 80's we cannot escape that we live in a dark time. The frenzy of technology seems entrenched everywhere. We have only one response to any problem—technology, power, control. Man is in danger of surrendering his free human essence to the computer and the analytic mind. Art education too is floundering in darkness. Renaissance theory breaks down in the face of new aims; old techniques no longer suffice. We still tend to the academic approach appropriate to the Renaissance—design principles, studio fundamentals, perspective and other techniques of representation—though it becomes obvious that these scientific rules do not guide the modern artist. The breakdown of theory has left a vacuum. So our students are often told, "Learn the rules first, then you can disregard them." There is no consensus as to what constitutes an appropriate art education for the Modern age. The great Post-Impressionist painters, Van Gogh, Cezanne and Gaugin were searching for a new end. They were compelled by intense inner drives which could not be adequately depicted by dramatic representation. "Nature is on the inside," said Cezanne. These men were called insane, childish, barbaric. New visions are often labeled perverse or pathological. In education we feel lost without the old guidelines, though it becomes obvious they are more hindrance than help to the contemporary imagination.

When old forms of thought and perception break down, artists and scholars often look to each other and to history to find some clue about

---

Howard McConeghey is a painter and past Chairman of the Department of Art Education at the University of New Mexico. He has been working consistently for twenty-five years on teaching art based on the image.

what is happening. Cezanne haunted the old masters in the Louvre and historians of art look to earlier ages of transition to explain changing styles. Or they look to psychology in an attempt to understand the artists' new mode of perception. As an art educator I find, for example, that the conventional model of art education is indeed losing its relevance. For a deeper understanding of the origins of the Renaissance academy and a clue as to what may now be emerging in its place, I would like to consider in some detail the work of E.H. Gombrich, a contemporary scholar of the Renaissance, in relation with James Hillman's archetypal psychology.

Gombrich's theories concern the history, "not of art but of image-making."[1] This makes his work especially relevant to art education which is best defined as the teaching of image making. Gombrich's notion of the transition which brought about the Renaissance differs from that of many scholars. While it was the Renaissance that suffered the Cartesian split between discursive reason and symbolic metaphor, Gombrich reminds us that it was also the Renaissance that kept alive the occluded tradition of the West which recognizes no split between subject and object, which preserves "the peculiar habits of the ancient world to 'hypostasize' abstract concepts."[2]

The Renaissance concern with representation was a radical change from the symbolic depiction of episodic narrative which had been the goal in Medieval art. Renaissance art can be understood as a means to a new end—the visual evocation of a mythical event. It aimed to render figures—often mythological—in a dramatic situation; to depict what events must have looked like to an eyewitness. For Leonardo,

> The elements of painted scenes must move those who look at them to experience the same emotions as those represented in the story, that is, to feel terror, fear, fright or pain, grief and lamentation or pleasure, happiness and laughter. If they fail to do this, the skill of the painter will have been in vain.[3]

This change to realistic representation reflected a change in attitude toward the world, a concern for the appearance of the world (mimesis), a concern for religious, mythical, or psychological drama. Gombrich does not emphasize the concomitant change that took place in the mode of art education. Obviously, however, the new goal of representation required careful observation of nature and new techniques for rendering the appearance of natural objects. It required the approach of an academy. The rendering of expression, of anatomy, of space and light would demand a new, more scientific mode of art education. Whereas apprenticeship to a master craftsman was an appropriate mode of education during the Middle Ages when the goal of art was episodic or narrative, the new representation, depending as it did on the observation of natural appearance, required the resources of scientific representation. This change in art education from apprenticeship to the academy was as dramatic and as closely related to the new end of art as the corresponding change in the image itself. The change in attitude came quite suddenly in the 16th century as the demand arose for intellectual artists capable of conceiving imaginative representations in historic, mythical or religious modes.

Gombrich indicates that art in the Modern period has an equally radical new end, that of expressing *psychic* nature. Art has moved from representing human drama to exploring the "inner recesses of the mind." The end of art has changed from episodic narrative in the Middle Ages, through the Renaissance goal of psychological evocation of an outer event, to the Modern aim of expressing the inner psychic image itself. Gombrich says, "When we arrive at an inner personal style, we have reached the frontier of what is usually called representation! For in these ultimate constituents the artist is said to express himself."[4] All or most twentieth century art, he tells us, tries to express the world of psychic nature where colors and shapes stand for feelings.

In his search for the means of expressing this inner reality, and in the attempt to achieve a valid reorientation, the modern artist sought inspiration from primitive methods. Gombrich claims that primitivism is the abiding form of the revolution against scientific representation and illusion.

> Primitivism... became perhaps an even more lasting influence on modern art than either Van Gogh's Expressionism or Cezanne's way to Cubism. It heralded a complete revolution in taste which began round about 1906, the year of the first exhibition of the "Fauves." It was only through this revolution that critics began to discover the beauty of the works of the early Middle Ages.... It was then that artists began to study the works of native tribesmen with the same zeal with which academic artists studied Greek sculpture. It was this change of taste, too, which led young painters in Paris at the beginning of the twentieth century to discover the art of an amateur painter. Henri Rousseau proved to them that far from being a way to salvation the training of the professional painter may spoil his chances.[5]

What led to a radical change of interest on the part of atists was the growing awareness that art offers a key to the mind as well as the outer world. "The language of forms and colors has come to be looked upon as right by nature. Our nature."[6]

Psychology and Meaning in Art

Gombrich's view of modern art as the discovery and expression of psychic reality naturally leads us to psychology. Gombrich acknowledges "...the necessity for historians of style to stage a counterraid across the psychologist's frontier."[7] Just across this frontier, closest to art, we find archetypal psychology, that psychology which most seriously and effectively deals with image.

James Hillman declares: "The image has been my starting point for the archetypal re-visioning of psychology."[8] Unfortunately Gombrich was unaware of this new vision in psychology. His formative works had already been written by the time Hillman's first full-length presentation of imaginal psychology, *The Myth of Analysis*, was published in 1972. That was also the date of the publication of Gombrich's important *Symbolic Images*. He had complained that psychoanalysis has contributed little to an understanding of artistic style, and that Gestalt psychology is too narrowly based on perception. I would like to suggest that archetypal psychology does offer a psychology of image-making which Gombrich, the "historian of image-making" would have found helpful. If modern art draws from the psychic image, if its concern is no longer the scientific representation of the outer human drama but the psychological grasp of the inner image, then a psychology consistent with this modern goal of art must be one which recognizes the importance of the image. Such in fact is the revisioned psychology that Hillman offers.

Re-visioning psychology, as twentieth century artists have revisioned art, means giving it an end more consistent with the "radical reorientation of all traditional ideas about the human mind"[9] which Gombrich was seeking. Psychoanalysis and Gestalt psychology obscured for him the nature and importance of the reorientation he was after. While they break with Renaissance techniques, they both retain Renaissance analytical modes of generalization and reduction. Gombrich complains that "The whole idea of the 'imitation of nature,' of 'idealization' or of 'abstraction' rests upon the assumption that what comes first are 'sense impressions' subsequently elaborated or generalized."[10]

In both art and psychology the basic terms of perception have lost their meaning. The old ideas of abstraction and idealization no longer hold. Rather, external experience rests upon contact with psychic image. Hillman tells us that the psyche can be comprehended "as a storehouse of qualities that are formal causes of experience, giving shape, color and significance."[11] (Gombrich, you will remember, says these shapes and colors stand for feelings.) The emphasis upon sense impression and visual perception can only be countered by a recognition that such feelings relate to a psychic reality—a mythopoetic seeing, feeling and hearing in archetypal patterns. Such a recognition does constitute a truly radical reorientation of all traditional ideas about the human mind and would seem to satisfy Gombrich's quest.

Hillman recognizes Freud's and Jung's thought as the roots of archetypal psychology and emphasizes the important influence of depth psychology, mythology and memoria:

> Freud and Jung have suggested that the unconscious enters into each mental act. This view of depth psychology gives a further correspondence between the unconscious and *memoria*. Aristotle held that no mentation could take place without the mental images given by imagination, the basis of memory.... The unconscious is always present, just as the past is always present.... Part of the soul is continually remembering in mythopoetic speech, continually seeing, feeling and hearing *sub specie aeternitatis*. Experience reverberates with memories, and it echoes reminiscences that we may never actually have lived.[12]

Experience echoes reminiscences that we may never have lived! It is not the external drama as seen in outer events so much as the psyche's inner experience of primordial or archetypal events that modern art and the art of children and primitives seek to express.

This awareness of the unconscious realm of psychic reality as the source of image bridges the frontier between modern art and archetypal psychology. Hillman calls the psyche "The imaginal part of ourselves," and insists that "fantasies and feelings are archetypal and thus right by nature—the nature of the psyche." He indicates that "we need a new way of looking, an imaginal way, a way that starts within the imagination itself.... We need a new imaginal ego-consciousness that is not estranged from the imagination and its fantasies."[13]

Some critics describe modern art as a relapse into barbarism and banality. I believe the failure to recognize the deep revolutionary significance of modern art may be a consequence of our inability to make subtle discriminations, for example between the meaning of the words "clarity" and "distinction."

> When *distinction* is not distinguished from *clarity*—Descartes made them interchangeable—we can have no underworld, no depth and shading, except as utter darkness in compensation. The best distinctions are the clearest, and the clearest are, of course, contradictions. Then metaphorical ambiguity can only mean dim-witted obscurity, for twilight has disappeared and psyche too, as it all but did for Descartes.
> Fortunately the underworld perspective offers another, a psychological mode of distinction, where sharp sight means *insight* into the thing at hand (not in comparison with something else) and where clarity means *precision* (of internal relations within images, not logical relations between them). A psychic approach to distinction works at the particularization of an event...by means of imagistic resemblances....[14]

In the Renaissance, clarity had to do with the clear representation of people in a dramatic scene, attendant on a concern for causing the viewer to experience the emotions represented in the story. The child and the modern artist, on the other hand, instinctively work for precision in expressing an inner psychic image and attempt to clarify the imaginal reality. To approach such works with the expectation of representational likeness is to see them as irrational and inarticulate. It is difficult for the analytic mind to understand the twilight zone of the inner image of primitives and modern artists. Art educators who cling to Renaissance academic techniques do so because it is a comfortable way to neutralize the disturbing effects and metaphorical ambiguity of imaginal expression. It spares one the confusion of participation in the troubling inner image. We are persistently tempted to exchange the suspense of the underworld image for the narrow but positive certainty of convention. When the artistic imagination begins to work on us, we have left the safe shore of tidy knowledge for the open sea of metaphorical shadow and depth. Art educators intent on establishing certainty and reliability tend to overemphasize rules and principles. The imaginal approach, however, requires a truly radical reorientation. The modern break with representation is not a degenerate spurning of rational perception. Rather it is an embracing of the syntax of soul. Max Beckmann, for example, held as an ideal "the imagination of space—to change the optical impression of the world of objects by a transcendental arithmetic progression of the inner being."[15] The modern mode demands a reorientation where sharp sight becomes insight and clarity becomes awareness of the internal relations within the psychic image. *We must become as precise in relation to inner nature as was the Renaissance in relation to the outer.*

An Art Education for Art with Expression as Its End

Such radical changes in art and psychology surely point to the need for an equally radical change in art education. The change in the meaning of Renaissance art demanded the change from apprenticeship to academy as the going style of art education. What change seems needed now in relation to the modern shift from representation to expression? What indications may be found for a new mode consistent with an art based in the image, with expression as its end?

One of the first art educators to make a complete break with past academic training was Franz Cizek. His Juvenile Art Class opened in Vienna in 1897. Cizek's curriculum was simple, "To let the child grow, develop and mature." Aside from its romantic aura, Cizek's curriculum was the beginning in art education of a focus on image-making as a valid expression of the psyche.

Cizek was a young artist in contact with the founders of the "Secession" movement in modern art in Vienna. He became so interested in the untutored drawings of the children in whose home he boarded that he established his school and carried on his study of the art work (which he called documents) of children from four to fourteen years of age. The break with Renaissance concepts of representation—and the expressive qualities of modern art, bright colors and expressive distortion—made *possible* the comparison of child art with the work of professionals. Child art could also be appreciated as an expression of the psyche.

As early as 1859 Herbert Spencer acknowledged the spreading recognition of drawing as an element in general education, and in 1887 the German Alfred Litchwark had recognized that the child "Simplifies according to laws which are valid for all times and all peoples."[16] But it was Cizek who first demonstrated both the aesthetic and psychological advantage of art education for children. Thousands of people visited the Juvenile Art Class during its forty-year span and exhibits of the children's work were widely circulated.

Art educators have scoffed at Cizek's method as "mere intuition." But Gombrich indicates that modern art comes from the inner image—which was the focus of Cizek's method.

While *academic* psychologists and art educators may find it difficult to justify Cizek's "intuitionism," archetypal psychology, founded on the image, has a different view of intuition and instinct. I think "instinct" applies better to what Cizek was doing than "intuitionism." First, his teaching was not so directionless as has been suggested, and second, by his idea that children's images come from an inner source he meant that they come from something more than mere intuition or hunch. Hillman suggests that instinct is more a metaphor than a concept: "Perhaps it is an idea in the original sense of that term where it meant 'to see,' so that by means of this word 'instinct' we are able to see certain kinds of behavior, both looking upon it as an observer and looking into it, insighting it, as a participant."[17] Jung tells us that images belong to the same continuum as instinct, and instinct as Hillman has shown, helps us to 'see' archetypally. "By working on imagination we are taking part in nature 'in here.' The method of this work, however, is not merely an activity of the conscious mind or will, though they play their roles."[18] The method, as artists of the modern period have indicated, is sensitivity to the intuitive and psychological reality of man's inner world; to the spontaneous and naive vision of the child and primitive within ourselves; to the images of the psyche.

Thus, while there is no consensus as to what constitutes an appropriate art education for the modern age, and while neither Psychoanalysis nor Gestalt psychology have proved adequate to our need for understanding image-making and image-reading, archetypal psychology does point to the imaginal realm as the place to begin our search. Following primitive and instinctual influences, which were also the inspiration for modern artists, archetypal psychology would

> ... let the insight contained within the fantasy appear of itself, in its own intrinsically intelligible speech. For try as we may, we cannot make insights with reason and will. Something imaginative is needed.... This imaginal background is given by *memoria*, as a kind of natural light that yields a consciousness about fantasy according to principles different from effort and will and the constraints of understanding. The imaginal ego reflects this imaginative background and this kind of consciousness. It is unlike the Cartesian ego, based on the *cogito* or the ego of will with which we are all too familiar.[19]

Art education must learn to read the image in its own "intrinsically intelligent speech"; to get in touch with the psychic realm of *memoria;* and "let the insight contained within the fantasy appear of itself." This will be a difficult task because it demands a new way of looking, a way that starts within the imagination itself. It requires a new imaginal consciousness. However, modern artists have insisted that only in the twilight of the inner realm can we find the image. "In a dark time, the eye begins to see"[20] as Theodore Roethke told us.

1 E.H. Gombrich, *Means and Ends,* London: Thames & Hudson, 1976, p. 7.
2 E.H. Gombrich, *Symbolic Images,* Oxford: Phaidon Press, 1972. p. 126.
3 Quoted from Gombrich, *Means and Ends,* p. 13.
4 E.H. Gombrich, *Art and Illusion,* Princeton University Press, 1961, p. 366.
5 E.H. Gombrich, *The Story of Art,* Oxford: Phaidon Press, 1954, p. 440.
6 *Art and Illusion,* p. 360.
7 Ibid., p. 27.
8 J. Hillman, *The Dream and the Underworld,* New York: Harper and Row, 1979, p. 5.
9 *Art and Illusion,* p. 27.
10 Ibid., p. 28.
11 J. Hillman, *The Myth of Analysis,* Evanston: Northwestern University Press, 1972, p. 176.
12 Ibid., pp. 176-77.
13 Ibid., p. 201.
14 *The Dream and the Underworld,* p. 84.
15 Max Beckmann, "On My Painting" in *Modern Artists on Art,* Robert Herbert, ed., Englewood Cliffs: Prentice-Hall, 1964, p. 134.
16 Quoted from Viola Wilhelm, *Child Art,* London: University of London Press, 1942, p. 8.
17 J. Hillman and W.H. Roscher, *Pan and the Nightmare,* Spring Publications, 1979, pp. xxiii and xxiv.
18 Ibid., p. xxv. (See also *Re-Visioning Psychology* by J. Hillman, pp. 224-45 regarding instinct.)
19 *The Myth of Analysis,* pp. 201-202.
20 Theodore Roethke, *Collected Poems,* Garden City, New York: Doubleday, p. 239.

Announcing
⚶ SULFUR ⚶

A Literary Tri-Quarterly of the Whole Art

Combustion. Inflamed language. And any of the numerous butterflies of the family Pieridae, with black-bordered yellow or orange wings. SULFUR on one level is an evolution of CATERPILLAR, a literary quarterly published and edited by Clayton Eshleman (with Robert Kelly as Contributing Editor), from 1967 through 1973.

SULFUR will appear April, October and January, beginning in the spring of 1981. A two-hundred page format, typeset and perfect bound, the magazine's production costs will be supported by the California Institute of Technology in Pasadena. Eshleman and Kelly will again be Editor and Contributing Editor respectively.

SULFUR's subtitle is to convey that what we feel is needed is a journal of the whole art — writing — as it presents and represents. In addition, SULFUR will publish translations, book reviews (polemical as well as evaluative), archaic, archetypal and alchemical "source materials," as well as music, art and photography.

In the first issue there will be the first of three presentations of the complete extant correspondence between Edward Dahlberg and Charles Olson; a 121 line section from Canto 84 suppressed by Pound; and ten unpublished letters from Hart Crane to Kenneth Burke.

There will also be poetry and prose by Kelly, Eshleman, Jerome Rothenberg, John Ashbery, Keith Waldrop, Michael Palmer, Gerrit Lansing, Diane Wakoski, Ron Padgett, Alan Williamson, Paul Blackburn, Lyn Hejinian, Tom Meyer, Michael Davidson, Theodore Enslin, a chapter from James Hillman's "Silver and The White Earth," and a previously untranslated letter by Antonin Artaud.

There will also be translations from the work of Leonardo Sciascia (Italy), Aimé Césaire (Martinique), Jacinto Cua Pospoy (Guatemala), and Hector Manjarrez (Mexico).

Mail check or money order to:
SULFUR
Box 228-77
California Institute of Technology
Pasadena, California 91125

Please send _____ single copies at $5.00 each.

Please enter my subscription for _____ year(s) at $12.00 per year (individual).

Please enter my subscription for _____ year(s) at $18.00 per year (institutions).

(Foreign subscribers add $3.00 for overseas postage.)

Name _____

Address _____

City _____ State _____ Zip _____

SHADOWS OF EROS:
NOTES ON DOROTHEA TANNING'S SURREALISM

NORMAN WEINSTEIN
(Boise)

> Out of imagination and reality something new is born and it is this very knowledge which is the miracle. The distinction between imagination and experience is no longer valid. But contrary to what one thought, it is not the world itself that falls to pieces as a result, but only the image of an enlightened world, which, although very familiar to us through force of habit, no longer satisfies.
> —Marianne Thalmann[1]

Surrealism developed as an artistic and philosophical movement in the years following the First World War. 1914 shattered the image of civilized Europe, a cracking of the public facade of reason and decency. While the surrealists created an extensive body of literature and painting to transfigure postmortem effects of the conflict, Freud and Jung probed the human unconscious to provide psychological keys to the event. The fact that the surrealists and the psychoanalysts never found a common ground is a curious and tragic paradox, given their common interest in dreams, fantasies, imagination, and the reconciliation of contraries within the soul.

The French surrealistic painter, André Masson, recently described a meeting between the leader of surrealism, André Breton, and Freud:

> ...when Andre Breton went to see Freud, they didn't get along at all. Freud said to Breton, not in these exact words but this is the gist of it: that which I want to cure, you, on the contrary, wish to expand.[2]

Exactly what was it that Breton and his artistic disciplines were attempting to expand? Breton's definition of surrealism in his first Surrealist

---

Norman Weinstein is the author of *Gertrude Stein and the Literature of the Modern Consciousness* (Ungar 1970) and two small collections of poetry. His reviews have appeared in *The San Francisco Review of Books* and *The American Book Review*.

Manifesto offers a clue:

> SURREALISM, noun, masc., pure psychic automatism which is intended to express, either verbally or in writing, the true function of thought. Thought dictated in the absence of all control exerted by reason.... Encycl. Philos. Surrealism is based on the belief in the superior reality of certain forms of association heretofore neglected, in the omnipotence of dream, and in the disinterested play of thought....[3]

Freud's unsatisfactory meeting with Breton should come as no surprise to the students of these movements. Surrealism spoke most powerfully to a generation of young artists intensely involved with sweeping cultural revolution. Freud's most loyal followers moved along the path of resignation and stoic adjustment to the cultural malaise. What Breton describes in his Manisfesto belongs to Freud's "Id."

Examining Surrealism in the light of Archetypal Psychology creates a different set of possible cross resonances. Breton's emphasis upon "the superior reality" of free associations, fantasies, and dream imagery corresponds with this definition of soul:

> the imaginative possibility in our natures, the experiencing through reflective speculation, dream, image, and *fantasy*—that mode which recognizes all realities as primarily symbolic or metaphorical.[4]

Archetypal psychology reminds us that the soul speaks a wild language, one riddled with contraries and paradoxes. This image of the soul, ambivalent, fluttering in its growth between dream and waking, sanity and madness, anima and animus, satisfies the surrealist definition of the imagination perfectly.

This study brings the language and ideas of archetypal psychology to bear upon one of the outriders of the official surrealist movement: Dorothea Tanning. Like many other women painters involved with Surrealism, she was largely ignored by Breton. Her husband, the famous sculptor and painter Max Ernst, attracted more of Breton's attention. Her paintings had their genesis long before Surrealism was born and continue long after its demise. Her link with the movement was forged largely through her marriage to Ernst and her involvement with painting oneiric imagery.

In working with her paintings I discovered that myth was indeed a viable tool for a critical sighting of her work. As well, I realized that several of Tanning's image clusters corresponded to imaginal movements within my own psyche; Tanning's art, as Jung insists all significant art must, speaks *transpersonally,* offers constellated images of universal significance.

My main interest lies in examining how the fiery inspiration of Eros moved Tanning to create art that transcends all the conventional notions of Eros. Tanning's portrayals show that the torch of Eros sometimes points down.

II.

Dorothea Tanning's reputation rests largely upon a series of canvases completed in the late forties and early fifties featuring pubescent girls wandering in surrealistic interiors. Nothing in the history of modern art—or traditional depth psychology—prepares us for Tanning's young girls.

In "Eine Kleine Nachtmusik" two girls dressed in tattered Victorian garb wander through a large corridor punctuated by several doorways, one slightly ajar. A stairwell leading to a lower level is blocked by a gargantuan sunflower with tendrils partially obstructing the corridor. The girls, one blond, the other brunette, are incompletely clothed. Their dress hangs in erotically provocative disarray. Long hair streams down a back like a cold river or defies gravity by rising in the air like a flame. Other young girls in Tanning's art sleepwalk to the night's music. In the terrifying "Jeux d'Enfants" they rip sheets of wallpaper off a bare wall revealing sexual portraits of genitals and pubic hair under the decorative surface. The nude girl in "The Guest Room" stands before an otherworldly gnome figure and in a bed a grown woman sleeps with a battered, deformed doll. In "Palaestra" six girls wander through a corridor full of closed doors, several girls levitating to the ceiling. The one whose head touches the ceiling is nude, the others in various stages of undress.

One could assume on the basis of these early canvases simply an obsession with awakening female sexuality. One could fantasize this involvement stemming directly from the artist's past. Tanning writes of herself in the third person:

> Dorothea was raised in an atmosphere of strict Lutheran piety. But at the same time there hovered over the Tanning roof a genre of extravagance which might

have been named "Keeping Up." Thus, while dancing and card playing were forbidden to the three little daughters of the house, they were to be found wearing lace, and velvet cloaks, and dresses that might have been Paris originals.'

Certainly the raw materials for these works existed in Tanning's personal memories. But they function like buckets dipped into that eternally flowing river of the imagination which both surrealist and archetypalist seek to tap. As Tanning herself states: "One of the goals for me in painting was to *escape* biography."

Tanning's girls are overwhelmed by sexuality (suggested by teasing undress or total nudity). They embody some of the demonic airs suggested by Hans Bellmer's "The Doll." But while Bellmer infuses his doll with sadomasochistic fetishism, Tanning's girls suggest an erotic curiosity and impulsiveness. Sex happens to these girls, shocks and unbalances, sends them to the ceilings. Who are Tanning's girls? Rather than speaking of them as symbols of an individual psyche, allegories of Tanning's own childhood and adolescent erotic confusions, perhaps they are crystallizations, imagistically of her *various* souls. The notion of a polycentric personality realized on canvas is hinted at in Tanning's interview from Alain Jouffroy:

> My personal space is so sumptuously furnished that there is not the least room for feeling exiled.... There is such a plethora, and everything out of place. Everything moves. Also behind the invisible door, another door. I suppose I should say that I live a double life.[6]

Later in the same interview Tanning speaks of living "a double life. Or triple or multiple."[7] Doors are the keystones of Tanning's pictures. As Lewis Carroll reminds us in *Alice in Wonderland* any doorway is a potential entrance to another reality, another level of consciousness. The various souls in Tanning's paintings flutter near thresholds, peek around doors slightly ajar, wander through endless corridors of shut doors searching for someone or something. In what is Tanning's most widely recognized canvas, "Birthday," the artist stands, breasts bared, before a series of open doorways. The maiden's positioning near the doors suggests the soul's fervor in wanting to cross the threshold into erotic fulfillment. Their long tresses, often defying gravity, intimate a desire to be swept away.

The longing is surely for Eros. But the mingling of erotic and fearful imagery, the static postures and raging stances declare that the embrace of Eros is not all sweet delight. We do well to remember that Freud, lifelong charter of Psyche in Eros' tangles, concluded his life meditating on the death wish, and that James Hillman has said: "Fear seems an inherent necessity to the eros experience; where it is absent, one might well doubt the full validity of the loving."[8]

Tanning's canvases show that Eros can sometimes be a god of the underworld, a sleeping monster, both animal and angel, dog as well as god. Dogs are everywhere in Tanning's work. The winged creature resting at the artist's feet in "Birthday" synthesizes characteristics of boar, porcupine, cat, eagle and dog. A pekinese—that classical 'lap'-dog—assumes a variety of conventional and non-conventional guises. In "The Rose and the Dog" it echoes the terribly sentimental gazing face of a child painted by a commercial artist like Keene. It wears a fully human face in "Maternity." In "The Blue Waltz" a girl dances with a serious looking pekinese her own size. We can note a strikingly similar use of the dog in Charles Olson's poetry. Charles Stein writes:

> The figure of the "Dog"...occurs with some frequency in the series, and the various meanings which this figure is given bear archetypal resonance. Like the serpent, the image of the dog connotes a bi-valued principle of energy which is both creative-daemonic and rabid-demonic.[9]

As Olson's dog is both bestial and heavenly so too is Tanning's image of Eros. In her vision Eros is also a force which dogs us, sniffs in embarrassing places, tripping and screwing the soul at every opportunity. The tears and terror of many of Tanning's girls are not a preparation for Eros; rather they are the experience of Eros *as* Thanatos, the god as rabid dog.

Tanning's experience of Eros is reminiscent of Orphism. The Orphics too noted some of the shadows of Eros, claiming in their cosmologies that Eros was born from Chaos. This genealogy of Eros may account for the presence in many of Tanning's pictures of peculiar unformed creatures—unformed in the sense that there is no hint of human proportion. These shapes often resemble sculptures created in clay or bread dough, or energies fashioned by closely wrapping metal sheets haphazardly together. In "Interior" and "Interior With Sudden Joy" these figures rest on spidery, thin leg forms. As Tanning says: "My paintings bristle with objects that have no relation to anything in the dictionary." These formless forms are not, I suggest, chaotic images, but are images of Chaos. Compelled to imagine the origin of Eros, Tanning repeated the Orphic genealogy.

The frightened sleepwalkers who wander through the halls, the winged animals and dancing partner dogs, the precise formlessness of Tanning's images of Chaos, imaginings of this dark truth: it is in our fears, our wounds, our chaotic emptiness, our private hells that Tanning would lead us. She says:

> I want to seduce by means of imperceptible passages from one reality to another. The spectator is caught (oops!) in a net from which he can extricate himself only by going through the whole picture till he comes to the exit. My dearest wish: to make a picture without any exit at all, either for me or for him.[10]

Tanning desires to seduce us through the doorways, down the corridors, into these chaotic regions so that we, like her, may know Eros.

Many of the themes here discussed coalesce in the painting "Interior With Sudden Joy." Six figures coexist in a dark room featuring one wall covered by a blackboard. Curiously, the French word for shame, *Honte*, is written on the board. Reading from right to left: the first figures are two adolescent girls in partial undress, their small breasts revealed, linking arms in a loving gesture. The girl on the far right has one arm linked to the other girl (her sister), the other hand pets the head of a large pekinese, its rear its only visible aspect in the picture. The next two figures merge into one another: a nude black girl in tight embrace with one of Tanning's Tanguy-like globular masses. Next to this entwined couple a woman stands in an open doorway, dressed entirely in black, the bottom half of her body obscured in smoke. In her hand she holds a glowing object. Whatever she is holding emits a pale white light that frames her face in ghostly luminescence.

I propose the following reading: the painting is "about" the soul's relation to Eros. All of the actions are happening simultaneously, deepening and complicating each other. On one level there are the caucasian girls, a curious mix of eroticism and eeriness. Both are dressed in old-fashioned, long, white nightclothes, their tops unbuttoned. One wears a chemise totally buttoned under her nightclothes, the other wears a fashionable low cut, flesh-tone bra. The chemise girl wears bobbysocks—that perennial symbol of adolescence; the other wears black nylons. A lit cigarette carelessly burns at the feet of the bobbysocked girl. One girl pats the pekinese while gazing away from the other figures; the other looks in the direction of the black girl locked in erotic embrace. Both girls are clearly toying with the outward trappings of being grown up, yet are still virginal and girlish.

The embrace of the black girl and the other worldly creature is a psychic deepening of the virgins and the pekinese. The virgins become a black nude woman, worldly wise—the anima is no longer so pure. Eros is no longer a force easily domesticated and house broken. Here the god is a terrifying ungainly form, plaster white, that suggests *anything but* unbounded sexual pleasure; or sexual pleasure as death. The relationship between virginal anima and cherubic pekinese is no longer a condescending pat; instead the black woman bends one of her knees slightly to allow for maximal genital contact with the alien form.

At the threshold of a *coniunctio,* a voluptuous union, is the final figure. Dressed in black, her marriage will also be a funeral, a death of psychic virginity, an awakening through death of soul into life. She looks frozen—perhaps already feeling the icy wind of Hell—her pose is an essential one, she is a soul iced in its own essence. Already occurring is the change of anima into psyche, a change signified by the smoke, and as Wheelwright has noted: "...smoke, cloud, and vapor are but different forms of the state of being of things intermediate between fire and water, and soul belongs ontologically in this area. Being vaporous a soul is also smoky...."[11] Finally, the light is a lunar light, pale and white, the self-reflective light of an awakening psychic consciousness.

Tanning's surrealistic art connects not only to Orphism but also to Neoplatonism, alchemy, and to archetypal psychology. This tradition imagines that the anima, the white virgin, the innocent young maiden is awakened into psychic life only through tortures. While the pathology must be valued for its own sake, it is not the end. The anima is tortured *out* of innocent girlhood and *in* to something else: the torture by Eros into the complications of beauty.

III.

These bodies are rather affirmation, symbolic perhaps, of voluptuousness, but also of the fierceness of a connection, of the amazing will of a being to affirm his most ancient roots upon the civilized plane.

—Dorothea Tanning[12]

The leap from Tanning's paintings of the forties and fifties to her most recent works exhibited at the Gimpel and Weitzhoffer Gallery in November 1979 in New York is a dizzying passage. In his 1974 interview with the artist Jouffroy attempts to establish discrete stylistic periods that Tanning's pictures can be classified within. Tanning rejects such categories:

> Each of my paintings is a station on the same track. I don't see any breaks or deviations—even temporary ones. The same preoccupations are obvious from the beginning, the same obsessions rise to the surface.... My paintings, and lately my sculptures, are part of the same search, with discoveries, storms, hilarity, sufferings, rebirths.[13]

Yet the links between works of different periods require a patient and critical eye to detect. The surface trappings of her surrealistic style are absent from her recent works. The adherence to sharply defined objects arranged in startling juxtapositions in realistic interiors (a style connecting her with various works by Ernst, Dali, Magritte, and Sage) is no longer present. Nude girls have vanished. Even the doorways are absent.

In place of those images, Tanning has created luminous adult bodies that are swirls of vortical physical energies. An inspirational figure for this transition toward energetic whirls of color might have been Matta. In any event, Tanning's dancing, gyrating, twisting bodies dominate each canvas so totally that they suggest that the very air and ground they inhabit are created by their movements, inscapes *made* by imagining. Bodies are no longer destined to wander through long corridors. Ecstatically they celebrate being alive in the flesh in a universe humming with Eros.

Consider, for example, the 1977 painting "Family Portrait." An earlier painting with the same title has a dark and forbidding atmosphere, and was dominated by a massive male figure with eyes totally concealed behind glasses. Like a stony faced Underworld deity, this 'god' voids life as he himself is devoid of it. But how different the later canvas! Three humans and one dog twist and turn in a kaleidoscopic swirl of ruddy flesh tones and pastoral greens. The sex of the two figures is obscured. The woman's figure is corpulent, luxuriously fleshy, a soul ripened and round by experience. Her abdomen and legs are bathed in a bright white light from an unknown source. Above the abdomen her body is wrapped in a greenish wash, a rich protoplasmic broth. The remaining two human figures merge simultaneously into the body of the pekinese and woman. Many of Tanning's later canvases celebrate a psychological universe, a world where the soul's sheer exuberance in being incarnated in matter gives life to the earth. In "Tango Lives" a male and female dancer, their bodies emanating a cool blue luminosity, dance a tango in celebration. Their long limbs gracefully punctuate a backdrop of green floor and chalky white atmosphere. The cobalt blues and ivories imply a subtle cultured eroticism, a contrast to the hot passionate sexuality of "A Family Portrait."

Given Tanning's adamant insistence that "each of my paintings is a station of the same track" what is to be made of this astonishing transformation? A way into this enigma is offerred by her novelette, *Abyss*, a wonderful surrealistic gothic fable in the tradition of Poe and E.T.A. Hoffman, where the haunting binding of Eros and Underworld is ambiguously stated.

The novelette is, at least in some respects, a reverberation of the Eros/Psyche myth. Destina, a seductive little girl living in a large mansion housing a number of her tutors and other boarders, reveals a secret treasure to Albert, a painter residing in the house. Her treasure is a "memory box," a wooden toy box that contains bits of animal, human and supernatural anatomy. Destina shares another secret: somewhere in the nearby desert she has befriended a panther. In attempting to confirm the existence of such an unlikely animal, and seduced by Destina's convincing tale, Albert meets violent and untimely death.

Albert's fate hints at the result of splitting Eros, as is so often done in life and in theory, into a physical and spiritual component. Albert's desire is ravenously physical:

> He dragged his eyes away from the table and looked at her face. There was a choking pain in his chest. His gaze devoured the little red mouth, the throat, the hair, the white dress, as his mouth had devoured the plateful of food.[14]

The reader's nose right away smells something rotten. Albert's desire is so engorgingly physical, without reflection, timing or culture. But at the same time the fascination with Destina is too puer, too spiritual. Falling in love with the fantastic animal of Destina's imagination, Albert must know if it is *real* or not, and it is this complex of to be or not to be that does him in. The division of Eros into dark and light, body and spirit, Tanning may be telling us, keeps the soul forever in a beguilingly white dress.

Destina's "memory box" recalls the box of beauty in the myth. A brief amplification may be appropriate here. The retrieval of the box of beauty from the Underworld, a terrifying task, is the last chore imposed upon Psyche by a jealous Aphrodite; but instead of delivering the box unopened to the feet of the goddess, as she had been instructed, Psyche lifts the lid herself. As her eyes close, she dives into a deep sleep. Hitting bottom she is rescued by Eros. Since Psyche finds the box in the Underworld, I suggest that the box is an underworld vision of herself, a vision that sees through the strawberry-and-cream appearance of the anima into the lacunae, wounds and weaknesses, the chronic conditions of the soul. This is a dark, dark eye that restores death to life. Death is recalled as intrinsic to life, running through the veins of the world's body like ice.

Yet the box contains beauty. When boxed in, bound by symptoms, afraid and suffering, and unable to keep the lid on for one second longer, it is then that the flesh unveils its beauty, the beauty of what is vulnerable and fragile. At just this bottoming out moment Eros appears: The celebration of this union is pleasure.

Heralded by Destina's "memory box," this transformation of anima into psychic beauty, a transformation occurring through an Underworld experience, a vivid pathologizing, is recorded by Tanning's canvases. Curiously, archetypal psychology appears today to be making a similar passage, that is, moving through pathologizing and an eye for shadow into an appreciation of the flesh of things, an *aesthesis*. Suddenly, the irony, if not the outrage, of using archetypal psychology as a means of interpreting Tanning's work shows itself. In their imaginings the archetypalists plod heavily where Tanning danced with grace and subtlety. Though that may be the importance of their work. Through painting and poetry the inferiority of psychology is discovered instead of the reverse.

"Still in the Studio" features a nude woman (Tanning?) at work in her studio. The studio is dark except for one overhead light pouring through one uncurtained window. The woman is leaning on her back over the drawing table with what appears to be a watercolor box (the box of beauty?) resting precariously over her breasts. He lower abdomen is disproportionate to the rest of her figure. In spite of the textual monotony and surface drabness of the studio space, the impact of the canvas is far from morose. The artist's body bathed in white light is clearly the dominating image. It is a psychic body. Its odd position suggests labor and repose, bodily indulgence and mental concentration, Eros and Psyche in precarious balance with pathology somewhere off in a dark corner of the studio, temporarily contained. The body placed where normally a sheet of paper would appear suggests that the artist's body is the original *prima materia* of the artisitc alchemical process, that the state of flesh unavoidably enters every moment in creating an artistic work. It is the drawing pad of the artist, Eros; the created image is the soul.

IV.

> I see eroticism as superb and triumphant, but what a dearth of spirit if that were all.
>
> —Dorothea Tanning[15]

Among the words subject to massive onslaught of cultural debasement, 'eroticism' has suffered ignobly. Media distortions create in the public consciousness a notion of indulgent recklessness, genital-bound, manic, sexual activity. The real roots of eroticism lie in the mythologem of the Greek god Eros, and those roots are dense and tangled. Eros is the lifeforce, the urge toward self-preservation, the libido. He is a God, linked, according to Jung, with that portion of a woman's consciousness between this material world and spiritual cosmos. Although a god of sexual pleasure, and upward transformation from innocence, Eros is also a child of Chaos.

Considering the range of Dorothea Tanning's art, I would insist on *all* the multifarious meanings of Eros. I don't want to split Eros into dark and light, body and spirit, Freud and Jung. I want to emphasize the advent of Eros in the frozen, fearful stances, seductively disheveled clothes and no-exit halls of Tanning's early work, while showing that Eros is also manifest in the dances, caresses, swirling movements and intense tonalities of the most recent work. No beauty without vulnerability, no love without fear, no life without death. "Each of my paintings is a station on the same track." Lines from a Robert Kelly[16] poem provide a fitting epigram:

> Eros was my master
> & now I wonder
> if I ever had another,
> he who shaped
> all these relentless subtle roads.

1. Maurice Nadeau, *The History of Surrealism,* tr. Richard Howard (New York: Macmillan, 1965), p. 89.
2. Deborah Rosenthal, "Interview with André Masson" in *Arts Magazine,* November 1980, p. 93.
3. Maurice Nadeau, *The History of Surrealism,* tr. Richard Howard (New York: Macmillan, 1965), p. 89.
4. James Hillman, *Revisioning Psychology* (New York: Harper & Row, 1975), p. x.
5. Elsa Honig Fine, *Women and Art*(New York: Allanheld and Schram, 1978), p. 210.
6. Dorothea Tanning, *Catalog From the Exhibition at the Centre National de l'Art Contemporain,* Paris, June 1974, p. 47. (The interview with Alain Jouffrey translated from the French for the author by Sandra Blackaby.)
7. *Ibid.* p. 45.
8. James Hillman, *The Myth of Analysis* (Evanston: Northwestern University Press, 1972), p. 81.
9. Charles Stein, "Olson and Jung: The Projection of Archetypal Force Onto Language" in *New Wilderness Letter* #8, Spring 1980, p. 52.
10. Dorothea Tanning, *10 Recent Paintings and a Biography* (New York: Gimpel and Weitzenhoffer Gallery, 1979), unpaginated.
11. P. Wheelwright, *Heraclitus* (Princeton University Press, 1959), p. 66.
12. *Tanning Catalog,* p. 47.
13. *Ibid.* p. 46.
14. Dorothea Tanning, *Abyss* (New York: Standard Editions, 1977), p. 43.
15. *Tanning Catalog,* p. 48.
16. Robert Kelly, *Kill the Messenger* (Santa Barbara: Black Sparrow Press, 1979), p. 21.

THE BENZENE UROBOROS:
Plastic and Catastrophe in *Gravity's Rainbow*

MICHAEL VANNOY ADAMS
(Easton, Pennsylvania)

> Apart from the python, the snake in general appears in Dahomean symbolism and art, though little in Yoruba. In the clay wall mouldings (bas-reliefs) and decorated cloths in the palace-museum at Abomey there are striking representations of brightly coloured snakes, red, blue, and white, the most sacred colours. The snake is curled in a circle, with its tail in its mouth; a very ancient and almost universal symbol of immortality and eternity.... by swallowing its tail it forms a circle...which goes round and round for ever, 'like a great ring,' or like 'first, and last, and midst, and without end.'...
> The coloured snake is not only called by the name of the principal snake Dā, but is also regarded by the Ewe as representing the rainbow, Aido Hwedo.
>
> Geoffrey Parrinder[1]

> Fate-the-rocket describes a parabola
> In darkness mostly, more rarely on a rainbow.
>
> Andrey Voznesensky[2]

From the title, *Gravity's Rainbow*[3] seems exclusively a novel of classical physics. And indeed Thomas Pynchon does combine Newton's theories of mechanics and of optics, his laws of mass and motion, light and color, in a metaphoric pun of immense imaginative complexity: gravity's rainbow is attraction's diffraction. Pynchon describes the trajectory of the visible spectrum; he plots the prismatic curve of a projectile, the plastic roiket that writes its iridescent, catastrophic way across the sky until gravity forces it to crash and explode at rainbow's end. The vapor from the exhaust of the rocket diffracts the white light of the atmosphere into red, orange, yellow, green, blue, indigo and violet, and as gravity's influence attracts the mass of the rocket in motion, the result is a rainbow. Pynchon's rainbow is not, like Noah's, the symbol of a covenant that God will never again destroy man in a diluvian catastrophe, but a symbol of the last judgment—that man may well destroy himself in a plastic one.

The author is Assistant Professor of English and Acting Chairman of American Civilization at Lafayette College. A version of this essay was presented at the Jungian Perspectives on Creativity and the Unconscious Conference, Miami University, Oxford, Ohio, June 1979.

As important as classical physics is to Pynchon, *Gravity's Rainbow* is also a novel of analytical psychology and organic chemistry. With C. G. Jung and F. A. Kekulé, Pynchon shares an intense interest in a self-consuming artifact: the uroboros, the self-devouring snake or dragon—an image Pynchon associates metaphorically with the plastic rocket that produces gravity's rainbow.

To the extent that Pynchon epitomizes the post-modern temper he is perhaps our most important contemporary novelist—and *Gravity's Rainbow* is his masterpiece. Jung requires no exposition or justification. But Kekulé is an instance of a person whose influence, direct or indirect, greatly exceeds his fame.[4] At a symposium to commemorate the hundredth anniversary of a discovery a sympathetic participant, George E. Hein, deplored the discrepancy between the truly remarkable contribution Kekulé made to science and the quite inadequate acknowledgement he received from society for it. Specialists in priority credit Kekulé with the discovery of the benzene ring, the indispensable prerequisite of the structural theory of organic chemistry, which Hein says "may be the most fruitful conceptual scheme in all the history of science." But "although he is considered the founder of a powerful and fantastically productive theory, Kekulé is essentially unknown except by chemists and professional historians."[5] An exception is Pynchon, who uses Jung's psychology and Kekulé's chemistry to construct a fiction that is scientific as well as artistic—and shattering to our complacent notions of "unconscious creation."

Kekulé and The Chemistry of Discovery

Evidence for the existence and vast creativity of the collective unconscious can be derived from Kekulé's discovery, the benzene ring, which appeared to him in a dream in 1865, leading to the foundation of organic chemistry as a field. In what Hein calls "a major address on creativity and the psychological processes related to discovery,"[6] Kekulé describes himself at work one evening in his study:

> I was sitting, writing on my textbook, but it was not going well; my mind was on other things. I turned my chair to the fire and sank into a half-sleep. Once again the atoms were dancing before my eyes. This time the smaller groups stayed discreetly in the background. My mind's eye, rendered more acute by repeated visions of the kind, could now distinguish larger images of manifold conformation. Long rows,

sometimes more closely coupled together; all in motion, twisting and writhing like a snake. But look, what was that? One of the snakes had seized hold of its own tail, and the image coiled mockingly before my eyes. As if by a lightning bolt I awoke...I spent the rest of the night in working out the consequences of the hypothesis.[7]

Anyone familiar with analytical psychology readily identifies the image of the snake seizing hold of its own tail. It is the uroboros, the central archetype of the collective unconscious and a universal symbol of transformation.[8]

Kekulé advises his colleagues to cultivate their private, perhaps involuntary visions, but he also cautions them to control their emotions and check and correct their claims, lest their "facts" prove to be mere figments of imagination—momentary enthusiasms, and embarrassments. In Kekulé's own words:

If we learn to dream, gentlemen, then maybe we shall discover the truth:
    And who doesn't think,
    To him it will be given,
    He has it without worries—
but let us beware of making our dreams public before they have been tested by the waking mind.[9]

Kekulé's proposition about the psychological processes involved in discovery entails the perhaps romantic (though not necessarily incorrect) notion that creation is often an intuitive, almost effortless unconscious event, that real originality is a gift, and that the so-called creator is not an active agent but a passive vehicle for the tenor of unconsciousness. Unless critical, reflective consciousness disciplines the dream, Kekulé says, the discovery may well prove to be a delusion, and genius self-indulgence. We shall see how Pynchon improves on Kekulé's warning—how catastrophic this creative unconscious can become even when checked and corrected.

The vision that reveals to Kekulé the hexagonal or ring form of the benzene molecule in so graphic a representation is an authentic case of a mantic archetype. A drowsy Kekulé dozes off into a dream or reverie; atoms couple and dance; as Kekulé focuses his mind's eye one of the images assumes uroboric form: the self-devouring snake dares Kekulé to draw the obvious inference and discover the molecular structure of benzene. What more dramatic documentation of a prophetic dream?

Kekulé the visionary scientist discovers the benzene ring—perhaps more properly, the collective unconscious reveals the benzene ring *to* him, but in a symbolic form, the theoretical meaning of which he must interpret for himself. The image that appears to Kekulé is a proleptic archetype; in this instance at least, the logic of scientific discovery is the illogic of oneiric divination.

It is highly significant that the uroboros, the most ancient image of the alchemical conjunction, or *coniunctio* ("what we now call chemical combination," Jung says), appears to Kekulé and leads to an important scientific discovery. According to Jung, the more "theriomorphic" the image of the conjunction (and with Kekulé the image is utterly reptilian), "the more obvious is the part played by creative fantasy and thus by the unconscious." In fact, Jung says, the discovery of the benzene ring is unique confirmation of the fantastic creativity of the collective unconscious and the alchemical imagination over almost two millennia. Jung says this about the role of metaphor in research, in reference to Kekulé's discovery:

> Since there can never be absolute freedom from prejudice, even the most objective and impartial investigator is liable to become the victim of some unconscious assumption upon going into a region where the darkness has never been illuminated and where he can recognize nothing. This need not necessarily be a misfortune, since the idea which then presents itself as a substitute for the unknown will take the form of an archaic though not inapposite analogy. Thus Kekulé's vision of the dancing couples, which first put him on the track of the structure of certain compounds, namely the benzene ring, was surely a vision of the *coniunctio*...that had preoccupied the minds of the alchemists for seventeen centuries....but in Kekulé's vision it reached its chemical goal in the end, thus rendering the greatest imaginable service both to our understanding of organic compounds and to the subsequent unprecedented advances in synthetic chemistry.[10]

The archaic analogy is so opposite as to be ironic, for it is not just any metaphoric ring that suggests the chemical structure of benzene to Kekulé but the alchemical uroboros, the self-devouring snake or dragon. It is as if the reptilian form of the *coniunctio* bides its time, conceals its secret over the centuries, and then in an annunciatory dream reveals the truth to Kekulé, who just happens to be the right person in the right place at the right time to receive credit for the "discovery."

Jung and The Alchemy of Individuation

"The dragon," Jung says, "is probably the oldest pictorial symbol in alchemy of which we have documentary evidence. It appears as the *ouroboros*, the tail-eater, in the Codex Marcianus...which dates from the tenth or eleventh century." The symbolic meaning is that the experimental method of the alchemists "is a sort of circle like a dragon biting its own tail."[11] Jung privileges the image of "the dragon devouring itself tail first." It is nothing less than "the basic mandala of alchemy."[12]

The ostensible object of alchemy is the transmutation of matter (*materia prima*) by various methods of refinement. In Jung's theory the alchemical method is a metaphor for a psychological process: the transformation of the psyche, or individuation.

Individuation involves an existential-ontological paradox—that man, the subject matter of the experiment, can only "become" what he already in a real sense "is"; that to complete one's development is merely to make actual one's potential; that the end is the beginning; in short, that the alchemical-psychological process is conspicuous for its circularity. It is therefore apt, Jung says, that the uroboros is an imagistic oxymoron: "In the age-old image of the uroboros lies the thought of devouring oneself and turning oneself into a circulatory process, for it was clear to the more astute alchemists that the prima materia of the art was man himself."[13]

The self-devouring snake or dragon is the intuitive expression of this dialectical development. "The alchemists, who in their own way knew more about the nature of the individuation process than we moderns do," Jung says, "expressed this paradox through the symbol of the uroboros, the snake [or dragon[14]] that bites its own tail."[15] The reason the uroboros occupies such an important position in analytical psychology as well as in alchemy is that it symbolizes in an especially concrete, concise, and visually impressive way the dynamics of individuation. One would of course expect the appearance of the uroboros, as for instance to Kekulé, to be creative. Let us see.

Time and Eternity

The uroboros has a history and a meaning prior to organic chemistry, analytical psychology and alchemy. One of the earliest records of the self-devouring snake or dragon occurs in *The Hieroglyphics of Horapollo,* an immensely influential pre-Champollion manuscript, which purports to decipher some of the most important Egyptian hieroglyphs, among them the uroboros. Marsilio Ficino, for example, mentions the symbol in his commentary on Plotinus, and interprets the hieroglyph by direct reference to Horapollo. The uroboros, Ficino says, has to do with time and eternity:

> Your thought of time, for instance, is manifold and mobile, maintaining that time is speedy and by a sort of revolution joins the beginning to the end. . . . The Egyptians comprehend this whole discourse in one stable image, painting a winged serpent, holding its tail in its mouth.[16]

The winged serpent, or basilisk, is the first hieroglyph that Horapollo interprets. The basilisk is an unreal creature, with the body and beak of a bird and the tail of a snake. Horapollo says that when the Egyptians symbolize eternity, "they draw a serpent with its tail concealed by the rest of its body."[17] In this gloss on the hieroglyph, the basilisk tucks its tail under its body—it does not hold its tail in its mouth. But in other representations the basilisk wraps its tail around its neck or touches its bird beak to a snake tail that is simultaneously a mouth.[18] The second hieroglyph that Horapollo interprets is the unwinged uroboros, "a serpent devouring its own tail," by which the Egyptians symbolize not time or eternity but the universe itself. Horapollo says that "the fact that it uses its own body for food signifies that whatever things are generated in the world by Divine Providence are received back into it by [a gradual process of] diminution."[19] George Boas, the translator of this passage, says that the image of a self-consuming cosmos is an allusion to "the doctrine of cycles,"[20] the periodic and perpetual turns and returns of the universe.

In all, the uroboros has at least four and perhaps more symbolic meanings—chemical, psychological, alchemical and hieroglyphical. To these Pynchon adds a radically subversive post-modern meaning that subsumes all previous conventional meanings under his own version of catastrophe theory. In the course of his reinterpretation, Pynchon reconsiders the role of unconscious inspiration in the creative process. *Gravity's Rainbow* is a critique of the contemporary human prospect, and in the uroboros Pynchon has a symbol to promote the catastrophic moral of his novel. According to Pynchon, the uroboros is by no means necessarily creative. *How it is used, not whether it is unconsciously inspired, is the issue.* Though the uroboros may be used to further the survival of man, Pynchon suggests that it is now being used in a way so egotistically destructive as virtually to ensure his extinction.

In *Gravity's Rainbow* Pynchon takes Kekulé's dream of the snake that devours itself, relates it to Jung's theory of the collective unconscious and raises a number of psychological issues; for example, the way in which a person (in this case a chemist) becomes the vehicle of a particular archetype, as if the image were meant especially for him:

> Look at this. There is about to be expedited, for Friedrich August Kekulé von Stradonitz, his dream of 1865, the great Dream that revolutionized chemistry.... It was nice of Jung to give us the idea of an ancestral pool in which everybody shares the same dream material. But how is it we are each visited as individuals, each by exactly and only what he needs? (p. 410)[21]

The ancestral pool is a convenient hypothesis, Pynchon says, but is it an adequate explanation? How in Jung's theory is the collective level related to the individual level, the general to the particular, the universal to the unique? Why does a transpersonal (or impersonal) archetype happen to have a personal meaning for Kekulé—just what he needs to perceive the benzene ring? If the essence of creativity is singularity, how can what we all share—the common, stock images of the collective unconscious—have such uncommon, even exclusive connotations as uroboros in Kekulé's case.[22]

Pynchon prefers to be provocative, to pose questions that may or may not have answers but are no less serious for all that. For example, he entertains the possibility that Jung's theory of the collective unconscious is no more adequate an explanation of the visionary experience than Plato's notion of an ideal dimension. Is not Kekulé's dream of the self-devouring snake, Pynchon asks, an archetype in Plato's, and not Jung's, sense of the word—an idea from another dimension, a spiritual reality separate from but parallel to this material reality? Pynchon suggests that "the cosmic Serpent, in the violet splendor of its scales," passes not from the unconscious into the conscious but from the spiritual into the material world, and appears to Kekulé as an archetype not so much in the psychological as in the philosophical—or religious—sense. Pynchon addresses this issue as if he himself were in Plato's timeless other dimension of ideas. He says, "after you get a little time in—whatever *that* means over here—one of these archetypes gets to look pretty much like any other." Only the most recent arrivals in eternity exclaim, " 'Wow! Hey—that's th-th' *Tree o' Creation*! Huh? Ain't it! Je-eepers!' " (p. 411). If one archetype looks pretty much like any other, how does a dreamer like Kekulé manage to identify an important image? Why is one archetype of no noticeable practical value, yet another of such energetic force and explanatory power that it startles the dreamer into sudden consciousness, an intense certainty of revelatory truth, indeed a portentous scientific discovery? Pynchon does not answer; he forces us to think.

Pynchon and Plastic

Pynchon recounts how Kekulé envisions the uroboric ring, the theoretical structure that eludes his critical intellect but seizes his creative imagination:

> ...Kekulé went looking among the molecules of the time for the hidden shapes he knew were there, shapes he did not like to think of as real physical structures, but as "rational formulas," showing the relationships that went on in "metamorphoses," his quaint 19th-century way of saying "chemical reactions." But he could visualize. He *saw* the four bonds of carbon, lying in a tetrahedron—he *showed* how carbon atoms could link up, one to another, into long chains....But he was stumped when he got to benzene. He knew there were six carbon atoms with a hydrogen attached to each one—but he could not see the shape. Not until the dream...(p. 412)

In the benzene ring Kekulé discovers "a basis for new compounds, new arrangements...new methods of synthesis," which enables experimenters to produce in their laboratories new molecules, artificial combinations that may not exist under natural conditions (p. 412). It is in reference to this synthetic system that one of Pynchon's characters associates the old serpent in the pristine, paradisaical garden with the new serpent in Kekulé's dream:

> "Who sent this new serpent to our ruinous garden, already too fouled, too crowded to qualify as any locus of innocence...something that Kekulé's Serpent had come to—not to destroy, but to define to us the loss of...we had been given certain molecules, certain combinations and not others...we used what we found

> in Nature, unquestioning, shamefully perhaps—but the Serpent whispered, *'They can be changed,* and new molecules assembled from the debris of the given....' Can anyone tell me what else he whispered to us? Come—who knows?..." (p. 413)

What else does the new serpent whisper to us in our polluted, overpopulated wasteland, the site of our ecologically perverse experience? Perhaps the word "plastic." For when the serpent whispers the word—whatever it is—he paraphrases what Pynchon calls "Plasticity's central canon: that chemists were no longer to be at the mercy of Nature. They could decide now what properties they wanted a molecule to have, and then go ahead and build it" (p. 249).

To succumb to the plastic serpent is to tamper with the world. The old Adam in us is the old Ego, not the new Self. The alternative to survival through individuation is sheer egotism—and extinction through temptation. No longer content with our God-given natural environment, we construct an artificial man-made one; its pervasively synthetic quality is a chemical realization of the alchemical objective—and an ironic comment on it.

Roland Barthes devotes a chapter in *Mythologies* to the phenomenology and semiology of plastic. According to Barthes, plastic is essentially "the stuff of alchemy." The production of plastic is "the accomplishment of the magical operation par excellence: the transmutation of matter." In fact, the product itself is less impressive than the property and process of plasticity. "So, more than a substance, plastic is the very idea of its infinite transformation," Barthes says. "In the hierarchy of the major poetic substances," plastic is "the first magical substance which consents to be prosaic." Barthes says that in plastic, "for the first time, artifice aims at something common, not rare." Unlike the gold of the old alchemists, the plastic of the new chemists is not precious but cheap and disreputable—as in the pejorative use of the word "plastic" to disparage anything artificial or unnatural. In short, Barthes says, "The hierarchy of substances is abolished: a single one replaces them all: the whole world *can* be plasticized..."[23] In *Gravity's Rainbow* Pynchon suggests that the whole post-modern world *is*, or is *being*, completely plasticized. Nature is at the mercy of the chemists.

Ancient usage associates the uroboros with what Mircea Eliade calls the myth of the eternal return.[24] The circular form of the self-consuming image suggests a cyclical model of the cosmos and of history. Pynchon is sympathetic to this interpretation, but he is realistic enough about our post-modern situation, and what he calls "the system," to be justifiably pessimistic about the use, misuse or abuse of the uroboros:

> Kekulé dreams the Great Serpent holding its own tail in its mouth...But the meanness, the cynicism with which this dream is to be used. The Serpent that announces, "The World is a closed thing, cyclical, resonant, eternally-returning," is to be delivered into a system whose only aim is to *violate* the cycle. (p. 412)

If the world is a closed thing, the serpent is a closed ring. To Kekulé, in his moment of almost mystical illumination, "what the Serpent means is—how's this—that the six carbon atoms of benzene are in fact curled around into a closed ring, *just like that snake with its tail in its mouth,* GET IT?" (p. 413).

The benzene uroboros is the ancient alchemical dream-come-true as a modern chemical discovery. Or is it? If it is, Pynchon says, then it is neither a good dream nor a bad dream but the worst nightmare imaginable: the ultimate ecological, historical and cosmological crisis. The synthetic system has only one aim, and that is to violate the life cycle with a death wish. The symbol Pynchon chooses to convey this meaning is the S-Gerat 00000 rocket, a secret missile made of a special experimental plastic, Impolex G; its research and development derive from the benzene ring Kekulé dreamed in 1865. The plastic rocket is the new uroboros, "beautiful Serpent, its coils in rainbow lashings in the sky..." (p. 721). Beautiful but catastrophic, as it crashes and explodes under gravity's influence. The trajectory of the plastic rocket is semicircular—a half not a whole circle, not a full or complete circle. Pynchon's plastic rainbow serpent and his plastic world are non-recyclable, nonreturnable, GET IT? Now the uroboros is not creativity but catastrophe.

Perhaps "plastic" is not the word the new uroboros whispers. "What's the *most* frequent word?" one of Pynchon's characters asks, and another answers, "death," as if the reply were just a casual fact of statistical life (p. 32). In this unconscious compulsion to repeat the word, Pynchon sees evidence of the death-wish, the self-destroying tendency of the synthetic system, whose express purpose is to violate—once and for all—the recreative, eternal return of the life cycle. Is this mood a temper or distemper on Pynchon's part—perhaps a case of post-modern paranoia (which not so incidentally is one of Pynchon's own most frequent words). Is Pynchon just paranoid, discontented with the current course of civilization, or has he good reason for being so pessimistic about the contemporary human condition?

The perspective Pynchon imposes on civilization is a prophetically catastrophic prospect implicit in a mantic archetype, the benzene uroboros. It is the art with which Pynchon uses science that makes this perspective real enough—and appalling enough—to give us pause. What is at issue is nothing less than our survival. If we continue on our egotistical course, persist in our perversity, and tamper with our world—as if it were infinitely transmutable and, more importantly, indestructible—then we willfully create the technological means to destroy ourselves in a plastic catastrophe. Kekulé dreams the uroboros, but organic chemistry is neither alchemy nor analytical psychology. No image from the collective unconscious is *per se* creative; every image requires interpretation, and as the example of Kekulé demonstrates, the technological application of that interpretation may be so destructive that it threatens man with extinction. To Kekulé the uroboros means one thing, benzene. And benzene means plastic. The benzene uroboros is not the beginning, the middle and end of things, the life cycle eternally returning. It is merely the end of things—the death-wish fulfilled.

---

1 *West African Religion* (London: Epworth, 2nd ed. rev., 1961), p. 52.
2 "Parabolic Ballad," trans. George Reavey, in *Modern European Poetry*, ed. Willis Barnstone *et al.* (New York: Bantam, 1978), p. 467. I thank Carolyn Marvin for directing my attention to this poem.
3 For criticism of *Gravity's Rainbow* see David Cowart, *Thomas Pynchon: the art of allusion* (Carbondale: Southern Illinois University, 1980); Douglas A. Fowler, *A Guide to Pynchon's Gravity's Rainbow* (Ann Arbor: Ardis, 1979); George Levine and David Leverenz, eds., *Mindful Pleasures: essays on Thomas Pynchon* (Boston: Little, Brown, 1976); Frank D. McConnell, *Four Postwar American Novelists: Bellow, Mailer, Barth, and Pynchon* (Chicago: University of Chicago, 1977); Edward Mendelson, ed., *Pynchon: a collection of critical essays* (Englewood Cliffs: Prentice-Hall, 1978); William M. Plater, *The Grim Phoenix: reconstructing Gravity's Rainbow* (Bloomington, Ind.: Indiana University, 1978); Mark Richard Siegal, *Pynchon: creative paranoia in Gravity's Rainbow* (Port Washington: Kennikat, 1978); Joseph W. Slade, *Thomas Pynchon* (New York: Warner, 1974); Thomas P. Walsh and Cameron Northhouse, *John Barth, Jerzy Kosinski, and Thomas Pynchon: a reference guide* (Boston: G. K. Hall, 1977); and Lawrence C. Wolfley, "Repression's Rainbow: The Presence of Norman O. Brown in Pynchon's Big Novel," *PMLA* 92 (October 1977), 873—889.
4 Kekulé (1829—1896) was appointed full professor of chemistry at the University of Ghent when he was 29. In 1860 he organized the first International Congress of Chemists. Eventually he was offered

the chair of chemistry at the University of Bonn. The year before his death he was enobled by William II of Prussia. Kekulé was known throughout his career as a theoretician who emphasized speculation rather than experimentation, conjectural models rather than laboratory tests. See the *Dictionary of Scientific Biography,* ed. Charles C. Gillispie (New York: Scribner's, 1973), VII, 279-283. Kekulé's great discovery was the structure of the aromatic compounds, of which the benzene ring was the most important: "The solution in this instance came to Kekulé in a vision—half awake, he saw before his eyes the animated image of a chain of carbon atoms, closing upon itself like a snake biting its own tail. He was instantly aware of the significance of such a closure. . .He arrived at a closed chain of six carbon atoms, linked alternately by three single and three double bonds and constituting the common nucleus of all the aromatic substances" (p. 281).

5 "Kekulé and the Architecture of Molecules," in Robert F. Gould, ed., *Kekulé Centennial, Advances in Chemistry Series,* 61 (Washington: American Chemical Society, 1966), p. 1.
6 Ibid., p. 2.
7 *Ber. d. deutsch, chem. Ges.,* 23 (1890), 1302; also in Richard Anschutz, *August Kekulé* (Berlin: Verlag Chemie, 1929), II, 942. I should like to thank Regina Zevas for her retranslation of the quotations from the German; cf. the previous translations by Francis R. Japp, "Kekulé Memorial Lecture," *Journal of the Chemical Society,* 73 (1898), 100, and Oswald J. Walker, "August Kekulé and the Benzene Problem," *Annals of Science,* 4 (1939), 40. See also Eduard Farber, "Dreams and Visions in a Century of Chemistry," in Gould, ed., *Kekulé Centennial,* pp. 129-139.
8 See the illustrations of the uroboros in Erich Neumann, *The Origins and History of Consciousness,* trans. R.F.C. Hull (New York: Pantheon/Bollingen, 1954), between pp. 32 and 33. See also Jorge Luis Borges and Margaritta Guerro, *The Book of Imaginary Beings,* trans. Norman Thomas di Giovanni (New York: Avon, 1970), pp. 234-235; Borges says of the uroboros: "Heraclitus had said that in the circumference the beginning and the end are a single point. A third-century Greek amulet, preserved in the British Museum, gives us the image which best illustrates this endlessness: the serpent that bites its own tail or, as the Argentine poet Martínez Estrada so beautifully put it, 'that begins at the end of its tail.' A story runs that Mary Queen of Scots had engraved on a gold ring the inscription 'In my end is my beginning,' meaning perhaps that real life begins after death. Uroboros (Greek for 'the one that devours its tail') is the learned name of the creature which became the symbol adopted by alchemists in the Middle Ages. The curious may read further in Jung's *Psychologie und Alchemie.*"
9 Op. cit.
10 *The Practice of Psychotheraphy, CW* 16, §353.
11 *Psychology and Alchemy, CW* 12, §404; see also the illustration of the uroboros.
12 Ibid., §165.
13 *Mysterium Coniunctionis, CW* 14, §513.
14 *Alchemical Studies, CW* 13, §105. Jung says that the logic of this transformation is life-cyclical. The turn (or return) into oneself is, symbolically, "the eternal cycle of birth and death. This cycle was represented in ancient alchemy by the symbol of the uroboros, the dragon that bites its own tail." See the frontispiece illustration and also those in *Psychology and Alchemy,* pp. 38, 53, 64, 103, 191, and 457.
15 *Aion, CW* 9, ii, §297.
16 Horapollo Niliacus, *The Hieroglyphics of Horapollo,* trans. George Boas (New York: Pantheon/Bollingen, 1950), p. 28.
17 Ibid., p. 57.
18 See the illustrations of the basilisk, ibid., between pp. 58 and 59, and in *Psychology and Alchemy,* p. 46. The basilisk that touches its bird beak to a snake tail is a detail from a twelfth-century French marble arch in the Metrogolitan Museum of Art.

19 *The Hieroglyphics of Horapollo*, p. 57. See the illustration of the uroboros between pp. 58 and 59.
20 Ibid., p. 58.
21 All parenthesized page references are to Thomas Pynchon, *Gravity's Rainbow* (New York: Viking, 1973).
22 Silvano Arieti raises this issue in *Creativity: the magic synthesis* (New York: Basic Books, 1976), p. 27.
23 *Mythologies*, trans. Annette Lavers (New York: Hill and Wang, 1972), pp. 97-99.
24 *The Myth of the Eternal Return; or, cosmos and history*, trans. Willard R. Trask (Princeton: Princeton University/Bollingen, 1954), *passim*.

Special Introductory Offer

NEW LITERARY HISTORY

A Journal of Theory and Interpretation

Ralph Cohen, editor

New Literary History is a journal that contemporary scholars in a variety of fields will welcome as an important contribution to the areas of aesthetic and literary study.

Centering on literary theory and interpretation *New Literary History* examines a variety of interdisciplinary theoretical models and their significance for literary history. Contributions from scholars in a variety of fields, including anthropologists, sociologists, historians, novelists, poets, philosophers, and linguists help to define and interpret the problems of literary study.

New Literary History is unique among literary journals because each issue is devoted to a particular topic or problem and offers in-depth analysis and a multi-faceted view of the question under consideration. The various points raised by the essays are brought together and analyzed through critical commentary.

NEW LITERARY HISTORY
November, February, May

☐ $12.00 Individual Rate (regularly $13.00)
☐ $25.00 Institutional Rate (regularly $26.00)

NAME _____

ADDRESS _____

CITY _____ STATE _____ ZIP CODE _____

Make checks payable to: **The Johns Hopkins University Press**
NEW LITERARY HISTORY
Baltimore, Maryland 21218

Unless otherwise noted, subscriptions will begin with the next issue. Offer valid for new subscriptions only. Prepayment required.

NX

A SOUL'S JOURNEY
Albert Camus, Tuberculosis, and Aphrodite

MICHAEL P. SIPIORA
(San Jose/Dallas)

> My chief occupation despite appearances has been love (its pleasures for a long time and finally its most painful transports). I have a romantic soul and have always had considerable trouble interesting it in something else.[1]
>
> Camus

Albert Camus, contracted pulmonary tuberculosis at the age of seventeen. The disease was to stay with him throughout his life. One of Camus' biographers, Germaine Bree, notes:

> Camus began to keep 'Notebooks' almost immediately after his first encounter with tuberculosis, and it is probably the reaction to his illness that made a writer of the passionate young Algerian.[2]

Philip Thody, another biographer, writes:

> Most critics have unhesitatingly stated that Camus's first attack of tuberculosis...[was] the crucial experience which turned him from an unreflective enjoyment of life to the long and sometimes anguished meditation on existence which informs his whole work.[3]

The *Notebooks* and early essays of the consumptive Camus lend themselves to imagining tuberculosis as a way of life; they tell the story of a journey of the soul.

The *Notebooks* are Camus' "meditation on existence," a journal which chronicles the progress of his work. Camus describes that work in the preface to *L'Envers et L'Endroit (The Wrong Side and the Right Side):*

The author received a Masters Degree in philosophy from San Jose State University and is currently a doctoral student in psychology at the University of Dallas. His article "Repairing, Furnishing, Decorating: Making a Home" will appear in the forthcoming issue of *Dragonflies*.

a man's work is nothing but this slow trek to rediscover, through the detours of art, those two or three great and simple images in whose presence his heart first opened.[4]

It seems that the young man's heart was opened by archetypal images, for his *Notebooks* embody a mythical mode of imagination, "The world in which I am most *at ease:* the Greek myth."[5]

Camus, brought up amidst ancient ruins on the North African coast, was a modern pagan Greek. His view of the world exhibits a Greek awareness, a way of seeing which does not need to go beyond things themselves, as they naturally are, to find the divine. His desire was to "restore to every being and every object its miraculous value."[6] And while he claimed "a sense of the sacred," he did "not believe in a future life."[7] Camus' university thesis, *La Métaphysique chrétienne et néoplatonisme*, shows him wrestling with the personifications of his Mediterranean heritage: Augustine and Plotinus.[8] He realized the difficulty of his situation:

> The truth is that it is a hard fate to be born in a pagan land in Christian times. This is my case. I feel closer to the values of the classical world than to those of Christianity. Unfortunately, I cannot go to Delphi to be initiated![9]

In his early youth Camus roamed the beaches and hills of Algeria enjoying what he called a "happy barbarianism."[10] Pursuit of the unreflective, immediate pleasures of the flesh filled his hot days. In this life full of passion, a life he embraced with abandon, Camus found his gods:

> Personally, I had no lack of gods: the sun, the sea, the night...But they are gods of enjoyment. They fill, but they also empty. With them alone for company, I should have forgotten the gods in favor of enjoyment itself. I needed to be reminded of mysterious and sacred things, of the finite nature of man, of a love that was impossible, in order that I might one day return to my natural gods with less arrogance.[11]

Illness proved to be the reminder he needed. The onset of tuberculosis was a turning point in Camus' life, because it forced him to take a reflective view of his hedonistic existence. (Jean Grenier, Camus' philosophy teacher at the *Lycée d'Alger*, was to cultivate this new sensitivity by giving his student a "first taste for philosophical meditation.")[12] This reflective turn was not away from his own nature or from the world. "The essential thing is not to lose oneself, and not to lose that part of oneself which lies sleeping in the world."[13] Rather, it served to temper his arrogance: "I don't go from one side of my nature to the other, but from the world to myself and from myself back to the world. It's a question of humility."[14]

Camus was led to discover his depths. His illness is true "pathologizing," a movement of the soul.[15]

> If there is a soul, it is a mistake to believe that it is given to us fully created. It is created here, throughout a whole life. And living is nothing else but that long and painful bringing forth. When the soul is ready, created by us and suffering, death comes along.[16]

At thirty-seven, having lived with his recurring affliction for twenty years, Camus made this single-line entry in his notebook: "Illness is a convent which has its rule, its austerity, its silences, and its inspirations."[17] Camus fell under this rule when quite young, experiencing its austerity in the severe shock of his consumption. Yet it was this austerity, the "convent's" rule of humility, which poised his reflections, reminding him of what he otherwise might have ignored. In the silence of reflection, Camus found the inspiration to be a writer. There was no need of Delphi. True to the archetypal images which first touched his heart, Camus' initiation was "not a demythologizing into 'hard' reality," but as Hillman puts it, "an affirmation of the mythical meaning within all reality."[18] The pathologizing of Camus' romantic soul does enact a fantasy of initiation. To whom, what mythical figure, god or goddess, might the "convent" of Camus' illness be dedicated?

*

> Others leave a flower between pages, enclosing in them a walk where love touched them with its wing. I walk too but am caressed by a god.[19]
>
> Camus

Pulmonary tuberculosis is a deterioration of the lungs caused by tubercle bacilli:

> ...the common result of the presence of the disease-products is to produce consolidations in the affected portions of the lungs, which, undergoing retrograde

changes (caseation), break down and form cavities, the result being the destruction in greater or lesser amount of lung-substance.[20]

Coughing, difficulty in breathing, spitting of blood, and fever are characteristic symptoms. Recurrent breath images in Camus' works testify to is place in his life. This omnipresence forced Camus to measure his life by means of writing.

> To give punctuation and regularity of breath, note down all of the events of my life: 'Today, I am twenty-seven,' and so on.[21]

Forcing him to write, Camus' illness kept him close to both words and experience, making an artist of him. In the nineteenth century consumption was romanticized as the disease of creative individuals, especially poets.[22] With the "slow rotting way"[23] of his lungs, Camus acquired that poetic sensitivity which above all else characterizes his work. "People can only think in images," observed Camus. "If you want to be a philosopher, write novels."[24] To Camus, writing was the forming of images. The *Notebooks* and essays gave reflected depth to his "gods of enjoyment."

In *The Origins of European Thought*, Onians provides a context in which to imagine the connection between soul and lungs. For the Homeric and Pre-Socratic Greeks, the lungs were in fact the place of a soul. The *thymos*, breath-soul, was located in the lungs. It was the breath of gods which inspired the souls of mortals:

> ...returning to Homer, let us note that it is not only emotion that the gods 'breathe' into men but also thoughts, devices relatively intellectual. This we might expect, since it is with his *thymos* and *phrenes* or, if our interpretation is right, his breath-soul and lungs, that a man thinks and knows no less than feels.[25]

It is a medical commonplace that tubercular bacilli gain entrance "by being taken into the lungs with the *inspired* air."[26] Double meanings open a door into the imaginal, and the word "inspired" is such an entry. According to Onians: "in the lexicons of Photius and Hesychius 'lung disease'...is explained as the 'disease of love.'"[27] In Homer too, love affected the lungs. "Well, do you not hold Love to be a god, the child of Aphrodite?"[28] asks Socrates in the *Phaedrus*. When a mortal is inspired by Eros there comes upon him "a shuddering" and "a strange sweating and fever seizes him."[29] Socrates proceeds to the effects of love:

> there comes a warmth, whereby his soul's plumage is fostered, and with that warmth the roots of the wings are melted, [then] the stump of the wing swells and hastens to grow.[30]

A sketch of the tubercular including "shoulder blades projecting like wings,"[31] is to be found in the Hippocratic Corpus. A nineteenth-century account of phthisis states that "the patient often complains of *flying* pains in the chest, shoulders and back."[32] Socrates' description of Erotic inspiration seems almost to suggest consumption. But these suggestions redirect us to Camus' own descriptions. That he chose to speak of his illness as a "convent" (one thinks of nuns!) prompts the question whether Camus' inspiration may have sprung from a feminine source. Might she be Aphrodite, mother of Eros?

Onians reports that for Euripides "love is the 'breaths (or 'blasts', *pnomí*) of Aphrodite.'"[33] Hesiod gives one version of Aphrodite's birth in which she emerges from the whirling foam surrounding the severed genitals of Ouranos when they fell into the sea. Hence the etymological meaning of her name as "foam wanderer" *(aphros-hodites).*[34] An account of the hemoptysis of tuberculars describes the blood as "frothy."[35] From the frothy *thymos* of the consumptive rises a goddess, the Goddess of Love. In her convent, perhaps, Camus undergoes his initiation.

Unique among the mythical gods and goddesses, Aphrodite makes her claim on mortals and immortals alike not through external means, but rather from the inside out. Her power, writes Friedrich, "consists mainly in inspiring compelling subjective states."[36] One sees Aphrodite by seeing through her inspirations, seeing her in the world by way of her own images. Camus had intimate knowledge of the Goddess' power. His reflection, turning back and forth from himself to the world, led him to see that it was neither he nor the world which counted, but "solely the harmony and silence which made *love* spring up between us."[37] The Goddess formed his subjectivity, for in "this extreme emotion"[38] Camus recognized his self.

Aphrodite is a close god unable to keep her distance. She is forever touching our private places, always taking up our personal space. The Love Goddess works her seduction on our subjectivity by possessing our eyes or heart, lungs or loins—or sometimes, as in Camus' case—by ensouling one she ravishes them all. A generative goddess, Aphrodite laid claim to Camus, creating his world in her image, her world in his imagination.

It is no coincidence that the descriptions of convents in Camus' writings are vivid images of Aphrodite's world.

> Late roses in the cloister of Santa Maria Novella and the women on a Sunday morning in Florence. Their uncorseted breasts, their eyes and lips leave you with a beating heart, a dry mouth, and glowing loins.[39]

Aphrodite has been called goddess of flowers, as flowers both of meadow and garden are a revelation of her world. Special among these is the rose, favorite flower of one of her favorites, the poet Sappho. Just as the hot blood in Camus' heart has been touched by the Goddess, the erotic rose is said to have received its color from Aphrodite's blood. Beautiful, desirable women lay open the heart of the Goddess' reality; they reveal her in her basic essence: provocative, sensual sophistication and a surge of ardor. The Love Goddess is vibrantly alive in the beauty, joy, and desire that breathe the air of that Sunday morning, an air heavy with the scent of roses.

In yet another convent, the little Gothic cloister of San Francisco on Majorca, Camus encountered a "new and yet familiar flavor"; he saw that "the world's face was smiling."[40] Camus recognized the visage of Aphrodite the "smile-loving," as one of her most common epithets names her. The smile of love is always fresh, each time it blossoms. It is an island that appears out of the churning sea of repetitious experiences. Such islands are Aphrodite's turf, moments of eternity that may vanish with the next turning of the tide. One of these moments held Camus in the convent's courtyard and made him witness to an epiphany of the Golden Goddess. Aphrodite disclosed her radiant presence in what he called a "unique play of appearances."[41] Golden hues enveloped the small courtyard: the "delicate, precious colonnade shone with the fine, golden yellow of old Spanish monuments...a fine, golden sun gently warmed the yellow stones of the cloister."[42] Pigeons flew overhead and rose laurels lay scattered around the yard.

Aphrodite's beauty is golden, shimmering in the light of the sun. She is a daylight, sunlit goddess whose world is aglow with warmth. While very much a figure of passion, she has another side which kindles affec-

A SOUL'S JOURNEY

tion and sensitivity. Face to face with the Smile-Loving Goddess Camus himself was "lucid and smiling."[43]

Again and again, Camus encounters the Goddess and she works her magic of passion on him. His essays and notebook entries are filled with Aphrodite's images, and very nearly her name:

> There is but one love in this world. To embrace a woman's body is also to retain, close to one, that strange joy which descends from the sky to the sea...[44]

> Every year, the young girls come to flower on the beaches.... For the man who looks at them, they are yearly waves whose weight and splendor break into foam over the yellow beach.[45]

It was, then, the Foam-Wanderer Camus unknowingly worshipped during his pleasure-filled youth on the sands by the sea, the same sea from which the Goddess herself was born.

Conventus, the Latin root of "convent," means "to come together." The Goddess' convent is not a place of withdrawal from the world, but the locus of the *coniunctio* of soul and world. Aphrodite is a goddess of union. She sparks the desire to unite, to fuse, to procreate. It is through this goddess of life that Camus imagines his impending death. He thinks of "flowers, smiles, the desire for women, and realizes that my whole horror of death lies in my anxiety to live."[46] Camus does not curse Aphrodite for his consuming inspiration; the thought of dying does not make him bitter. But the Love Goddess has her curse on him, and so he is "jealous of those who will live and for whom flowers and the desire for women will have their full flesh and blood meaning."[47] Jealousies, envy, and rivalries are a dark side of love, even love inspired by a goddess.

Camus' second series of essays, *Noces (Nuptials),* is a pagan celebration of life on the Algerian coast. It is no surprise that Aphrodite presides over this celebration. Patroness of courtesans, her realm also includes the arts of passionate child-begetting love in the marriage bed. "The world is beautiful," Camus wrote in these essays, "and outside of it there is no salvation."[48] Many years later he was to admit, "I cannot live without beauty. That's what makes me weak in the face of certain people."[49]

There are those over whom Aphrodite has no power.[50] Camus may have meant that his weakness was seen only by those "certain people." Aphrodite too, though uniquely beautiful among the immortals, has been seen as weak by certain of her peers. In the eyes of some, love is a comic escape or a distracting folly in a life of hard struggles. Beauty is a threat to the routine of daily commerce; to those whose souls are bloodless or austere, passionate physical love is not even a weakness. It is ugly, degenerate, filthy. Yet the faces of these "certain people" are again the faces of our own soul when we have been shunned or slighted, deceived or betrayed, or simply frightened by Love's power. Even with all the dangers, Camus preferred to live in Aphrodite's proximity: suffering his weakness yet finding his strength, his salvation, in the fatal embrace of "insistent beauty."[51] And as for the Goddess herself, she does not hesitate to take a mortal lover when the longing moves her.

Camus saw himself as an artist rather than a philosopher, because he thought "according to words and not according to ideas."[52] Aphrodite's delicate and divine splendor shows forth in the golden words of the poet. Poetic inspiration belongs to her, along with her attendants the Graces and Muses. No wonder that the young Camus took up the pen as it is Aphrodite who sustains the passion that exudes from his works.

One finds two sorts of love or desire in Camus' writings. There is an array of images which pulsates with physical desire, a love that glows in the loins. This sensual desire—the Greeks called it *himeros*—was part of Camus' embrace of his embodiment, his zest for a life of the flesh.[53] On the other hand, or better yet, "in the other lung" breathed Camus' hard-felt desire for "mysterious and sacred things." Both of these belong to the perennial Aphroditic world as described by the Platonic tradition. As Plotinus observes: "Now we say that Aphrodite is double; one the heavenly, we say is the 'daughter of heaven,' and the other one 'born of Zeus and Dione....' "[54] The love of Aphrodite, daughter of Zeus, is that of passion and erotic desire, and so she is called the earthly. The heavenly Aphrodite is "innocent of any hint of lewdness."[55] Her love, Plotinus tells us, is "the activity of soul reaching out after good. So this love here leads each individual soul to the Good...."[56]

L'Enver et L'Endroit holds a unique place in Camus' unfinished opus. These were his first essays. First in more than chronology, they were his self-proclaimed "source,"[57] first in the ordering of his heart (*thymos* is often mistranslated as heart). Camus hoped that the reader of his essays would "feel, between the first page and the last, a secret movement which gives them unity."[58] When *L'Enver et L'Endroit* was reissued some twenty years later, Camus added a new preface. Not his best work, he said (at twenty-two "one scarcely knows how to write"), but "there is more love in these awkward pages than in all those that have followed."⁵⁹ In the same preface he shared his dream of a future work:

> On the day when balance is established, I shall try to write the work of which I am dreaming. It will be like *L'Enver et L'endroit;* in other words, a certain form of love will be my guiding support.⁶⁰

The secret movement in Camus' first little book of essays belongs to the world of Aphrodite; it is a movement of the forces she creates in the soul. Awkward, maybe; when is young love not awkward, stumbling, fumbling for words? But even at that young age, Camus knew something essential about his art, that creativity requires the breath of the Earthly Aphrodite, the passion and desire which she gives. He also knew that the earthly should be balanced by the Heavenly Aphrodite: "A spectacular virtue that leads to denying one's passions. A higher virtue that leads to balancing them."⁶¹

*

> It is not so easy to become what one is, to rediscover one's deepest measure.⁶²
>
> Camus

There is an archetypal figure for the journeying consumptive soul: the puer. Tuberculosis is a puer disease, an affliction of the young, the weak, the aspiring. It is a puer wounding which gives the breath an odor reminiscent of Philoctetes.⁶³

"Every minute of life carries with it its miraculous value, and its face of eternal youth,"⁶⁴ Camus once observed. The face of eternal youth, the face of the *puer eternus,* can be recognized in many of Camus' images. In one of the rare descriptions Camus gave of his illness, there is the story of the mythical puer, Icarus:

> ...foreseeing death from the mere sight of a handkerchief filled with blood is being plunged suddenly and effortlessly into time in a dizzying way: it is the fear of what's ahead.⁶⁵

Like the consumptive whose lungs are "melted" in caseation, Icarus' wings are melted when he flies too close to the sun. Plunging dizzily from sky to sea, Icarus reenacts the birth of Aphrodite, as does the tubercular's spitting of frothy blood.

In typical puer fashion it was Camus' illness, his wound, which set his soul journeying. Reminded "of a love which was impossible," Camus wandered on his path. Years later, Camus listed "love of the remote"[66] as a theme he wanted to pursue. *Pothos* was the Greek word for such desire for distant, unattainable things or persons. Socrates defines it as a longing that is "expressive of the desire of that which is not present but absent, and in another place."[67] It is Camus' yearning for the sacred, his nostalgia for the images which first opened his heart. Hillman imagines *pothos* as "the boyish urge to come home and be safe in the harbour of Aphrodite. Aphrodite would then be the image of what the puer in each of us longs for...."[68] *Pothos* is the inspiration of the Heavenly Aphrodite, as *himeros* is that of the Earthly. Plotinus tells us that Heavenly love is the soul's reaching out after the Good which is also the Beautiful. The Good and the Beautiful are personified by Aphrodite whose image Camus searches for and so to her belong his simple and great images. Camus' *pothos* is "a desire that would return desire to its source in the archetype."[69]

Camus' wandering was not without its dangers; he found himself set upon by dogs. Aphrodite has been symbolized by both the dog and wolf, and as Helen testifies in the *Iliad*, the Love Goddess can be a real bitch. Camus tried to fight the canines that tore at his chest: "My most constant temptation, the one against which I have never ceased fighting to the point of exhaustion: cynicism."[70] The Greek *kynikos*, from which "cynic" comes, means "dog-like." The dogs unleashed by Aphrodite Uranos are cynicism itself. According to Plato, those inspired by the Heavenly Aphrodite prefer "the more vigorous and intellectual bent,"[71] and as Camus observes: "the temptation shared by all forms of intelligence: cynicism."[72] Aphroditic Inspiration and cynicism are two sides of the same Aphroditic world.

Even when their bite is not fatal, the dogs of cynicism leave teeth marks on the wanderer's soul. Those who are afflicted with tuberculosis in their youth and survive the disease are generally marked by it. In his essay, "Puer Wounds and Ulysses' Scar," Hillman stresses the importance of the scar in understanding Homer's *pothos*-driven wanderer. Ulysses' scar is, as is cynicism for Camus, a reminder of death and uncertainty. It is little wonder that Ulysses, whose glance across the sea was like Camus' toward Algeria, was a favorite.

Calypso offers Ulysses a choice between immortality and the land of his birth. He rejects immortality. Therein lies perhaps the whole meaning of the *Odyssey.*[73]

The scarred-lung Algerian approves Ulysses' choice: "The world is no secret for the wise man. Why does he need to stray into eternity?"[74]

*

> Yes, I know all this and I've also learned or nearly learned the price of love.[75]
>
> Camus

Camus said he would "achieve nothing"[76] if he did not manage to rewrite *L'Envers et L'Endroit.* He never did rewrite that work, never wrote the one he was dreaming of. But he did imagine his dream in sketches found in the *Notebooks* and elsewhere. The dream was his work as an artist, his "slow trek" of rediscovery. It was a journey of the imagination which sought a balance between the two Aphrodites, a fusion of *himeros* and *pothos.* His art was a dream of giving imaginal embodiment to that carnal knowledge of the divine he carried in his chest.[77]

Camus' scar, received in Aphrodite's convent, was part of his initiation. "Initiation refers to the transition from only-puer consciousness, wounded and bleeding, to *puer-et-senex* consciousness, open and scarred."[78] Illness brought puer and senex together for Camus. Aphrodite's breath brought to him the wisdom of *puer-et-senex* consciousness expressed in "that 'most widely cherished Renaissance maxim' *festina lente* (make haste slowly).'"[79] "Do not forget: illness and decrepitude," wrote Camus. "There's not a minute to be wasted—which is perhaps the contrary of 'one must hurry.'"[80] The integrity of puer and senex shines most brightly in Camus' "lucidity." Far from the clearheadedness of the rationalist who has his world neatly arranged in separate unambiguous categories, Camus' lucidity was an awareness of the deep ambivalences, the polarities and absurdities that confront us. Lucidity means the rediscovery of both sides of the world, the recovery of two faces in love's imagination.

Camus' belief that "the world is no secret for the wise man" did not prevent him from recognizing mystery: "The limits. Thus I shall say that there are mysteries it is suitable to enumerate and to meditate. Nothing more."[81] To enumerate and to meditate on mysteries is to take the unfamiliar as measure. Camus' writing, his wandering on the path of tuberculosis, was a measuring of his existence.[82] Scarred and open,

Camus searched after his gods, for as Proclus pronounces: "every god is a measure of things existent."[83] Aphrodite initiated Camus' barbarous soul so that it might make poetry.

> The poet makes poetry only when he takes the measure, by saying the sights of heaven in such a way that he submits to its appearances as to the alien element to which the unknown god has 'yielded.' Our current name for the sight and appearance of something is 'image'... by such sights the god surprises us.[84]

Of course it is hard to believe these things about Camus. After all, he was an existentialist caught in a heroic ego. But surely the truth is something like our story. Did not Camus himself say:

> The end of the absurd, rebellious, etc. movement, the end of the contemporary world consequently, is compassion in the original sense; in other words, ultimately love and poetry. But that calls for an innocence I no longer have. All I can do is to recognize the way leading to it and to be receptive to the time of the innocents. To see it, at least before dying.[85]

1 Albert Camus, *Notebooks 1942-1951*, trans. Justin O'Brien (New York: Harcourt Brace Jovanovich, 1978), p. 235.
2 Germaine Bree, *Albert Camus* (New York: Columbia University Press, 1964), p. 6.
3 Philip Thody, *Albert Camus 1913-1960* (New York: Macmillan, 1961), p. 17. Camus' own view on the subject: "I wanted to be a writer when I was about seventeen, and at the same time I was vaguely aware that I would become one." "Replies to Jean-Claude Brisville," in *Lyrical and Critical Essays*, trans. Ellen Conroy Kennedy, ed. Philip Thody (New York: Vintage Books, 1970), pp. 357-58.
4 *Lyrical and Critical Essays*, p. 17. I have slightly altered Kennedy's translation in light of other translators' renderings of the same passage. This procedure has been followed in subsequent quotations.
5 Camus, *Notebooks 1942-1951*, p. 249.
6 Camus, "Love of Life," in *Lyrical and Critical Essays*, p. 54. Camus' desire is expressed within the context of being "soul-sick" while traveling.
7 "Replies to Jean-Claude Brisville," p. 364.
8 Vide. Roger Quilliot, *The Sea and Prisons*, trans. Emmett Parker (n.p.: University of Alabama Press, 1970), pp. 85-87.
9 "Interview with Albert Camus," in *Lyrical and Critical Essays*, p. 357.
10 Camus, cited by Thody, *Albert Camus 1913-1960*, p. 16.
11 Camus, "On Jean Grenier's *Les Iles*," in *Lyrical and Critical Essays*, p. 328.
12 Camus, "Encounter with Albert Camus," in *Lyrical and Critical Essays*, p. 350.
13 Albert Camus, *Notebooks 1935-1942*, trans. Philip Thody (New York: Random House, 1965), p. 25.
14 *Ibid.*, p. 76.
15 Barbarians were so called by the Greeks, because their speech sounded like "bar-bar," a chatter of empty sounds, unintelligible. Empty like Camus' first gods, the barbarian soul has no depth; there is

no reflection, image disappears in hedonistic pursuits. Tuberculosis is the path on which Camus' barbarous soul was to seek its gods' images.
16. Camus, *Notebooks 1942-1951*, p. 224.
17. *Ibid.*, p. 41.
18. James Hillman, "Senex and Puer: An Aspect of the Historical and Psychological Present," in *Puer Papers* (Dallas: Spring Publications, 1979), p. 29.
19. "The Wrong Side and the Right Side," in *Lyrical and Critical Essays*, p. 60.
20. *Encyclopaedia Britannica*, s.v. "Phthisis" (New York: Scribner's, 1889), vol. XVII, p. 855.
21. Camus, *Notebooks 1935-1942*, p. 176.
22. *Vide* Susan Sontag, *Illness as Metaphor* (New York: Farrar, Straus and Giroux, 1978), pp. 18 and 32.
23. Camus, *Notebooks 1942-1951*, p. 39.
24. *Notebooks 1935-1942*, p. 10. Also see Quilliot, *The Sea and Prisons*, p. 84.
25. *The Origins of European Thought* (New York: Arno Press, 1973), p. 56.
26. *The New International Encyclopaedia*, s.v. "Tuberculosis" (New York: Dodd, Mead, 1910), vol. XIX, p. 524, my italics.
27. *The Origins of European Thought*, p. 37.
28. Plato, "Phaedrus," 242d, trans. R. Hackforth, in *Plato: The Collected Dialogues* (Princeton: Princeton University Press, 1978), p. 490.
29. *Ibid.*, 251a, p. 497.
30. *Ibid.*, 251b, p. 497.
31. E.D. Phillips, *Aspects of Greek Medicine* (New York: St. Martin's, 1973), p. 69.
32. *Encyclopaedia Britannica*, p. 857, my italics.
33. *The Origins of European Thought*, p. 55.
34. *Vide*. Paul Friedrich, *The Meaning of Aphrodite* (Chicago: University of Chicago Press, 1978), p. 202. Besides Friedrich's excellent book, I have drawn from works by Kerényi and Otto for the portrait of Aphrodite.
35. *The New International Encyclopaedia*, p. 522.
36. Friedrich, p. 101.
37. "Nuptials at Tipasa," in *Lyrical and Critical Essays*, p. 72.
38. Camus, "The Wrong Side and the Right Side," p. 60.
39. Camus, *Notebooks 1935-1942*, p. 55.
40. Camus, "Love of Life," p. 55. Aphrodite, whose favorite loci are islands and mountain peaks, must have had a strong liking for Camus as she smiles at him even in the desert: "Millions of eyes have looked at this landscape, and for me it is like the first smile of the world.... It assures me that nothing matters except my love, and that this love has no value for me unless it remains innocent and free." "The Desert," in *Nuptials*, p. 103.
41. *Ibid.*
42. *Ibid.*
43. *Ibid.*
44. "Nuptials at Tipasa," p. 68.
45. *Notebooks 1935-1942*, pp. 190-191.
46. "The Wind at Djemila," in *Nuptials*, p. 78.
47. *Ibid.* Camus' envy is Aphroditic; it arises from a desire for life and love, not material possessions. *Vide* "Preface," in *The Wrong Side and Right Side*, p. 7.
48. "The Desert," p. 103.
49. *Notebooks 1942-1951*, p. 71.
50. Three of the goddesses, Athena, Artemis, and Hestia, are immune to Aphrodite's spells.
51. "The Wind at Djemila," p. 78.

52 *Notebooks 1942-1951*, p. 113.
53 Hillman defines *himeros* as "the physical desire for the immediately present to be grasped in the heat of the moment." *"Pothos:* The Nostalgia of the Puer Eternus," in *Loose Ends* (Zürich: Spring Publications, 1975), p. 53. Also see Friedrich, pp. 99-100.
54 Plotinus, *Enneads, III, 1-9*, Loeb Classical Library, trans. A.H. Armstrong (Cambridge: Harvard University Press, 1967), III. 5.2, p. 175.
55 Plato, "Symposium," 181c, trans. Michael Joyce, in *Plato: The Collected Dialogues*, p. 535.
56 Plotinus, *Enneads, III, 5.4*, p. 183.
57 "Preface," p. 6.
58 *Notebooks 1935-1942*, p. 34.
59 "Preface," p. 6.
60 *Notebooks 1942-1951*, p. 234. A slightly different version appears in the actual preface.
61 *Ibid.*, p. 270.
62 "Nuptials at Tipasa," p. 67.
63 The mention of Philoctetes is not farfetched. As the Achaeans had to have Philoctetes with them in order to take Troy, many Frenchmen waited for Camus' return to the political arena after his self-imposed silence. Philoctetes made it to Troy. Camus died on the way to the arena.
64 *Notebooks 1935-1942*, p. 10.
65 *Notebooks 1942-1951*, p. 67.
66 *Ibid.*, p. 268.
67 Plato, "Cratylus," 420a, trans. Benjamin Jowett, in *Plato: The Collected Dialogues*, p. 455.
68 "Pothos," p. 56.
69 *Ibid.*, p. 60.
70 *Notebooks 1942-1951*, p. 249.
71 "Symposium," 181c, p. 535.
72 *Notebooks 1935-1942*, p. 93.
73 *Notebooks 1942-1951*, p. 13.
74 *Ibid.*, p. 198.
75 "Preface," p. 13.
76 *Ibid.*
77 Note how Camus defines "image" in his graduate thesis: "the attempt to express the undefinable nature of feeling by what is obvious and undefinable in concrete things." *Notebooks 1935-1942*, p. 103.
78 "Puer Wounds and Ulysses' Scar," in *Puer Papers* (Dallas: Spring Publications, 1979), p. 122.
79 Hillman, "Senex and Puer," p. 35.
80 *Notebooks 1942-1951*, p. 79.
81 *Ibid.*, p. 126.
82 Another dimension of Camus' "measuring of his existence" is to be found in his repeated concern for ethics. The fusion of *himeros* and *pothos* can be seen as a participation in the world's "unique play of appearances." Such vital participation is where Camus' ethical sensitivity must be located. Aphrodite may be in his ethics as well as his art: "One must encounter love before having encountered ethics. Or else one is torn." *Notebooks 1942-1951*, p. 199.
83 Proclus, *The Elements of Theology*, trans. E.R. Dodds (Oxford: Oxford University Press, 1963), Prop. 117, p. 103.
84 Martin Heidegger, "...Poetically Man Dwells..." in *Poetry, Language, Thought*, ed. and trans. Albert Hofstader (New York: Harper and Row, 1975), pp. 225-6.
85 *Notebooks 1942-1951*, pp. 157-8. Camus died in a late-night car accident while on the way to catch a train for Paris (City of Love). He was forty-six years old. "My whole work," Camus often said, "is ironic." *Ibid.*, p. 249.

SOCRATES AND STORIES

DAVID A. KOLB
(Lewiston, Maine)

Socrates made men think about the basis of their beliefs and values; after trying him for corrupting the youth and upsetting the order of life, they condemned him to die. In prison, he talked with his disciples about life after death, then drank the hemlock and was silent. So the story goes. It is historical; we take it literally. I want to argue it is a myth, and it can guide us in approaching Plato's other myths. There was indeed a man Socrates, son of Sophroniscos of Athens. He was born around 469 and died in 399 after being condemned by the city during the tumultuous times after the Peloponnesian War. He was married, had children, perhaps worked as a stonecutter. He was short and ugly but brave and incredibly hardy, a heroic soldier when heroism was demanded. He had aristocratic friends and spent much of his time in conversation in public places or at his friends' homes. He asked questions and talked about virtue, love, and justice. When he was younger he may have studied the new physical theories of the day; when he was older he had little to do with such topics. He may or may not have taught something like Plato's Theory of Forms. He did not approve of democratic government. Some of his students went on to become famous philosophers and virtuous men, others became notorious tyrants and traitors. When brought to court he defended himself but refused to engage in easy rhetoric or to accept exile. He died nobly.

This Socrates seems an interesting person, but not yet the shining figure we all know. That figure exists in the words of Plato, not the pages of the historians. A more strident, less captivating Socrates, less poetic and creative, more the moral preacher, exists in the words of Xenophon, our other contemporary source for Socrates' life. The quest for the historical Socrates provides only limited illumination. Because Socrates existed and really did die for his convictions, his life obtains added cachet,

---

The author, having studied with the Jesuits and at Yale, is now Chairman of the Philosophy Department at Bates College.

though we are not sure precisely what those convictions were that he died for. It is the story Plato tells that gives significance to his life. Plato said that "There is not and never will be a written work of Plato's; what are now called Plato's are those of a Socrates become young and beautiful."[1] *This* Socrates fascinates us by his irony and his seriousness, his detachment together with his erotic dedication to his hearers and to truth, his ability to weave words and thoughts, while eyeing the goal and judging fairly his own ignorance.

> I tell you that to let no day pass without discussing goodness and all the other subjects about which you hear me talking and examining myself and others is really the very best thing that a man can do, and that life without this examination is not worth living.[2]

To foster this examination of life Socrates questions, argues, goads, laughs, teases, accuses, anything at all that will move his hearers. Beyond what he says shines the beauty of the quest and the beauty of the good embodied in him.

> What Socrates reminds me of is one of those little statues of Silenus you see for sale, an ugly little man holding a flute in his hands, but when you open the figure up there are images of the gods inside.[3]

What attracts us is this picture of the wise old man who is a playful erotic child. This rich significant Socrates enfolds the historical facts. He is the Inquirer, a mythic figure who structures our lives into a journey from ignorance and confusion in search of ever wider knowledge and deeper grounds, until at the end we come into the luminous presence of what is in its fullness. Socrates argues for theories in high metaphysics, but his significance transcends those theories. It is his image and his quest that open a conversation which allows such theories.

In pursuing his inquiries Socrates does the things we have come to expect of philosophers. He analyzes concepts, seeks principles, tests methods, attacks views by pointing out inconsistencies and providing counter-examples, and so on. In the game of *logos*, he knows all the moves. But at times he announces he is leaving the *logos* and entering the *mythos*. Then he tells stories. The stories range from little anecdotes to grand and glorious visions of the fate of the soul.

In the *Phaedo* we hear of the immense earth in one of whose murky hollows we live, while above on the true surface live men who see the stars as they really are. Our souls will be carried about and purified by the great interior rivers of this world until the time for their rebirth. In the *Phaedrus* we see the great procession of gods and souls above the world, and the fall of the soul which loses its wings and descends to our confused realm, only to find its wings again through love. In the *Republic* we are told of judgment after death, and how souls must choose lots for their next lives. And there are many more stories.

These myths puzzle me. Socrates insists on the need for conceptually clear principles; he attacks Homer and the usual Greek myths for telling lies; he announces that he is continuing the ancient quarrel between poetry and philosophy. Then why does he tell myths? They have been variously interpreted as persuasive rhetoric, metaphysics for the masses, substitutes for argument, mystical intimations. Later I will suggest how they ground the significance of the realm of *logos*.

But the point to notice now is that when people argue about the place of the myths, they take the story of the way of philosophical inquiry as a literal description. The myths jar us because we think too easily of a historical figure, Socrates, recommending a literal way of life, yet telling odd stories. I proposed above that the historical figure is enfolded within a mythic personage that gives him significance. Now I want to convince you that inquiry itself is a mythic journey. *Philosophy is as mythic as is the figure who is its first proponent, Socrates.*

I do not mean that when Socrates argues about the nature of mathematics or the analysis of some ethical concept he is telling a myth. His arguments have to be judged in their own terms according to their subject matter. When he argues, Socrates is not telling a myth, but he is enacting one. Socrates and his interlocutors argue about metaphysics and the good life. Later thinkers argue against Socrates' conclusions. They do not wish to say what he said, but they willingly do what he did. They have accepted his story of the path of inquiry.

This path stretches from ignorance to total knowledge. We are to take nothing for granted. We seek complete illumination by circumscribing areas of obscurity and penetrating to their basic principles. Plato believed the world was structured so as to make such a goal possible. Values could be founded upon contact with what truly is, the Forms which are the pattern and ground for all being. Such is Plato's story of the philosophical path.

Other thinkers may deny the metaphysics, deny values can be founded, deny complete illumination is possible, restrict knowledge to the physical sciences which Plato considered unworthy of the name "knowledge," and, despite all these changes still describe their inquiring in Socratic terms.

How can this be? Socrates tells a story that shows how our inquiries and curiosities may be seen as approaching a goal, "holding ever to the upward way." The Socratic journey to knowledge encourages us to emphasize and link together feelings and episodes which we may not have noticed or may have considered marginal: questions of definition and grounds, desire for a knowledge beyond our opinions and our history. We can see stretches of our thought as having a direction. We can distinguish stages, and progress toward a goal of completely grounded knowing. This creates unity in our intellectual life; it makes into a connected story what otherwise might have been only scattered curiosity, and gives a sense of advancing through stages of increasing illumination.

Even when the final goal is declared impossible it does not lose its power to polarize our inquiries and create internal distinctions and stages in our intellectual life. Plato also offers us guides for behaving well on the journey: erotic attraction to the good, communal dialogue, impartial questioning, openness and the refusal to insist on one's own opinions, a desire for grounded certainty. These guides in their internal stages take precedence over the end; its very existence becomes a belief to be tested according to the requirements of the journey. This acquires its own autonomy and structure from its stages, whether dialectic, ethical or erotic. A final higher knowledge can provide the structural point of reference for stages on life's way.[4] Our cognitive life becomes a unity, a *way* when the story gives it direction.

The Socratic path of inquiry thus seems less literal. It looks like a story we tell ourselves to give unity and structure to our actions, a story we find ourselves within. We find ourselves *within* its horizon and its direction for our activities, and we find *ourselves* there, called unto unity by the narrative and its patterns. It is a myth we live.[5]

Apollo at Delphi declared Socrates the wisest of men. After his condemnation Socrates' execution was delayed while Athens sent a ship to Delos to commemorate the victory of Theseus over the Minotaur, the end of sacrifice to the half-beast. Socrates' quest is for a victory of light to render all things clear. His is a myth of the spirit with the goals of the spirit: unity, simplicity, transparency, grounded clarity and purified necessity. The shifting polysemic soul will become uniform. Socrates tells us in the *Apology* to care for our souls, but this care is the transformation of soul to spirit. The images in the cave are to be left behind for clear vision above where what-is stays fixed in its pure identity. Socrates lives a mythic turning away from myth. He makes us live the story of the transcendence of all stories. His story lets us see the stages of our thought as liberation from ego but also from soul and its images. Soul is to be spirit. Plato's practice may belie this story, but this is the tale he tells.

In Plato's eyes there was little choice; the only alternatives to the Socratic spirit were blind confusion in the old stories, or the willful chaos lurking behind the fashionable scepticism of the Sophists. What startles is that after so long we still agree with him. While there are many myths of gods and soul, the cognitive quest remains much as Socrates defined it. It seems odd to call 'story' this quest which brooks no competition. As I pointed out earlier, thinkers who reject all Plato's doctrines tend, in terms of method, to be wayfarers on the Socratic path.

Other cognitive routes have been suggested from time to time, those leading to mysticism or placing poetry above principles, but they remain less significant. How has Socrates triumphed? Has he really defined *the* way minds can inquire? *His is a myth which takes itself literally*, and when we are taken up in it we define ourselves in its terms. It gives professional identity to groups who tell it to themselves—a story which has become the official identity of science and philosophy, woven into our intellectual institutions and practice. What would a university or a laboratory look like without the Socratic story of ever firmer grounds and more total vision?

The times are changing. David Hume preached sceptical contentment with ungrounded custom; Nietzsche taught everlasting conflicts of interpretation; Heidegger talks of an inquiry that listens without seeking any overall goal, partial illumination that is not part of a full vision to come. Post-structuralism, hermeneutics, semiotics, tales from the East, there are many cognitive stories nowadays that do not lead to the Socratic path.[6]

We are not sure how to handle these stories, for judging and integrating the new is done by means of this path they challenge. The new stories have not yet changed our institutional or personal identity as inquirers, but they are present. No longer is it a choice between Socrates and sceptic terror. Whether the Socratic myth will be successfully challenged we do not know; what myth of inquiry might take its place we cannot tell. That no single myth reign supreme is scarcely imaginable.

No matter what happens, the recent multiplication of cognitive stories brings home to us how Socrates' inquisitive path is a mythic journey. He embodies a story which provides stages for a life of inquiry, imaginatively compelling, though it has never been self-evident that our inquiring must be unified in only one story.

If this is true it lessens the contrast between Socrates the pure inquirer and Socrates the teller of myths. The myths which crown Plato's dialogues need not be rhetorical flourishes; they belong to the Socratic myth and as such they too provide stages on life's way.

Socrates' myths are placed strategically to influence our present, not to give us news briefs about a future life. They tell us how to live here.

> Now perhaps all this seems to you like an old wife's tale and you despise it, and there would be nothing strange in despising it if our searches could discover anywhere a better and truer account, but as it is you see that you...cannot demonstrate that we should live any other life than this, which is plainly of benefit also in the other world.[7]

> Now Glaucon the tale was saved, as the saying is, and was not lost. And it will save us, if we believe it....we shall hold ever to the upward way and pursue righteousness with wisdom always and ever.[8]

The myths are not facts about future events to be taken into account in some utilitarian calculation, but stories about the movement of life. They turn moral theories into life-plans. The myths encourage us to emphasize and link together feelings and episodes we may have not noticed or have considered marginal: feelings of emptiness and insecurity or impurity, desires for wholeness and harmony, desires for more than the senses provide.

We can live these stages of moral growth, which supply their own internal contrasts within our present life, even if the otherworldly goal is left aside or taken metaphorically. It is enough that the goal makes it possible for us to discern stages and direction in our lives. Just as Socrates' goal of total knowledge can serve to structure inquiring though the goal is unattainable, the purity and harmony of the myths he tells function as reference points. Our life becomes a *way* when the story gives it direction.

In fact Plato's myths can remain in force even if the literal metaphysics is denied. This independence of Plato's metaphysics and cosmology may surprise us, since the myths are usually treated as nothing more than Plato's metaphysics in rhetorical fancy dress. The myths seem to receive their force from the metaphysics, but the situation is reversed. Imagine that all Plato's metaphysics is literally true: the Forms, the half-real world of the senses, the afterlife, and so on. Is it self-evident how such a world would be lived? Perhaps we would live in terror, or boredom; perhaps we would find the whole structure irrelevant to life as we do much of modern physics. The question how such a world would be lived, what impact it would have on us, could only be settled by living, by finding ourselves in stories that weave the structure of the world into patterns and stages of our lives. This would be to find ourselves and our identities in a myth which digests the metaphysics and gives it significance. *The impact of the metaphysics comes through the myths*.

For all this, Plato's myths of the soul have not survived as living forces except where they have been incorporated into Christian stories. They *could* function like Heracles and Oedipus, but seldom do. Perhaps this is because for adventures of the soul we know there are multiple stories—Plato's, Odysseus', Heracles', the path of duty we hear in Marcus Aurelius, the Christian story, the hero of science, the revolutionary, the Nietzschean man of power and so on. No one story in this multitude commands exclusivity at all costs. We are accustomed to an Alexandrine plurality in our culture and our changing visions of our lives. We are less inclined to cling to one story of the soul, and Plato's myths give way to other, perhaps richer models.

We are not as literal about our moral career as we are in our cognitive life. There Plato's meta-myth has more than survived; Socrates reigns supreme. Will the day come when we shall see as many stories structuring our cognitive curiosity and inquiring as we do the stages of moral, emotional, and spiritual life? No story tells us what will happen next.[9]

1 Plato, *Letters* 314e. The second letter, from which this quote is taken, is one of the several most likely to be genuine.
2 Plato, *Apology of Socrates* 38a. The excerpt is from Socrates' speech to the jury after his condemnation.
3 Plato, *Symposium* 215b. Alcibiades is telling of his fascination with Socrates.
4 The phrase of course refers to the title of one of Kierkegaard's books.

5 The Socratic myth would seem to be confirmed by the steady progress of our knowledge of the world. But to claim that our growing practical mastery and our science can only be interpreted within the Socratic story begs the question.
6 Kant argued that we cannot escape the drive to tell only one story about ourselves and the world. If the tendency is indeed inborn, it remains open how we are to respond to it. Whether our tendency to metaphysics and monotheism leads to earnest dedication, playful teasing or dogged renunciation depends on what story we find ourselves within.
7 Plato, *Gorgias* 527a.
8 Plato, *Republic* 621c.
9 If Socrates' story of the transcendence of all stories is itself another story, if the "upward way" is one of many, there is room for all the myths. Still it might be objected that prior to all stories is the structure or structuring which opens the space that makes stories possible. Nothing said here denies this, as long as the structure or structuring is not taken as the matrix for a uniquely privileged Socratic upward way to attain its ineluctable flowering.

HOW JUNG COUNSELED A DISTRESSED PARENT

WILLIAM McGUIRE
(Princeton)

During the winter of 1936, an American woman traveled to Zurich to consult C.G. Jung about her seriously disturbed son. After returning to Paris, which was then her home, she wrote the following letter to a close relative:

>   Feb. 24th, 1936
> ...I went to Zurich and stayed with Mary Foote—really, I have got the grandest friends. Mary gave me her room and her bed. She slept on a couch in the dining room, but besides that, she gave me love and deep understanding and such wonderful courage. Mary is a tower of strength when you get down underneath her shell of shyness and reserve. I went to see Jung with such a load of photographs and documents that it seemed absurd, but I thought it would be worse to have too little than too much. I was with him for an hour and a half; it seemed about five minutes. Of course, he is the great wise man of the world, a sort of sage. Big, fat, old, bespectacled, the kind of man who gives you all his attention and allows nothing to distract him from what he has before him. No telephone in his office. I guess not, it is all quiet and solemn and eternal, exactly what you need. I can't tell you all he said because there was, naturally, too much, but he at once saw and understood everything and went slowly, ponderously to work to help me. There was nothing more for Jobic[1] but there really was a lot for me. We didn't talk about me, at all, or...the other boys, nothing of that—we talked exclusively about Jobic. Everything that I needed to be told I was told, and with

---

William McGuire, executive editor of the *Collected Works of C.G. Jung* and editor of *The Freud/Jung Letters*, has completed *The Bollingen Wheel*, an account of the Bollingen Foundation and related personalities (including Mary Foote), which Princeton University Press will publish. He is currently involved in editing Jung's English seminars, of which the first volume, *Dream Analysis (1928-1930)*, will shortly be published as a corollary to the *Collected Works*, by Princeton University Press and Routledge & Kegan Paul.

such insight and spirituality that I, at last, understood—not only understood but accepted.

The man is inspired, really. I suppose you can't be a great confessor and want to bring God into the lives of suffering humanity without learning a lot.

He believes in God—he lives with and works for God but he calls it the Universal Unconscious—it is just the same as our God but he makes you feel Him in a different way and in a way that is more acceptable to the modern mind. To me, so familiar with the psychoanalytical jargon, it was like a sermon at High Mass. Quite extraordinary. When I think of Dr. Hunt and his stressing of all the filthy sexual stuff it seems as though I had sat and talked with the devil. Jung on the other hand took Jobic's pure, beautiful side and brought it out into a complete, radiant, conquering thing. It made me think of that phrase in Tom's letter that sent me crying like a baby. "Some men and women yield without a struggle, just sink complacently into comfortable slavery. But was there ever more evidence of a struggle, a fierce, tearing fighting back, than in Jobic's case."

Jung told me that those first photographs of Jobic, the very early ones, when he was eleven months old, showed what he was going to become. "But" I said "children aren't born with dementia praecox, are they?" "No" he said "but some children are born with a predisposition to it and in this case it is unmistakable, nothing could have saved him." Then he showed me step by step in the photographs, Jobic's eyes, those piercing exaggerated eyes. In other words, Jobic was born with the split-personality which is schizophrenia. He couldn't meet the world, he was turned in, too busy in the unconscious to have any interest in the world—too busy with God and things eternal, with intuition—it is hard to explain, but to Jung the unconscious is the eternal. Jung said Jobic couldn't learn to read because he had not time, was not interested. Why should he learn to read when his unconscious was so full of things to do and think. All his trouble was [that] he was being constantly pulled back into a reality which had nothing to do with him.... You see, when the high side is very high the low side is very low, and Jobic fought alright, all his papers and diaries show that. How he fought—and how he kicked and sputtered as he fought.

Jung said that even if he had had him as a patient years ago he could have done nothing. Psychoanalysis can do nothing in cases of psychosis—patients don't stay cured when they are insane. Perhaps when I had my cataleptic fit at the altar rail before Jobic was born it was Jobic already trying to escape reality, dragging me with him that time, as he always has and always will drag me with him. Perhaps when he almost died under the tonsil operation he was trying to escape reality, always, always running away. Then you come down to his big break-up at the Mill. He had the pistol in his hand, he wrapped it up in Paul's trousers, threw it on the floor and ran away. Anyway, he won out. So now what a blessing it is that he is where he does not have to fight so much. Where he has friends, where he can do as he likes, where he is safe and can rest. I have a note here this morning from the head nurse of the Villa Saint-Luc. She says "Il parait satisfait de l'endroit qu'on lui a donné pour ses expériences. Ce dernier est dans le jardin ce qui l'oblige à rester dehors et à prendre l'air." He is trying out some ideas on the rapidity with which cement dries, and they let him do what he likes and help him all they can. Well, after my talk with Jung, Mary and I got in the car and went all across Switzerland to Lausanne, and near there we visited a sanatorium for mental cases and talked to a very eminent medical man. He said Jobic was incurable. He said that at his place they give exactly the same treatment as the one Jobic is getting from Cosse. It is called "treatment de shock à la sulfosine"; they also give *sels d'or* and so does Cosse.

This Swiss place was more expensive than the Villa St-Luc and Jobic would loathe it. They make the patients do bead work and little ash trays of metal and leather work. Mary almost died, she said "Imagine Jobic with all his taste being forced to do that"—no, where he is is best. There is only one other insane boy at the Villa St-Luc and they are fond of him, they say Jobic is always good, always polite, likes everything and gives them no trouble at all. There, if he wants to turn in on his unconscious they let him, he can stay in bed and brood, nobody minds. If he wants to paint they will be delighted—they are human beings and like all French people they take an individual care of him.... His sense of guilt and of conflict must have died down, and he probably is happier than he ever has been in his life before. He doesn't like his family, they never do, so he is well away from us and we from him.

There is a lot more Jung said but I cannot write it, nor even tell it ever, I think. That was for me—it makes all the difference in the world. I am content. I am happy that the long hard struggle for us both is over.

Now comes a long peace, just a slow day by day working out of what must be, but I am sustained by the inner light and very happy....

*

The writer was Eleanor Keyes Du Vivier—Mrs. Joseph Du Vivier. She was born in 1878 and lived in New York City most of her life, except for the years 1921 to 1938, when her husband's law practice established the family in France. The Du Viviers—there were four sons—spent several summers in Fontainebleau, and there, in 1924, they met Mary Foote, the American portrait painter, then in her early fifties. In 1928, Mary Foote was to find her way to Zurich, where she entered analysis with Jung, became the editor of Jung's Seminars, painted his portrait, and remained for nearly thirty years.[2] A portrait of Eleanor Du Vivier was commissioned, and during August Mary Foote worked on it in her studio in Fontainebleau. The two women became close friends and remained in touch during the years that followed.

The eldest son, Jobic (a Breton diminutive, his family nickname, which he later adopted legally, thus—significantly—escaping his father's name), was born in New York in 1908 and educated in the United States and France. He studied art at Fontainebleau, and for a time he lived in the monastery at Mount Athos and in Florence. He became a gifted painter of fresco, and his work was displayed at the Colonial Exposition in Paris, 1933. Jobic was asked by the Curé in Montereau, a town a little southeast of the Forest of Fontainebleau, to decorate a small church there, and he executed frescoes in the apse and choirloft and a decorated crucifix, but his mind broke before he had completed less than half of the frescoes for which he had drawn cartoons. And Jobic, or perhaps his family, privately published a monograph he had written on the technique of fresco, illustrated with remarkable drawings, maps, and charts that depicted, in almost obsessive detail, the tools of the art, atmospheric and light conditions affecting fresco painting in France, the incidence of frescoes throughout Europe, and sketches of Michelangelo's frescoes on the ceiling of the Sistine Chapel. Photographs of Jobic's frescoes at Montereau, as well as his cartoons for frescoes that he never carried out, suggest work of notable originality, feeling, and power, as well as technical brilliance. Clearly Byzantine in influence, they also combine something of the Pre-Raphaelite aestheticism of Burne-Jones with a mysticism reminiscent of Blake. And the monograph—actually, the first chapter of a projected book—is learned, idiosyncratic, witty, written with a special literary flair. His career was promising—more, it was well on its way. But Jobic suffered "crises" of psychic instability even in childhood. Violent episodes in the spring and summer of 1935 caused the family to institutionalize him. Once he escaped from the sanatorium, wandered for days around the countryside and along the roads, and was at last found in a wretched state.

In early 1936, Mrs. Du Vivier, who had confided to Mary Foote her son's difficulties, came to the decision, at her prompting, to consult Jung. The appointment was set for 11 o'clock the morning of February 20. Mrs. Du Vivier had arrived in Zurich the day before, driven from Paris by her chauffeur, and stayed at Mary Foote's apartment on the Plattenstrasse, not far from the house of the Psychological Club, on Gemeindestrasse. As she wrote in her diary, "Mary put me in her room and her lovely soft bed. After dinner I went to bed early with that very amusing second volume of Mabel Dodge's Life." (Mabel Dodge Luhan had been one of Mary Foote's friends in her worldly pre-Zurich days.) The day after the interview with Jung, the two ladies motored to Lausanne to inspect the sanatorium that both thought inappropriate. Jobic was kept on where he was, at the Villa St-Luc. Later in the year Mrs. Du Vivier went to New York, and she had one more encounter with Jung, when he spoke on the question "Is Analytical Psychology a Religion?" at the Plaza Hotel in New York on October 3.[3] On October 7, when Mrs. Du Vivier sailed for France on the *Queen Mary*, her friend Mary Foote was also aboard, after a rare visit to the States.

In spring 1937, Jobic was subjected to a bizarre surgical procedure introduced by a French physician, Rambaud, as a treatment of psychic illness. It involved an operation designed to "clear out all the sinuses" by removing deviations of bone. In Jobic's case it was not effective; whether other cases so treated enjoyed benefit we do not know. Jobic remained in the sanatorium, generally in a calm though delusional state. In another letter, his mother wrote of a visit to him.

> He told his nurse to leave us alone and then he said, looking straight at me: "Tell me, Mother, is this a crazy idea I have that I am the heir to the French throne?" "Yes, it is," I said quietly. "Have I many crazy ideas like that?" "You have two or three." "Then it is not true that I am an illegitimate son and that the mob is trying to destroy me for my pretensions to the throne of France." "No, that is all your imagination," I said quite seriously and quietly. Since then he has given up that idea completely. And so, little by little, at each visit we clear up some point that has been bothering him and he takes my word for it, just like that. He knows I have never lied to him.... I follow him along the fantastic road trying to see it as he does until the thought breaks.... He said one day, "Will you bring me back my soul? I have lost it." "Why, yes, of course, where did you lose it?" "I lost it at the Gare Saint Lazare... near the checking room." "But where, try and remember, did you check it?" "You'll find it in a slot machine," he said. "All right, I'll go to the Gare Saint Lazare. I'll put fifty centimes in the slot machine and bring you your soul." Then he looked at me with all his senses normal and smiled very sweetly. I said, "It is just like Alice in Wonderland." "Oh no, it's much worse than that," said he.

Jung's counsel had the evident effect of reconciling Mrs. Du Vivier to her son's hopeless illness, and perhaps Jung also helped her to reach Jobic. She was a devout Catholic, and Jung addressed her spiritual consciousness.

Throughout the war years, Jobic remained in a sanatorium, occasionally stirring to paint a fresco, ever more fantastic, on a wall of the establishment. He died in 1956, his mother in 1962. Her keepsakes contained a newspaper clipping about Jung's death the year before. Jobic's frescoes are on the walls of the church in Montereau, his cartoons for those he never executed are at Newton College of the Sacred Heart, near Boston, and his mother's portrait by Mary Foote is in the family's possession.

*

In the same period, possibly in the same year, there seems to have been another and similar consultation in Küsnacht. The American poet Robert Lowell, in an autobiographical poem, "Unwanted," which he composed a year before his death in 1977, wrote:

> That year Carl Jung said to mother in Zurich,
> "If your son is as you have described him,
>   he is an incurable schizophrenic."[4]

"That year" was apparently around 1935-37, when Lowell was a student at Harvard and a patient of the psychiatrist and poet Merrill Moore, as he discloses in the same poem.[5] Moore (1903-57) had a somewhat ambivalent interest in Jungian psychology, and he may have referred the poet's mother, Charlotte Winslow Lowell, to Jung. Indeed, Moore may have met Jung at the Harvard Tercentenary Conference in September 1936. The details of the encounter of Jung and Mrs. Lowell, who died in 1954, are still to be unearthed. Though there is a similarity in external circumstances between the two distressed mothers and in psychiatric terms between the two disturbed sons, as well as in aesthetic disposition between the young men themselves, the outcomes of their fates and their art are so dissimilar as to raise that recurring enigmatic question about the relation of mental illness and artistic creativity. The closing lines of Robert Lowell's poem put the question in another way:

> Is getting well ever an art,
>   or art a way to get well?

---

1 Joseph Du Vivier, Jr. (1908-1956). I am indebted to his brother, Mr. David Du Vivier, of Princeton, for informing me of the case and giving me access to family papers in his possession.
2 See Edward Foote, "Who Was Mary Foote," *Spring 1974*.
3 See *Spring 1972* for the notes of Jung's talk, edited by Jane A. Pratt. The occasion, however, is incorrectly dated 1937, and the error was carried over in a republication of the notes in *C.G. Jung Speaking*, edited by William McGuire and R.F.C. Hull (Princeton and London, 1977), pp. 94 ff.
4 *Day by Day* (New York, 1977), p. 122. Copyright© 1975, 1976, 1977 by Robert Lowell. Quoted by permission of the publishers, Farrar, Straus, and Giroux, Inc., New York.
5 Cf. Steven Gould Axelrod, *Robert Lowell: Life and Art* (Princeton, 1978), pp. 22, 241.

Mal Occhio The Underside of Vision

by Lawrence DiStasi

The author remembers the rituals of "mal occhio," the evil eye, as practiced in and around his family. He then ranges far afield to examine the rituals and beliefs of the evil eye in other cultures and times. The writings of Freud, Jung, Sir James Frazer, Norman O. Brown, Joseph Campbell, and many others illuminate the dim origins of "making evil eye."

Over 50 illustrations show the various amulets and charms used to ward off mal occhio. MAL OCCHIO has been produced by the award-winning Yolla Bolly Press.

"A book to learn things from, and enjoy. At last some psychology from the South Side: images, gestures, and *cupiditas*." — James Hillman

160 pages, 6 × 9, *illustrations, photographs, bibliography*
Cloth, $12.50

NORTH POINT PRESS • P.O. Box 6275 • Berkeley, California 94706

SCHOPENHAUER AND JUNG

JAMES L. JARRETT
(Berkeley)

Suppose a student of the writings of C.G. Jung were given the pedantic task of citing chapter and verse for the following texts:

> As life becomes more and more unconscious, the nearer it approaches the point at which all consciousness ceases, the course of time itself seems to increase in rapidity. In childhood all the things and circumstances of life are novel....[1]

> Up to our thirty-sixth year, we may be compared in respect of the way in which we use our vital energy, to people who live on the interest of their money: what they spend to-day, they have again to-morrow. But from the age of thirty-six onwards, our position is like that of the investor who begins to entrench upon his capital.[2]

> Everything that is really fundamental in a man, and therefore genuine, works, as such, unconsciously; in this respect like the power of nature. That which has passed through the domain of consciousness is thereby transformed into an idea or picture; and so if it comes to be uttered it is only an idea or picture which passed from one person to another.[3]

> I know of no greater absurdity than that propounded by most systems of philosophy in declaring evil to be negative [i.e. privative] in its character. Evil is just what is positive; it makes its own existence felt.[4]

> ... If only one individual were left in the world, and all the rest were to perish, the one that remained would still possess the whole self-being of the world, uninjured and undiminished, and would laugh at the destruction of the world as an illusion. This conclusion *per impossibile* may be balanced by the counter-conclusion, which is on all fours with it, that if that last individual were to be annihilated in and with him the whole world would be destroyed. It was in this sense that the mystic Angelus Silesius declared that God could not live for a moment without him, and that if he were to be annihilated God must of necessity give up the ghost.[5]

Professor Jarrett offers seminars at Berkeley on Jung, phenomenology, value theory, etc. His latest book is *The Humanities and Humanistic Education*. Having worked with Jungians in Zürich, London, and in the Bay Area, he is now nearing completion of a book-length Ms. on the philosophy of C.G. Jung.

"What bad luck!" the student might utter. "As it happens, I can't think *exactly* where even a single one occurs!" Still, he plunges in bravely enough, and confident, especially if he has access to the general index of the *Collected Works*, that he can rather quickly run down the sources.

But no—not in *those Collected Works*. They are, in fact, all from Schopenhauer.

Indeed, the list of Jungian-sounding quotations from Schopenhauer could be extended almost indefinitely, including the theory of "individuation," Eastern wisdom, the relating of "good consciousness" to the Moral Law and Instinct, citations of Jacob Boehme and the *I Ching*, and so on; though in truth in some cases the similarity would be but superficial. Yet considerable similarity of idea between the two thinkers is demonstrable. Though one must beware of arguing *post hoc*, Schopenhauer indeed was a profound influence, to be ranked alongside of Kant and Freud, and ahead of even Nietzsche and William James.

All his life Jung had a love/hate relationship with philosophy. When the philosophers indulged in verbal acrobatics and logic-chopping, when their speculations cut loose from the moorings of experience, he would cry out, "I'm not a philosopher, I'm an empiricist, a phenomenologist." Yet he was fully aware of the irony of his protest; empiricism and phenomenology are themselves philosophical positions, orientations, schools, methodologies, as are the mechanism and positivism he so despised. Early Jung came to see that nothing is more dangerous to a psychologist than being grounded in a wrongheaded philosophy, but the corrective movement is *not* in eschewing philosophy, becoming a non- or anti-philosopher, for this is to give over criticizing one's own assumptions, one's "personal psychic premises," the great philosophical tasks. A psychologist *is* a philosopher, consciously or unconsciously—but here as everywhere, the influences that remain dark are potentially full of mischief. "Ideas that we do not know we have have us."[6]

Long before he ever heard of Freud, Jung had encountered a number of theories of the unconscious. From his rather desultory research in the history of philosophy he knew of Leibniz's *petites perceptions*, the subliminal registrations of organisms (even of inorganic substances), and had been thunderstruck by Kant's revelations of the things-in-themselves—space-less, time-less, cause-less entities within and without the psyche. (He was to remain, in important ways, a Kantian throughout his life.) He knew too some of the speculations of Kant's followers like

Schelling and Herbart, and he was impressed with the work of a minor but daring thinker named C.G. Carus, who in 1846 had published *Psyche*, a book in which he discourses on the development of the soul from the unconscious. Eduard von Hartmann's *Philosophy of the Unconscious* (1869) was no doubt much discussed among the intellectuals of his set. Jung, who is open about his intellectual debts, described the study of Kant and Schopenhauer as "mentally my greatest adventure." (*CW 18:* §485) "My ideas of the unconscious," he once told a seminar, "first became enlightened through Schopenhauer and Hartmann."[7] Again, "the great find" was Schopenhauer, for here at last was someone who saw that not all was well in the "fundaments of the universe."

> He was the first to speak of the suffering of the world, which visibly and glaringly surrounds us, and of the confusion, passion, evil—all those things which the others hardly seemed to notice and always tried to resolve into an all-embracing harmony and comprehensibility.[8]

Jung would have had Schopenhauer call that blind will which is at the core of every being *God*, and felt that here for once Schopenhauer's courage failed him, though Schopenhauer, neither theist nor pantheist, saw only obfuscation in the identification. *The World as Will and Idea*, Schopenhauer's great work, epitomizes his philosophy in the very title: Will and Idea (Representation), noumena and phenomena, "things" in their primordial state and as appearance, the Unconscious and the Conscious.

As Jung was to insist against Freud, there are no *ideas* in the unconscious; yet the fountainhead of our deepest ideas and feelings is the unconscious. As Schopenhauer put it:

> But ordinarily it is in the obscure depths of the mind that the rumination of the materials received from without takes place, through which they are worked up into thoughts; and it goes on almost as unconsciously as the conversion of nourishment into the humours and substance of the body. Hence it is that we can often give no account of the origin of our deepest thoughts. They are the birth of our mysterious inner life. Judgments, thoughts, purposes, rise from out that deep unexpectedly and to our own surprise.... Consciousness is the mere surface of our mind, of which, as of the earth, we do not know the inside, but only the crust.[9]

Or as he says elsewhere, "Everything that is really fundamental in a man, and therefore genuine, works, as such, unconsciously...."

"Accordingly, any quality of mind or character that is genuine and lasting, is originally unconscious."[10] Here he speaks of transformation into an "idea or a picture"—the conscious, phenomenal constructs. "Only that which is innate is genuine and will hold water...."[11] What is concocted without coming up from the unconscious is affectation, superficiality.

The unconscious, the primordial part of all being, is the surge of will, desire, want, lust. As with plants and animals, so too with man; but in the latter there emerges that precious function which nearly all philosophers have desperately wanted to make fundamental, even absolute: the intellect. However much our cognitive functions may represent our only hope of escaping the engulfing maw of the will, they are derivative, secondary. "The will is the substance of man, the intellect the accident; the will is the matter, the intellect is the form; the will is warmth, the intellect is light."[12]

Between the abstracting intellect, the reason and will itself stands immediate sensation or feeling. Indeed, Schopenhauer does not always distinguish between willing and feeling. In a linguistic aside not unlike the sort that Jung often indulged, Schopenhauer writes:

> A true feeling of the real relation between will, intellect, and life is also expressed in the Latin language. The intellect is *mens, nous*; the will again is *animus*, which comes from *anima*, and this from *anemon*. *Anima* is the life itself, the breath, *psyché*; but *animus* is the living principle, and also the will, the subject of inclinations, intentions, passions, emotions; hence also *est mihi animus*—for "I have a desire to," also *anima causa, etc.*; it is the Greek *thymos*, the German "Gemüth," thus the heart but not the head.[13]

He adds that our very identity lies in what lies below consciousness: "It rests upon the identical *will* and the unalterable character of the person.... In the heart is the man, not in the head.... Our true self, the kernel of our nature, is what is behind that, and really knows nothing but willing and not willing, being content and not content, with all the modifications of this, which are called feelings, emotions, and passions."[14] In an early work he makes the same point, but suggests that a range of will-states is open to our immediate inspection: "Introspection always shows us to ourselves as *willing*. In this *willing*, however, there are numerous degrees, from the faintest wish to passion...."[15] But important as the passage is from lower to higher consciousness,

Schopenhauer is far from thinking that development of the intellect demands the attrition of will. "The higher the consciousness has risen, the more distinct and connected are the thoughts [Cf. Jungian "differentiation"], the clearer the perceptions, the more intense the sensations. Through it everything gains more depth: emotion, sadness, joy and sorrow."[16]

Jung, who ranks high among the world's thinkers who have been notably imagistic, pictorial, in their cognitive processing, will have found an ally in Schopenhauer in this respect too. The "Vorstellung" sometimes rendered "Idea" in the title of his main book, means literally "placed before," and is perhaps most nearly adequately translated "representation." (In a letter to R.F.C. Hull, his English translator, Jung discusses the difficulties of rendering both *Idee* and *Vorstellung*.)[17] These phenomena, representations emerging from unconscious willing, and known immediately—that is, intuited—are largely pictorial, though we have the ability, of course, to make representations of representations—that is, concepts.[18] "Imagination is an essential element of genius."[18] "Imagination" is presumably meant to include both simple imaging or mental picturing and the extension of the mind beyond the immediately given. The poet (who shares with the nonacademic philosopher Schopenhauer's highest praise) is characterized as one who, starting with mental images, exhibits "the art of bringing into play the power of imagination through words."[19] As writer, Schopenhauer (again like Jung) conjures up pictures continually—in severe contrast to his antithetic rival Hegel.

But the highest function of the artist is to help extend the mind beyond concrete objects and pictures, to the Platonic Ideas. This has two consequences, subjective and objective. In the first, the result is an "enhancement of consciousness to the pure, will-less, timeless subject of knowing."[20] That is, to rescue the will-driven soul from futility one must abandon the phenomenal ego for a state of contemplation. In music we come closest to being presented with the will itself, the Unconscious itself, to regard contemplatively and hence escape for a time being its tool.

Jung recognized early the affinity between his own "primordial images" or "archetypes" and the Platonic Forms, for in both cases they are seen as at once ultimate creative forces in the universe, the engenderers of what boils up into consciousness, and ultimate though ineffable objects of knowledge. "In Plato," he says, "an extraordinarily high value is set on the archetypes as metaphysical ideas, as 'paradigms' or models, while real things are held to be only the copies of these model ideas." (*CW 8:* §275)

Jung speaks variously of the archetypes, calling them "dominants of experience" (*CW 8:* §423), says they "organize images and ideas," are an "inborn disposition to produce parallel images," configurations (*CW 9*, ii: §179), and "forms in which things can be perceived and conceived."[21]

Readers will not have failed to notice Schopenhauer's use of different words to name mental functions, and will have been put in mind of Jung's famous four functions. This needs to be looked at directly.

A most promising statement is this: "... The direct opposite of rational knowledge is feeling...."[22] One is struck not only by the differentiation of feeling from thinking, but also his pitting them against each other as "direct opposite(s)." Both Jung (*e.g., CW 6:* §723-29) and Schopenhauer were much struck with the exceptional ambiguity of "Gefühl":

> For the most diverse and even antagonistic elements lie quietly side by side in this concept; for example, religious feeling, feeling of sensual pleasure, moral feeling, bodily feeling, as touch, pain, sense of colour, of sounds and their harmonies and discords, feelings of hate, of disgust, of self-satisfaction, of honour, of disgrace, of right, or wrong, sense of truth, aesthetic feeling, feeling of power, weakness, health, friendship, love, etc. etc. ... There is absolutely nothing in common among them except the negative quality that they are not abstract rational knowledge.[23]

This, indeed, he makes the definiens of the concept, but he goes on to propose *empfindung* (sensation) as more precisely designating bodily feelings—and this is exactly what Jung does. One might better say that when Jung uses *empfindung* to name a distinct function he employs it somewhat broadly; a "sensation type" may be more distinguished by his attention to the account books than by his emphasis on the bodily senses. But what is left over still does not correspond to Jung's notion of "feeling," which for Schopenhauer has nothing to do with emotion and everything to do with sense of *value*. Though rational knowledge, *wissen*, also does not correspond exactly with Jung's thinking, *denken*, Schopenhauer wants to distinguish between *reason* and *understanding* in the Kantian manner. "Intuition," a common word in Schopenhauer's vocabulary, appears however only as a translation of *anschauung*, which means "immediate presentation," in William James's phrase, knowledge by acquaintance, and has little to do with dwelling in the realm of the possible, as in Jung, who stresses the Latin *in-tuire*, to look in.

Another theory that brings to mind the Jungian four categories is found in Schopenhauer's 1813 *On The Fourfold Root of The Principle of Sufficient Reason*. Here the principle "Nothing is without a reason for its being" is found by the young Schopenhauer to take four different forms: the logical, the physical/causal, the mathematical, and the moral. It would be disingenuous to pretend that these correspond to Thinking, Sensing, Intuiting, and Feeling, as Schopenhauer in turn mentioned Aristotle's quadratic analysis of "cause" but made no claim for a correspondence. Still, they do constitute a modification of the Kantian categories (which derive directly from Aristotle), in being *a priori*, necessary ways of interpreting the raw data of experience. And Jung in turn accepts the Kantian (and Schopenhauerian) inbuilt forms without which there can be no movement from the chaos of the unconscious to the relative orderliness of consciousness. We will return to this point of categories and forms presently.[24]

Schopenhauer makes less capital than Jung of the clash of opposites as the source of energy, going in this respect hardly farther than the scattered commonplace that opposites illumine one another.[25] Perhaps Hegel had so thoroughly preempted this anti-thetic way of thinking that it was strictly out of bounds for his rival. Yet some opposites were crucial for Schopenhauer: subject/object, inner/outer, will/body, which overlap significantly. The great point is that he resolves this sort of dualism precisely as Spinoza (not one of Schopenhauer's favorites) did, by a double-aspect theory. "The act of will and the movement of the body are not two different things; ... they are one and the same, but they are given in entirely different ways—immediately, and again in perception...."[26] The body is the objectification, the outward manifestation, the visible representation of the will. (The intellect is the other, opposite aspect of the brain.)

It may be worth recording the striking similarity of Jung's position:

> For what is the body? The body is merely the visibility of the soul, the psyche; and

the soul is the psychological experience of the body; so it is really one and the same thing. *(CW 3:* §41-2)

Elsewhere he speaks of "the mysterious truth that the spirit is the life of the body seen from within and the body the outward manifestation of the life of the spirit—the two being really one. ..." *(CW 10:* §195)

For Schopenhauer man knows himself as a conscious individual, a phenomenal being; and as thing-in-itself, the unconscious realm that lies below individuation. He liked to cite the authority of Kant for the first, of the *Vedas* for the second.[27] Jung would have said Yea to both the distinction and the documentation. He would also have resonated most affirmatively to Schopenhauer's citation of dreams as best illustrating "the identity of my own being with that of the external world.... For in a dream other people appear to be totally distinct from us, and to possess the most perfect objectivity, and a nature which is quite different from ours, and which often puzzles, surprises, astonishes or terrifies us; and *yet it is all our own self.*"[28]

Schopenhauer was, indeed, more interested in dreams than most philosophers have been. One other reference may be of interest: mentioning that we sometimes perform certain unusual actions without knowing why, Schopenhauer says that these are aftereffects of forgotten fate-portending dreams, the dynamics being very much like that exhibited by instinctive behavior.[29]

On the related topic of *differentiation*, for Jung the great *Logos* function which leads out of unconsciousness, there is one important passage in Schopenhauer which may have influenced the budding metapsychologist:

> Why is our consciousness brighter and more distinct the further it extends towards without, so that its greatest clearness lies in sense perception, which already half belongs to things outside us—and, on the other hand, grows dimmer as we go in, and leads, if followed to its inmost recesses to a darkness in which all knowledge ceases? Because, I say, consciousness presupposes *individuality*; but this belongs to the mere phenomenon.... Our inner nature, on the other hand, has its root in that which is no longer phenomenon, but thing-in-itself, to which, therefore, the forms of the phenomenon do not extend; and thus the chief conditions of individuality are wanting, and with these the distinctness of consciousness falls off. In this root of existence the difference of beings ceases, like that of the radii of a sphere in the centre; and as in the sphere the surface is produced by the radii ending and breaking off; so consciousness is only possible where the true inner being runs out

into the phenomenon, through whose forms the separate individuality becomes possible upon which consciousness depends....[30]

Withdrawing into the center as "in sleep, in death, to a certain extent in magnetic or magic influences" is becoming part of the undifferentiated will, wherein (as in Aristotle's " active reason") the only claim to immortality resides. Schopenhauer cites the *Bhagavadgita* as authority, explaining that "mystical and figurative language...is the only language in which anything can be said on this entirely transcendent theme."[31] Here Schopenhauer anticipates Jung's use of the concept *symbol*, "For when something is 'symbolic,' it means that a person divines its hidden, ungraspable nature and is trying desperately to capture in words the secret which eludes him."[32] The symbol is necessarily paradoxical, its purpose being to synthesize opposites that for the purely rational mind must remain forever apart.

In the same spirit, Schopenhauer says "...With me the ultimate foundation of morality is the truth which in the Vedas and the Vedanta receives its expression in the established, mystical formula, *Tat twam asi* (This is thyself), which is spoken with reference to every living thing, be it man or beast, and is called the Mahavakya, the great word."[33] Later he specifically sets the "principle of individuation" over against the *Tat-twam-asi* principle,[34] and though individuation does not have the same meaning in the two authors, it is fair to say that both see human development as from the undifferentiated unconscious into the light of logic and reason and then farther on to a mystical contemplation of the abiding forms and symbols.

For both thinkers Plato was in this last regard the great exemplar in Western thought—in Schopenhauer he is constantly "the divine Plato"—but they agreed in finding Buddhist and Hindu spiritual wisdom far more advanced than anything in our tradition. But for both the great objects of our contemplative regard are also the great engenderers and shapers of our intelligible life. Schopenhauer called them *Urbilder* or *Musterbilder*, "prototypes" or "archetypes." Speaking of Plato's parable of the cave, he writes: "The real archetypes ... to which these shadows correspond, the eternal Ideas, the original forms of all things, can alone be said to have true being (*ontos òn*), because they *always are, but never become nor pass away.*" In this instance, Jung specifically notes the similarity of his own thoughts to those of Schopenhauer, prefacing a lengthy quotation from *The World as Will and Idea* with the remark, "I would ask the reader to replace the word 'idea' by 'primordial image,' and he will then be able to understand my meaning." (*CW* 6: §752) "Primordial image," it will be remembered, was the expression which in Jung's development modulates into "archetype." And archetypes are the contents of the collective unconscious, hence innate, the great forms which organize our experience. Interestingly, both authors specifically allow that Locke was right in his attack on innate ideas, since in his context "ideas" are mental representations of material reality, and therefore can be learned only in experience. But they agree further that Locke overdogmatized in saying that nothing is innate. Schopenhauer puts it, "Locke goes too far in denying all innate truths inasmuch as he extends his denial even to our *formal* knowledge—a point in which he has been brilliantly rectified by Kant...."[35] For Jung as for Schopenhauer the archetypes, the primordial images, the prototypical Ideas are the forms into which is poured the material content, with its individual and cultural qualities.[36]

"Night after night," Jung wrote, "our dreams practice philosophy on their own account." (*CW 12:* §247) He meant, of course, that the dreams furnish the raw material of philosophy, but a huge job awaits the conscious reflective mind. Once noting that an "imbecilic locksmith" he encountered had had some marvelous visions that were extraordinarily Schopenhauerian, he quickly adds that the difference was that for the patient in the mental hospital "the vision remained at the stage of a mere spontaneous growth, while Schopenhauer abstracted it and expressed it in language of universal validity.... A man is a philosopher of genius only when he succeeds in transmuting the primitive and wholly natural vision into an abstract idea belonging to the common stock of consciousness." (*CW 7:* §229)

An exhaustive comparison of the two thinkers would reveal other similarities. For instance, both put great stress on personality as a determinant of experience. Both claimed to be empiricists. Schopenhauer made slight anticipations of the concept of *persona*. Neither had much use for "society" as an explanatory concept—and thus were conspicuously outside the Hegelian-Marxian-Weberian tradition that has predominated in the last hundred years. And so on. But enough has been said to suggest the profound similarities.

Influence is a hard matter to prove. No doubt some similarities are little more than coincidences. Others may develop from a common propensity and an attraction for a common tradition (Plato, Kant, the East).

Jung took great delight in finding in his predecessors anticipations of his own ideas—"... There is not a single important idea or view that does not possess historical antecedents" (*CW 9,i:* §69), he once wrote—though no doubt it was often the case that Gnostic and alchemical adumbrations of his thought parallel ideas he had independently developed. But Kant and Schopenhauer got to him in his most formative stage, apparently giving direction to some of the concepts which were to prevail throughout his career albeit deepened, extended, and given local habitation in his phenomenological reflections on his clinical practice and perhaps even more on introspection. Jung continually pays tribute to Schopenhauer as an original and great mind who courageously broke free from the crushing weight of the rationalistic tradition, who dared speak of the pre-rational unconscious. We can imagine Jung, after the disappointments of his father's library, coming upon the scandalous Schopenhauer, an unabashed introvert, far more interested in spiritual than material phenomena, a freethinker, a celebrator of Eastern religion, one who knew evil to be real and unrelenting, and who found in contemplation of the great eternal forms some surcease from the will-driven life.

Is it true, as I suspect, that the young analysts who today so eagerly follow Jung's lead into the world of fairytale and myth, adept in horoscopes and the Tarot, stop short when beckoned into the philosophic mansions? If they take as their justifying text Jung's protest that he is "not a philosopher but an empiricist," they are stuck with the letter but remain empty of the spirit; for did not Jung explicitly hold that it is necessary for psychotherapists "to be philosophers or philosophic doctors"? (*CW 16:* §181) This, for the excellent reason that it is often important to enter into philosophical discussions with patients on problems of epistemology, ethics, metaphysics, in making progress toward a Weltanschauung. In a late talk to the New York Psychology Club, Jung said quite simply, "I am speaking just as a philosopher."[37]

---

1 *The Complete Essays of Arthur Schopenhauer*, trans. T. Bailey Saunders (New York: Wiley Book Company, n.d.), *Counsels and Maxims*, "The Ages of Life," p. 131. (Cited hereafter as *Essays.*)
2 *Ibid*, p. 128.

3 *Essays, Studies in Pessimism*, "Psychological Observations," pp. 45-6.
4 *Essays, Studies in Pessimism*, "On the Sufferings of the World," p.1.
5 *Essays, Human Nature*, "Human Nature," p. 28. Cf. *The World as Will and Idea*, trans. R.B. Haldane and J. Kemp (London: Routledge & Kegan Paul, 1883), Vol. I, p. 167. (Hereafter *WWI*.)
6 James Hillman, "Anima II," *Spring 1974*, p. 113.
7 Unpublished typescript of the notes of Cary F. de Angulo on the 1925-26 seminar, p. 3.
8 *Memories, Dreams, Reflections*, New York: Vintage edition, p. 69.
9 *WWI*, III, p. 328.
10 *Essays, Studies in Pessimism*, "Psychological Observations," pp. 45-6. Cf. *Schopenhauer's Fourfold Root of the Principle of Sufficient Reason*, trans. E.F.J. Payne (Open Court, 1974), p. 122.
11 *Loc. cit.*
12 *WWI*, II, p. 412.
13 *WWI*, II, p. 459. Readers of Jung may well fix on "anima" and "animus," but it is evident that Jung's use of these words to designate the contra-sexual soul is not Schopenhauerian.
14 *Ibid*, p. 460.
15 *Fourfold Root*, p. 168.
16 *WWI*, III, p. 17.
17 *Letters*, II, pp. 460-1.
18 *The World as Will and Representation*, trans. E.F.J. Payne (Falcon Wings Press, 1958, repr. Dover), Vol. I, p. 40. (Hereafter WWr.)
19 *WWR*, II, p. 424.
20 *WWR*, I, p. 199.
21 *Memories, Dreams, Reflections*, p. 347.
22 *WWI*, I, p. 66.
23 *Loc. cit.*
24 C.A. Meier remarks at the end of a similar comparison that the parallel is best not overdone. *Bewusstsein*, Walter-Verlag, Freiburg im Breisgau, 1975.
25 *WWI*, I, p. 268, 474.
26 *WWI*, I, p. 170.
27 *Essays, Human Nature*, "Human Nature," p. 27.
28 *Essays*, "Genius and Virtue," p. 86 (emphasis added).
29 *WWI*, Ch. 27.
30 *WWI*, III, p. 74.
31 *WWI*, III, p. 75.
32 *Letters*, I, p. 123.
33 *Essays, Human Nature*, "Human Nature," p. 24.
34 *Essays, Human Nature*, "Character," p. 79.
35 *Fourfold Root*, p. 139.
36 See *Memories, Dreams, Reflections*, p. 347.
37 *Spring 1972*, p. 147. On Kant, Jung and philosophy see also Stephanie de Voogd's article in *Spring 1977*, pp. 175-182.

COUPLING/UNCOUPLING
Reflections on the Evolution of the Marriage Archetype

ROBERT M. STEIN
(Beverly Hills)

Behind the human drive toward coupling are images of the sacred marriage of a divine couple and the soul's sense of incompletion. As powerful as the human need for coupling is the need to be free and unattached. In other words, the archetype behind the urge to be bound in marriage contains an opposite drive (as do all archetypes) to be unbound and separate. The tension between the needs to be coupled and to be single has become an increasing problem in our times. That the bonds of marriage no longer seem to hold, or at least function creatively to nourish the soul, is largely a consequence of our lack of connection to the changes occurring within the marriage archetype. Our urban-industrial society wreaks havoc on marriage, family and kinship community. As a consequence nuclear families atomize and couples become increasingly dependent on each other and their children for intimacy and security. This dependence has put enormous pressure on the marriage relation to fulfill all needs for intimacy and security, of course intensifying the soul's need to be free.

Since the 1960's we have seen sexual freedom, open, multiple or communal marriages, unmarried unions, democratic or patriarchal communes, religious and non-religious communities, explored. And it appears that in spite of the external changes, psychologically the younger generations have encountered the same oppressive patterns in their relationships, and seem just as incapable as older generations of resolving the polarization between the need to be bound and attached, and the need to be free and unattached. The 60's revolution has not reaped many new fruits in marriage and relationship. When the tension between the op-

---

The author, a practising Jungian analyst, presented this paper at the VIII Congress of the International Association for Analytical Psychology, San Francisco, September 1980. Other writings by Dr. Stein have appeared in *Spring* (1970, '71, '73, '76).

posites becomes unbearable, separation or divorce is still the prevailing solution.

Let us briefly review some of the ways in which the polarization *within* the marriage archetype has been dealt with historically. In our Western monogamous culture the dominant pattern has been the illicit, extra-marital love affair or prostitution. In polygamous cultures, multiple marriages or concubinage, in primitive societies polygamy, ritual orgies, ritual sharing of wives are some of the patterns. Much has been written about comparative cultural patterns of marriage. My intention is only to show that none of these solutions attend to the soul's need to be separate, free and unattached. An illicit love affair is eventually as binding and confining as legitimate marriage. The same can be said for multiple marriages in a polygamous culture. Though all these patterns allow for variations on the theme of coupling, and may relieve the oppressive tension of the exclusive, monogamous marriage, they hardly speak to the other pole of the archetype. They do little to heal the split. Neither does the more modern pattern of sequential marriage and divorce. The need to be coupled soon returns in full force, and a high percentage of divorced people remarry.

The Hieros Gamos: Zeus and Hera

The incestuous sacred marriage (Hieros Gamos) between Zeus and Hera presents a model for human monogamy. It is told that they celebrated their mating for three hundred blissful years. Only after the royal honeymoon was over did Zeus begin his wandering infidelities. Hera is recognized in Greek religion as the Goddess of Marriage, as the guardian of the sacrament of coupling. Her jealousy, wrath and vindictiveness toward her husband's infidelities with other Goddesses and mortals are well known. To the present day the myth of unfaithful husband and abandoned, faithful wife, devoted to the sanctity of the marriage bed, continues to be enacted, though changes are evident as a result of women's liberation and cosmopolitan sexual mores. One argument to support the apparent difference between masculine and feminine archetypes is that women need the stability and security of a permanent relationship in order to raise and educate children. But men seem to have an equally strong instinctual need to raise and educate children. Studies of animals with their young suggest it is so for them too. I question the notion that women are more concerned about permanent coupling than men. Even among the Olympian deities the Goddesses, including the Mother Goddess, Demeter, have as much need to be free and uncoupled as do the males. Unless we believe that Zeus entered into marriage with Hera only in order to satisfy his lust, we must assume that the great Father God was equally committed to the Hieros Gamos.[1]

The relation between Zeus and Hera can be viewed from the perspective of the marriage archetype splitting after three hundred years of blissful union. Among mortals once the honeymoon is over, typically (archetypally) one spouse remains secure and content while the other begins to feel dissatisfied with bondage, unfree to pursue fantasies and desires (sexual and otherwise) which don't involve the spouse. Jung uses the metaphor of the container and the contained as a way of viewing this phenomenon.[2] He sees one partner as having a more complex nature than the other. "The simpler nature works on the more complicated like a room that is too small, that does not allow him enough space. The complicated nature, on the other hand, gives the simpler one too many rooms with too much space, so that she never knows where she really belongs. So it comes about quite naturally that the more complicated contains the simpler."[3]

The notion of one person as more spiritually developed[4] or psychologically complex than another is such fertile soil for moralistic judgments that I have not found it very helpful. When Jung says, "It is an almost regular occurrence for a woman to be wholly contained spiritually in her husband, and for a husband to be wholly contained, emotionally, in his wife," the concept grows ambiguous.[5] Another objection I have to the container-contained model is that it implies that the simpler nature must become more psychologically aware and developed so the more complex partner will not feel so confined. I agree that a psychologically creative marriage requires the partners to pursue a path of psychological development, but I disagree that marriage or any relationship can contain the soul.

For these reasons I prefer the notion of the split archetype as a way of understanding the soul's inherent need to be both fully coupled (contained) and uncoupled (uncontained). Seen from the perspective of the split archetype, we begin to appreciate how the Zeus-Hera archetypal marriage tends to plunge the feminine into a rigid Senex position and the masculine into the mercurial Puer position. In the traditional monogamous patriarchal marriage, the feminine aspects of the soul become locked into coupling and carrying the responsibility for upholding the sanctity of the marriage bond. The free, unattached creative spirit becomes identified with the masculine, particularly with the eternal young boy, the Puer. As long as the polarity within the marriage archetype remains, the development and creativity of the feminine will remain stifled in both women and men. If the feminine is always a function of a responsiveness to the quick of life, to the movements of the soul in the moment (as I believe it is), to make it the responsible guardian for a rigid patriarchal marriage is surely oppressive to soul and the flow of life.

Philip Slater sees the Zeus-Hera relationship as a reflection of the patriarchal structure of Greek marriage;[6] Kerényi sees the Greek (human) marriage as modeled on the divine Zeus-Hera one.[7] Whichever way we toss this coin, we end up with a pattern of marriage which has prevailed in most cultures. Slater goes so far as to say, "the history of all known civilizations, including our own, is patriarchal."[8] Let me suggest that another archetypal split is there in these opposing views of Slater and Kerényi, important to examine because if the Gods are responsible for determining the patterns of human relationships, it leaves little room for affecting the Gods or archetypes. On the other hand, if archetypes merely reflect human customs and behavior they are depotentiated and man correspondingly inflated. That human attitudes and behavior can effect transformation within an archetype is essential to an evolutionary perspective and not inconsistent with an archetypal psychology. The danger in this evolutionary perspective is that the great powers which inform and regulate the cyclic patterns of human and cosmic life will be depotentiated, resulting in a desacralization of life. Lopez-Pedraza suggests that human nature has two parts, a part that does not change and a part that moves.[9] This notion allows for the possibility that archetype and instinct can participate in change while at the same time allowing for the eternal, unchanging nature and power of the Gods. I see the soul's painful struggle with coupling relationships as a challenge to transform the marriage archetype (Zeus-Hera) through a process of deliteralization that will restore the original unity of the instincts to be coupled and uncoupled, but on a new level of consciousness.

Hand in hand with the need to be coupled goes the need to be uncoupled, always there as soon as the coupling instinct moves us toward another person. Seen from this perspective, the freedom the soul needs is to be able to experience being *simultaneously coupled and uncoupled*. Only then are the inherent polarities of the archetype experienced as complementary rather than splitting. How is it possible to experience oneself bound and committed and at the same time separate, free and unattached? Is it possible to honor the traditional marriage vows and still feel free to behave as a single, unattached person?

Some Dynamics of the Monogamous Patriarchal Marriage

In a monogamous culture, by definition, only one marriage at a time is allowed; if I desire to have an intimate relationship with another woman the coupling instinct soon enters and my marriage is immediately threatened. The soul-splitting tension this rather common situation creates can become unbearable and destructive. It results in a holding back in both relationships even if the tension is resolved in the traditional manner by maintaining a dayworld legitimate marriage and going underground with the other person. Even with this resolution the pressure to choose one or the other is always present. For a man this tension is experienced as a terrible pull between two women (internally between two polarized aspects of the feminine), and the fact that the split is *within the marriage archetype itself* gets lost. Instead of dealing with the soul's need to be free and unattached, the split is experienced as being between Wife-Mother and Adventurous, Exciting, Mysterious Other Woman. This tricks each woman into deeper identification with her role, which becomes increasingly oppressive to all parties involved. The phenomenon is similar when it is a woman who takes a lover: Husband becomes identified with Husband-Father, the lover with Adventurous, Exciting, Other Man. This soap-opera pattern has accompanied the marriage commitment for a long time. Because of this, I believe the split within the marriage archetype has been largely overlooked.

Deliteralization and Unifying the Split Archetype

What is missed in the Western love affair as well as in polygamous systems is the soul's need to be both married and unmarried. If we can now begin to view the need for extramarital intimacy as arising from this polarization within the marriage archetype, perhaps something new may emerge. While the need to feel free and unattached within my marriage may lead me to seek an intimate involvement with another woman, won't I experience this polarity with the other woman? If so, won't it be more to the point if I focus on the split within my soul which has led me toward the other woman in the first place? I resist being coupled to the other woman as much as I resist being coupled to my wife, yet experience the desire to be coupled to both. If I can resolve this conflict in either relationship, it may lead me to a resolution in the other. If I can experience being bound and coupled, free and uncoupled with the other woman, perhaps I can achieve that state with the woman to whom I am literally married. Here is a clue to a possible resolution, a deliteralization of the marriage bond as well as a deliteralization of the soul's need to be free and unattached. Let us explore some of the consequences.

By maintaining the connection to both the desire to be coupled and the desire to be uncoupled, both poles of the instinct (archetype) can be experienced and lived as complementary rather than as divisive opposites. Connection implies separation. In this instance it means that one separates oneself from identifying with either the desire to be coupled or uncoupled while maintaining awareness of both needs. This move is an essential step toward deliteralization.

Literalization is the result of identifying with one particular need, feeling, attitude, idea, viewpoint, God, etc. If we identify with the need to be coupled, fulfillment is only possible through actual marriage (or its equivalent). Only when this need is filled will I become aware of the opposite pole, the need to be uncoupled, which I can also only experience by my identification with its opposite. In other words, if I experience coupling only literally, I experience uncoupling only through the literal act of flight and divorce.[10]

Extramarital Sexuality

Both love and sexuality fare ill under restrictions which limit them to one primary relationship. As soon as coupling occurs, the need to be free and unbound is close at hand. If the need for extramarital erotic involvement is primarily an expression of the other pole of the marriage archetype (as I have suggested) perhaps the vow of sexual fidelity may serve to facilitate rather than hinder the soul's quest for freedom—which is not necessarily reached through satisfying every impulse and desire. Spiritual freedom, as the great religions teach, follows the difficult path of being able to let go of worldly and literal attachments. We know how important sexual restrictions have been in the development of culture, and I have no doubt that the universal restrictions on extramarital sexuality were useful for the soul's development. To simply suggest the elimination of sexual restrictions would seem foolhardy.

I think the dialogue and struggle with the archetype, the God, behind the restrictions on extramarital sexual activity are fundamental to soul-making. For one thing, the desire for fidelity and exclusiveness belongs to the soul's experience of uniting, of coupling, with the beloved. When a culture does not honor this numinous experience, the sacramental mystery of sexual union is profaned. Cultural taboos and restrictions on sexuality originate with the soul's need to sacralize sexuality and life. Still, something seems terribly oppressive to the soul's development in the traditional marriage structure. Something new is needed; I have no doubt that whatever emerges will include a new relationship to the archetype behind the urge for sexual fidelity as well as corresponding changes in the marriage vows and ceremony.

The Church

Marriage, as an institution, is primarily concerned with ensuring the stability and permanence of the relationship, and tends to inhibit or restrain urges toward freedom and uncoupling, so long as it is being determined by the Zeus-Hera archetype. Love is particularly threatening to the exclusivity of the marriage bond because it is a powerful spirit which can not be limited to one relationship. The Church believes that God's nature permeates the world with an all encompassing universal love as well as with an intensely focused love for the particular. Jesus has the capacity to share in both God's universal love (agape) and his special love for the particular individual (eros), but we ordinary mortals seldom have this capacity. For the majority of people marriage is the way. Those chosen to follow the path of agape must forsake that aspect of their natures which binds them to a particular person. The Church seems to believe that when love is consummated in sexual union, the two people are less free to serve God's universal love. Thus, the religious must take a vow of celibacy and not marry to be free to serve the many.

The Church's position here has considerable psychological and empirical validity. Whenever one experiences a strong soul connection with another person, the image of the Hieros Gamos is released. If this union is consummated in the flesh, the soul feels bound to its mate in a sacred marriage which conjures a powerful desire to love and serve the beloved eternally. The body of the beloved is experienced as a sacred, numinous incarnation of God. Lovers experience both an intense love for the God embodied in the beloved, as well as the bliss of God's personal love for them. When lovers merge through erotic union, the soul commits itself forever to serving God through the beloved. For the lover to be cut off from the beloved may seem like being cut off from God. In these notions the Church is expressing a deep understanding of the soul's nature, and the vow of sexual fidelity which incorporates into the marriage ritual is an expression of this wisdom. In the ordination ceremony a priest, in his symbolic mystical marriage to the body of Christ which is his Church, dedicates himself to serving God's love for the Christian community. The religious, just because they are not bound to a particular person, are free to be intimate and loving with many people—free to live the other pole of the marriage archetype in their human relationships.

Sexual Fidelity

Why does love consummated in sexual union seem to bind two people together and make them no longer free? What is there about the coupling instinct which demands sexual exclusivity? Is it possible to transcend these instincts, transform the archetype, so that the soul may live its need to be free, unattached and unencumbered by limitations on its capacity for love and sexuality? "The pair," as Scripture says, "shall become one flesh." At the moment of union, souls feel bound together in a sacred marriage. The desire to love, cherish, serve, protect and be sexually faithful to the beloved belongs to the total experience. Traditional rituals reflect these human sentiments. In spite of these basic emotions, these psychological truths, which support the traditional marriage vows, it seems essential that modern couples have the freedom to explore other intimate relationships, which may or may not involve sexual intimacy. Won't the soul feel sinful, guilty, if it transgresses the vow of sexual fidelity? I believe that as long as the Zeus-Hera structure of the marriage archetype remains the dominant image of marriage within the soul, the answer is yes. A new image and model is needed that will allow for the possibility of experiencing the Hieros Gamos with more than one person while still honoring the sentiment and psychological truth expressed in the traditional marriage vows.

Much of the suffering one encounters in psychotherapeutic practice relates to the soul's frustration and despair from not being able to unite with its mate. Those who are married tend often to be painfully dissatisfied with the quality of the conjugal connection. Single people long to find their mate or, disillusioned, struggle with their fearful ambivalence about fulfilling the soul's need for coupling. In his book *Marriage, Dead or Alive*, Guggenbühl,[11] speaking of the soul's suffering in marriage, takes the position that marriage is a vessel for salvation, not for happiness and well-being. He believes that individual development may need to be sacrificed for the individuation process which is contained in the marriage relationship. He also states that marriage is *but one* of many paths through which people individuate. Of course each soul must follow a unique path of individuation, but it seems to me that the soul's need for a mate, to be coupled and to share its life with another person, is basic to the human condition and not to be compared with the various paths people must follow for individuation. The fantasy of finding completion through union with another person serves mainly to drive the soul toward its own completion, toward fulfilling its unique destiny. Relationship, love and intimacy, the complexities of human involvements are a *sine qua non* for the soul's development. Attention to relationships, to the care of the love the soul feels toward another soul is, therefore, crucial to everyone's individuation.

Marriage and Community

The marriage archetype is also responsible for binding people together into community through the sacrament of the mystical marriage of God with his faithful followers—for the Jews, for example, the union of Yahweh with Israel, for the Christians the union of Christ with his church. Communal life is not only sustained and renewed by the sacrament of marriage, but really only begins when a people are united in a mystical marriage to a common God—the Olympian family did not exist before the Hieros Gamos of Zeus and Hera. *To feel coupled and belonging to a community is, therefore, an even more basic expression of the marriage archetype than the need to feel coupled to another person.* As Jung puts it,

> Everyone is now a stranger among strangers. Kinship libido which could still engender a satisfying feeling of belonging together, as for instance in the early Christian communities—has long been deprived of its object. But being an instinct, it is not to be satisfied by any mere substitute such as a creed, party, nation or state. It wants the *human* connection. . . .[12]

Because communal life has broken down for most of us, the modern marriage relation has been burdened with having to carry most of the kinship needs of the soul. To be cut off from its communal roots is perhaps the most threatening experience the soul can have. As long as the kinship libido is primarily attached to one's spouse, the fear of uncoupling will always be greater than the need to change. Since containment in community is so essential to the life of the soul, meeting the challenge of changing the deeply rooted patterns of marriage is overwhelming, and I believe doomed to failure, without communal support. Perhaps small *groups* of people using the archetypal perspective will help deepen our understanding of the sacramental mystery of marriage and sexual union, and facilitate the emergence of communal rituals which will enable the soul to honor its need to be both *free* and *faithful*.

---

1. In his excellent paper "Hera: Bound and Unbound" in *Spring 1977*, Murray Stein (following Kerényi) presents the thesis that the mating instinct belongs to a feminine aspect of the soul (Hera). His view is that Hera's pain, fury, jealousy, vindictiveness are not owing simply to Zeus's infidelities, but to his not allowing her to fulfill her basic need to find "perfection" and fulfillment in *gamos*. He suggests that if Hera's basic need for the Hieros Gamos is fulfilled, her destructiveness can be contained and bound. Besides ignoring the three hundred blissful years Zeus and Hera lived in complete fulfillment of the Hieros Gamos, I find his viewpoint tends once again to attribute the vicissitudes of the soul's passion for union, as well as its painful frustrations and jealous rages in relationships, to the feminine. Such a view keeps women in their traditional role of being responsible for the relationship needs of the soul in marriage. I believe the mating instinct to be primarily informed by the *complete* image of the Hieros Gamos (incest archetype) rather than only one pole of the archetype. (For a more complete study relating the mating instinct to the psychic internalization of the Hieros Gamos and to the incest mystery, see my book *Incest & Human Love: the betrayal of the soul in psychotherapy*, Penguin Books, Baltimore, 1974, now distributed by Spring Publications.)
2. C.G. Jung, "Marriage as A Psychological Relationship," *CW* 17.
3. Ibid., para 333.
4. Ibid., para 331c.
5. Ibid., para 331c.
6. Philip E. Slater, *The Glory of Hera*, Beacon Press, Boston, 1971.
7. Carl Kerényi, *Zeus & Hera: archetypal image of father, husband and wife*, Princeton, 1975.
8. Philip E. Slater, *Footholds*, E. P. Dutton, New York, 1977, p. 68.
9. Rafael Lopez-Pedraza, *Hermes and His Children*, Spring Publications, 1977, p. 89.
10. Nathan and Sandra Schwartz, in a paper titled, "On the Coupling of Psychic Entropy and Negentropy," *Spring 1970*, also develop the view of a split in the marriage archetype, but imagine the split in terms of "profane time" and its entropic, disordered correlate, and the unifying order of "sacred time."
11. Adolf Guggenbühl-Craig, *Marriage—Dead or Alive*, Spring Publications, 1977.
12. C.G. Jung, "Psychology of the Transference," *CW* 16, para 445.

FRAGMENTARY VISION:
a Central Training Aim

ANDREW SAMUELS
(London)

I am going to present an approach to training which I think will at first seem quite inimical to analytical psychology. In part I am reacting to my own training; in part to what I see and hear, particularly in the group of trainees and junior analysts from several countries which has been meeting regularly. This is certainly not a paper about psychological theory—it is an attempt to make proposals about how to organize training for analysts and back up these proposals with some psychological reflections. I shall be arguing against the current tendency to concentrate in an unrealistic and counterproductive way on the idea of wholeness. I imagine this started as an attempt to differentiate analytical psychology from other groups of psychotherapists but the notion has developed a life of its own.

My contention will be that in many circumstances such a whole person view is alike inconsistent with practice and theory and on occasion destructive to analysand and analyst. I am thinking of a spiritualised *folie à deux* in which erotic and aggressive interaction is denied. Some of the risk of this can be overcome by adopting what I call a *fragmentary vision* of the psyche and by deliberately training students to develop this type of vision. A slogan at the outset—"bits are beautiful." Actually I point out that bits are inevitable and that bits form the basis of practice.

The pluralism of Karl Popper and William James is a precursor of this approach, and I shall touch on this, albeit sketchily.

Conflict-Oriented Training

In many respects our various international gatherings serve as paradigm and stimulus for this way of thinking since one is healthily deprived of

---

Andrew Samuels is a Professional Member, Society of Analytical Psychology and Lecturer and Supervisor, Westminster Pastoral Foundation, London Centre for Psychotherapy and Richmond Fellowship. This paper was originally presented at the VIIIth Congress of the International Association of Analytical Psychology, San Francisco, September 1980.

the familial support for one's ideas that is often available at home—where even virulent disagreement within the local group can function as a matrix-strengthener. The international context is the best training ground of all for a fragmentary vision point of view. As Popper has said, the place for any beginning seeker after knowledge to go is *where the disagreements are*. If you allow that psychological theory and practice develop organically, in a process, then just where current practitioners cannot agree represents the state of the art. Here you can be sure of being in the presence of the best minds and talents and the most contemporary viewpoints (that is, the most contemporary synthesis of what has gone before and view of what might happen next).

This notion of what a trainee should do opposes the apparently more sensible and customary view that you should start with what is known and agreed, and when that has been mastered or at least understood, engage in the grown-up disagreements. Of course the arena where talented and experienced people differ is a heady place to enter, dizzy-making, frightening, fragmentary. But a training program basing itself on conflict rather than consensus has its points.

For instance, I should suggest that next year's training in the various centers commence with the arguments entered into at the International Congress in San Francisco, not with Jung's early dealings with Freud or whatever usually comes first. Not only would such a program attract the bolder soul to analytical psychology because of its danger, it would serve as an appropriate analogue to the ongoing personal analysis of the trainee. In analysis the beginning is also where the conflicts are, where the forces of the psyche are fragmentary, not in agreement with each other.

Another point in favour of exchanging linear training for conflict-oriented training is that the latter continually puts the student in a problem or rather a problem-solving situation. He has to decide which of several views is more reliable and suits him best—often quite a problem. He will still be at the growing tip of some line of inquiry, stretching back to Jung and beyond, but directly in touch with the complexity and fragmentation of the psyche. His first experience as a trainee is to *choose*. Popper says, "We do not know how or where to start an analysis of this world. There is no wisdom to tell us. Even the scientific tradition doesn't tell us. It only tells us where other people started and where they got to."[1]

A further example: instead of studying the works of Freud, Jung, Klein in a sensible order, one might start with Hillman's attack on the developmental approach in *Loose Ends* or Fordham's attack on Neumann in his last C.G. Jung Lecture. Here you have two excellent minds at work; what turns them on, energises them, is worth being close to. Such arcane conflicts are supposed too much for the student to bear. It wouldn't matter if some aspects of these disputes were over students' heads; they will understand more in time and even linear syllabi are not absorbed in a linear manner. *Starting at the beginning is no guarantee of comprehension.* The assumption that students are not equipped to make choices and handle problem areas needs to be questioned. Accepting the fragmentary nature of the problem situation, adopting a conflict model for learning, compels the student to resonate more fully with didactic material. If fragmentation has to do with conflict then it has to do with wholeness, so the idea of wholeness is at least notionally present.

For the teacher too there are advantages in starting where the problem or conflict is—particularly if he has been teaching for some time. For even old arguments are more stimulating and refreshing than rehashing consensus theories on a more or less chronological basis. By plunging into the chaotic and fragmented world of the conflict or argument the student cannot avoid learning what has been said by others before him. It seems to me that in doing so one pays more respect to the history of knowledge and of dynamic psychology in particular.

And again, I think this approach fits with the unfolding of an analysis which is irregular and unpredictable. I remember one of my fellow trainees being quite upset that we hadn't got to some subject or other which she thought might apply to her analysand. I say this because I want to defend my position against a possible charge of irresponsibility; it might be thought a student trained in the fragmentary way would be somehow less well prepared to undertake clinical work than one whose professional development has been linear.

In general, there are three places to start a training—at the beginning, where you're told, or you can look for where the explosion is and start there.

Against Holism

I do not doubt the sincerity of those who wish to relate in a whole way to whole people or live in a world experienced as inextricably united or to feel whole. Though I doubt such things are possible to the extent wished for, these are acceptable ideals I partly share. I simply doubt that they are an appropriate base for psychology in its attempts to put its insights and understandings at the service of others. In a recent paper June Singer summed up the idea behind the stance:

> that it is holistic means we see entities first as wholes and only secondarily do we examine the parts...every science, every religion, every philosophical system...helps those who use it gain a holistic and organised picture, involving phenomena too vast and complex to be grasped if approached piecemeal.[2]

Jung seems aware of the dangers of this. In "Depth Psychology and Self Knowledge" he writes

> if the goal of wholeness and of realizing the personality originally intended for him should grow naturally in the patient we may sympathetically assist him toward it. But if it does not grow of itself, it cannot be implanted without remaining a permanently foreign body. Therefore we renounce such artifices when nature herself is clearly not working towards this end. As a medical art, equipped only with human tools, our psychology does not presume to preach the way to salvation.[3]

Since first writing this paper I have been heartened by what Guggenbühl-Craig has to say on this topic.

> Unfortunately, when we talk about the Self, there is too much said about qualities like roundness, completeness, and wholeness. It is high time we spoke of the deficiency...of the Self. Today we have succumbed to the cult of the complete, healthy and round, to mandala-like perfection.[4]

Firstly, holistic thinking tends to be utopian, covertly reformist if not revolutionary (Jung's "preaching"). One common variant of the holistic theme is the "unus mundus." Sometimes I think that Latin functions like a mantra for believers. There is a certain moral compulsiveness that gets attached to holism. In the field of personal relationships this overlooks the fundamentally fragmented nature of human contact. We are *not* with our partners all the time and with our analysands even less. I shall say more about analytic sessions and what they mean later on; for the moment I would say that holism seems an attempt to deny that the outcome of one's growth or of a relationship is uncertain. We do make mistakes and miscalculations and we *can* learn from them. In the development of our theory and its application we need trial and (very much) we need error. The inevitability of error compels us toward accepting a pluralist world-view which could be flexible, adaptable and human. For one immersed in fragmentation the holistic aspects will look after themselves. Would not this imply a trust of the self that the thrust of holism does not?

Those who measure cognitive dissonance have shown how a person aims to organise his inner and outer world as harmoniously as possible. This I take to be a way of dealing with anxiety rather than satisfying a holistic impulse. Thus the individual will give greater weight to select aspects of his perceptual field to fit his relatively stronger needs. A deprived person will see parent figures everywhere or be overwhelmingly conscious of their absence. The perceptual field alters to avoid a sense of fragmentation or confusion; even gross inconsistencies are accommodated. Sometimes this smoothing over is not a positive phenomenon. I suspect a good deal of holistic thinking is of this kind; current interest in astrology and acupuncture, for instance, may perform this butterknife function for some people. We could go on to say that psyche is meant to be experienced in a fragmentary way. Wholeness exists before birth perhaps or after death. Wholeness is therefore a spiritual matter while fragmentation remains the affair of the psyche.

Fragmentation, Anxiety, Training and Cults

I now wish to apply this to training. Though the trainee is an adult who has had experiences in profusion, a degree of regression seems inherent in the training situation due to the various entanglements of the student's continuing analysis, supervision and interaction with fellow-trainees. The trainings I know about attempt to isolate this regression on the part of the trainee both from anxiety in general and from the fragmentation process in particular. I am thinking of the whole range of syllabi, seminar themes, reading lists, feedback sessions and all the other thoughtful, caring experiences most of us have been through. I wonder if all this might inadvertently take the creative sting out of fragmentation. A denial of fragmentation may be built into the integrated training program. Since doing away with the fragmentation process is impossible, some sort of response to the anxieties of the trainee *is* needed. I am thinking of some sort of peer group experience whether with a leader or not. This proposal has already been adopted in at least one training centre but I am not sure if this is for the same reason—to relieve anxiety without running from fragmentation.

I fear that the attempt to protect the trainee from fragmentation may have contributed to the formation of cult-like bodies within our little world of analytical psychology. I refer first to a pattern which you might call the cult of the seniors. I may be a part of it, having been invited to give this paper perhaps because I am a Congress virgin as it were, and have not spoken at one before. Choosing an all-new team suggests, after all, an oppressive awareness of the same old faces. The paradox is that of planned novelty.

Being in a cult implies obedience. There is too much obedience in the Jungian world today and the idea of fragmentary vision is deliberately set against it. There is a serious danger of any training program becoming an obedience cult. I may be accused of being naive or ahistorical but I am struck by how many of our groups cluster around leader figures. The leaders may be remarkable people but the phenomenon as a whole is worth examining. I am thinking of Fordham in London, Adler (also London), von Franz in Zürich, Henderson in San Francisco, Dieckmann in Berlin, Hillman anywhere.... I don't think this results from conscious fostering, but would argue that it protects the trainee from fragmentation. For the need for strong leader figures has a lot to do with the desire to avoid the anomalous. The leader sorts out issues by arranging competing ideas in a hierarchy of acceptability. The desire to avoid fragmentation leads groups to erect leaders as combination censor and safety net. It is a misconceived attempt to acquire parenting.

A cult is characterised by a belief system based on ideas which have become standard within the group. The group is hence relatively closed, and backed up by a degree of police power over the members. Indeed the key element can be summed up in that word "membership." There are two things involved here, (a) the status of belonging to a group to which not everyone can, and (b) the hurdle one must cross to obtain status (a). The quality of the status must be in part an effect of what happens at the hurdle.

Individuals of a certain turn of mind and personality "decide" to become analysts. Even a person without the slightest notion of becoming an analyst at the start of his analysis has to make a decision at some point. There are then a series of stages or phases the individual passes through. For a variety of reasons (I wonder if the reader has noticed this) these stages usually get referred to as "years"; "she's a second year trainee" or "he qualified a year ago" or "the third year group are monsters." This calendric approach can be seen as a massive defence against fragmentation because the implication is of an orderly, logical, in control sort of process, a symbol of the dangerous tendency to mass produce our new analysts.

And yet our courses, my course, are not unhealthy or sterile places to be. Most of the members of the International Juniors group speak highly of their training and this cannot all be put down to identification with the trainers or flattery or professional protectionism. I think that what happens for many (it happened to me) is that at a certain point one takes up a fragmentary stance toward the training. This can take the form of doing less or even more work than is required or otherwise varying the task in an attempt to individualize it. For me this usually happened in the form of reading everything in a journal or book but the required piece. In particular I liked the obituaries. What this says about my psychopathology is neither here nor there. Of the 1974 year (!) at the S.A.P. nearly all report a similar experience. Seminar leaders note: if you want a paper read, recommend one adjacent.

What does membership really mean? The opportunity to relate to people and share feelings and ideas does not depend on membership. Even adequate practice does not depend on it. But membership, while not logically crucial, has emerged as the universal procedure for societal recognition. I do not want to tackle the question of why this is so, but merely to suggest that this may have something to say to us about the way we run our trainings on the human level. There is clearly a desire for a true *membership* which is a community of equals, of peers. In London over the past few years there has been a substantial growth in the number and variety of small, informal peer discussion groups. Some have felt that these sap the vitality of more formal meetings and that these groups are too subject to favoritism. I think that membership as lived in these groups is what is truly desired in our general move toward institutional membership. I envisage such groups as preventing our slipping back into the safe and easy world of linear, consensus training.

Fragmentary Vision and Analytic Practice

Translating the vision of fragmentary training into reality does, as I have just hinted, risk the re-emergence of linearity. Another way to meet that danger might be to entrust a part of the training to those who have only just qualified. This does happen to a limited extent but I am thinking of making the teaching of new trainees a part of the immediate post-qualification experience. The relative uncertainty and unknowingness of the new teachers, together with their freshness and enthusiasm, would act as an antidote to linearity.

When the idea of a general education for all was mooted in nineteenth-century England there were a number of schemes proposed, and some actually set up, in which the older pupils were given responsibility for teaching the younger. It was felt that the closeness of the older children to the problem of learning made them suitable teachers. Of course there were economic factors. The schemes did not survive partly because of the disapproval of schoolteachers who were beginning to organise as a profession, with rules governing membership and so on. If this idea were applied to analytical training a permanent stake in fragmentation would be acquired, and there would be advantages for the new teachers.

Student teachers and peer discussion groups are fragmentary answers to fragmentary questions. The important thing is that there should be an oscillation between anxiety and security, a mixture of cosiness and danger. That mixture fits all the great vortices of life— feeding, sex, marriage—all are cosy and all are dangerous.

I should now like to consider the way in which the fragmentary approach has most conditioned our practice, the general procedure of dividing work into sessions. Whether we offer our analysands one hour, fifty minutes or what, whether once, twice or five times per week does not alter the fact that the work goes on in a bitty way. Of course it could not be otherwise in practice. But practice generates its own truths, its own symbolic life and psychological meanings. The sessional nature of our work makes us face the great theme of parts and wholes, makes us think about the possibility of treating the whole person or training the whole person. The sessional approach involves separation; out of separation comes individuation. Separation as a psychological theme is accentuated by the sessional approach, which, as essentially fragmentary, has something to do with individuation.

One aspect of the session/fragment approach has great relevance to training for analysis. I refer to the attempt of the analyst to commence each session as if it were a fresh event or fragmentary phenomenon, trying to forget all that is known about the patient and all that the analyst wants to achieve in his work. The purpose of this is to plug into the psyche as directly and spontaneously as possible and release the analyst's intuitive capacities, in particular his capacity to observe and make use of his various countertransferences. It is in order to use these countertransferences that the analyst tends not to speak first but rather to wait and react. Various practical measures follow—very little note-taking, working on written productions from the patient only in the session in which they are introduced, and so on.

What I am describing is derived from Bion's work. He states that the analyst

> must impose on himself a positive discipline of eschewing memory and desire. I do not mean that 'forgetting' is enough. Only by doing this can analytic intuition be enhanced. . . . By rendering oneself artificially blind through the exclusion of memory and desire . . . the piercing shaft of light can be directed on the dark features of the analytic situation.[5]

There is a rather surprising feature in all this. It follows that it is a good thing for an analyst to be slightly too busy in his daily routine so that he does not dwell too much on any one analysand's material or on any one area of interest. This presents special problems in the training situation since the number of analysands seen under the training umbrella is very small. Given this and the understandable conscientiousness of the beginning analyst, the conditions for unanalytic unfragmentary excessive recording of case material and dwelling on it are created. It would seem to be necessary then to assess potential trainees on the basis in part at least of how busy they are likely to be during their training. If they are just a bit too busy then they will have less difficulty with the analytic attitude; but if they have no other therapeutic investments at all then they do run the risk of creating a nonanalytic style for themselves. In a way, the ideal candidate for training should be less than fully committed to it.

Fragmentary Vision and Pragmatism

It has occurred to me that a pragmatic coloring can be put on most of this. Fragmentary vision does resemble pragmatism as I (probably imperfectly) understand that approach. William James said "ideas become true just so far as they help us to get into satisfactory relations with other parts of our experience."[6] So, for example, the psychological theories we learn in training are not to be seen as answers to questions of human nature but as instruments to guide future action and practice. Pragmatism involves a type of democratic procedure in which a man is free to decide which of various conflicting hypotheses to accept. If his rational examination of the alternatives cannot help him make a decision then he is free simply to follow his own inclination. I hope it can be seen how this fits in with the notion of a conflict oriented training. The truth of an idea will be in whether or not it has fruitful consequences. This sums up the essence of fragmentary vision. (Note: written before reading *Spring 1980*, Taylor on Jung and James.)

Summary

Fragmentary vision seems inherent in analysis, fundamental to both its theory and practice, but unrecognised in any specific sense in its training. The adoption of a fragmentary approach to training would be justified to avoid excesses of linearity on the one hand and holism on the other. This involves challenging the training structure and I put forward certain specific proposals to increase the amount of fragmentary vision in a training program and prevent backsliding to more conventional models, viz:
(a) the abandonment of consensus based training and the chronological approach; these would be replaced by a training centred around contemporary arguments or disputes in the field. This may be termed "conflict oriented training";
(b) training would tend to use books and papers written with polemical intent;
(c) the abandonment of fixed curricula, syllabi and other pedagogical devices and the institution of peer groups to focus on resultant student anxiety;
(d) the utilization of recently qualified analysts as teachers for their very lack of certainty. This should be part of the qualified members' final training stage;
(e) the selection of candidates who are not too committed to the training and who have a rather full life already;
(f) a conscious attempt to avoid installing strong personalities as cult leaders;
(g) informal groups should be promoted within the overall life of the training institute.

1 K.R. Popper, *Conjectures and Refutations: the growth of scientific knowledge* (London; Routledge and Kegan Paul, 1972), p. 129.
2 J. Singer, "The Use and Misuse of the Archetype," *Journal of Analytical Psychology*, Vol. 24, No. 1, p. 10-13, 1979.
3 C.G. Jung, "Depth Psychology and Self Knowledge," *CW* 18, p. 97.
4 A. Guggenbühl-Craig, *Eros on Crutches* (Spring Publications, 1980), p. 25-26.
5 W.R. Bion, "Attention and Interpretation," *The Seven Sisters* (London: Tavistock, 1977), p. 31.
6 W. James, *Pragmatism* (Fontana Library of Philosophy, 1962; orig. Longmans, Green, 1911).

BOOK REVIEWS

von Franz, Marie-Louise. *Projection and Re-Collection in Jungian Psychology.* La Salle, Ill.: Open Court Press, 1980. Pp. 253. $15.00.

On the cover of the September, 1980 issue of *Psychology Today* appeared a painting of a man with the top half of his head removed, revealing in place of the brain a movie projector casting detailed fantasy images through his eyes onto a screen. The appearance of this image indicates the pervasiveness of the fantasy of psyche as a mechanism contained in the skull, projecting images onto an external world.

Yet scholarly reflection on projection *as a theory* has been minimal. This is why Marie-Louise von Franz's new book on projection is particularly important. A translation by William Kennedy of *Spielgeungen der Seele: projektion und innere sammlung* (Zürich: Kreuz Verlag, 1978) this book, in both clinical and metapsychological insight, expands the inquiry beyond the two other recent major studies of projection in depth psychology. Sami Ali's *De la Projection: une étude psychoanalytique* (Paris: Payot, 1970) is a Freudian interpretation of projection as a narcissistic regression and lowering of perceptual organization. Rudolf Bühlmann's *Zur Entwicklung des Tiefenpsychologischen Begriffs der Projektion* (Zürich: Juris, 1971) is a history of the theory as an *idea*, from Freud's early neurological concept to Jung's alchemical discoveries.

Von Franz weaves a fabric rich with insight into the soul-work of projections, individually and culturally. She amplifies Jung's differentiation of five levels of awareness of projection (*CW* 13; 247ff) into a typology quite helpful in disclosing both the psychological implications glimmering in religious hermeneutics and the archetypal images hiding in scientific theory. She shows how early forms of allegory, seen as a withdrawal of projections, can move myths out of concrete descriptions of external world, not into mere rationalistic paraphrase, but into the realm of psyche. In von Franz's hands the imaginal background of matter as known today is disclosed by the withdrawal of projected archetypal images of infinite sphere, particle, divine number and force field. We see shadow daimons delude through projection's terrors, anima/animus lovers seduce through projection's raptures, and Self's redeemers clear away illusions.

When von Franz sticks closely to the images—daimon, Psyche, Hermes, eye, mirror—the important foundation of the inquiry into projection is unconcealed: dissolving projection's naive concretisms and descending into the twilight of the underworld. It seems that the more vitality discovered in the fruitful ambiguity of the images, the less determinate become von Franz's theoretical guides, whether ego, shadow, anima/animus, Self and its unified field, or the transfer of psychic "stages" into historical process.

Yet the most difficult issue for anyone approaching the problem of projection theory is, as von Franz puts it, "the still-open question of exactly *where* projections come from" (p. 20). Is the source of projection psyche as internal subjectivity, like a movie projector contained within the skull? Or does "projection" disclose phenomena not captured in the literalized either/or of the subject/object dichotomy? Projection theory raises this question as its archetypal riddle, for the theory is the tool with which psychology attempts to overcome the illusions and dilemmas of naive concretism or archaic *participation mystique*. Like Jung, von Franz knows that the fantasy of psyche as contained subjectivity is inadequate, for archetypal images lead beyond personal subjectivity, so "outward-material and inner-spiritual are only characteristic labels" (p. 91). Both Jung and von Franz are compelled to speak of some trans-subjective world or *unus mundus*. Yet the image of "withdrawing projections" makes the inner/outer differentiation difficult to re-imagine. So, knowing the language of inner subjectivity to be inadequate to the phenomena, von Franz represents a collective dilemma when she writes of a "purely inner psychic happening in the...subject" (p. 51).

This difficult, uncomfortable use of an inadequate formula in projection theory has been questioned, most clearly for archetypal psychology by Wolfgang Giegerich in his article "Der Sprung nach dem Wurf: Über das Einholen der Projektion und den Ursprung der Psychologie," *Gorgo* 1(1979), p. 49-71. He criticizes projection theory as a theoretical construct of ego-psychology, founded on the archetypal images of geometric space, physics and the Cartesian subject/object dichotomy.

The work, then, seems to be to remain within the *experience* called projection, so well understood by von Franz, and let the imaginal, archetypal background of the theory itself emerge. Von Franz has begun this work by letting images such as eye and mirror speak. So this book is an important contribution to un-covering the underworld of projection theory.

Lee Bailey (Syracuse)

Everson, William. *Earth Poetry: Selected Essays & Interviews*, 1950-1977. Ed. Lee Bartlett. Berkeley: Oyez Press, 1980. Pp. 251. $10.95 cloth, $4.95 paper.

For nearly four decades William Everson's poetry has dramatized the journey of a soul oscillating between orthodox Catholic devotion and a gnostic erotic mysticism that transcends conventional religious labels. Of all the possible categories Everson's poetic gift can be subsumed under, two spring to mind: Dionysian and Archetypal. Dionysian—since Everson's sensibility is a contemporary version of John of the Cross. Wildness, passionate speech, indulgence in self-inflicted rounds of high-pitched pleasure/pain, a thirst for psychic release—these qualities are central to Everson's artistic process. And he is archetypal since,

> It seems to me that the more profoundly the poet adheres to the creative unconscious, to the archetype, the more he will emerge as a curse to the complacent mind of the everyday world, because of the nature of ego structure. (p. 107)

Everson directs his attention to three archetypes in this collection of essays and interviews: poet, prophet and shaman. He considers the Poet archetype as representing those constellations of psychic powers that permit a person to tap unconscious materials and render these in linguistic form. The Prophet archetype directs the artist toward awakening his/her community to psychic and political revolution. The Shamanic archetype empowers the artist to transcend the societal lattice to return with a transformative vision.

Everson's dialectical love/hate affair with the Dominican order propels him to move from poet as prophet toward poet as shaman—a move curiously bound up with his outer garb. A poem in *Man-Fate* traces the spiritual journey from lay monk to shaman by recording the sensation of wearing a buckskin jacket rather than black robes.

The talks collected in *Earth Poetry* provide an intensive backdrop to the man and his poetry. Lee Bartlett's editing is attentive and sharply focused. The danger of editing any of Everson's writing is simply being overwhelmed by purely autobiographical data. The man has had a richly textured artistic and spiritual life. And he has a penchant for self-dramatization. His subject is most often himself. Yet his true subject is soul. Whether Everson talks about his falling away from the church in personal terms, about the poet as shaman, or about ecological issues, he colors each with a Jungian orientation.

One of the most moving lectures in *Earth Poetry* is a piece written for the National Water Commission on water conservation. He discusses water in terms of its participation in the feminine archetype while simultaneously addressing a spectrum of pragmatic political issues related to California water usage, and somehow manages to relate the phenomenon of water to his own development as a poet. It is a tour de force of archetypal analysis translated into the "hard" arena of "buy and sell."

BOOK REVIEWS

Earth Poetry is captivating reading for anyone interested in exploring the psychological underpinnings of postmodern American poetics. It represents another imaginative advance for the most significant religious poet to emerge from the West Coast since Robinson Jeffers. The book's title reminds us how the most deeply spiritual literature of our age founds its ground upon earth.

Norman Weinstein (Boise)

Diel, Paul. *Symbolism in Greek Mythology: Human Desire and Its Transformations.* Tr. Vincent Stuart, Micheline Stuart, and Rebecca Folkman. Boulder and London: Shambhala, 1980. Pp. 218. $15.00 (hardback).

A photograph on the rear inside flap depicts the author, dressed in rough hiking gear, looking down upon a glacial field: an appropriate attitude for a psychologist whose favored mythic pair is Zeus and Hera ("the supreme couple," he calls them) and whose intention in this book, his first translated into English, is to "elevate" psychology to a science by means of hieroglyptic analysis of the gods—mythic deities as allegorical symbols of human psychological life.

From his alpine perspective, Diel surveys the mythical expressions of man's fiery excesses—the overblown exaltation of human imagination represented in the story of Icarus and his family—and man's icy depravities, represented by Poseidon ("related to Satan"), Dionysus ("a hell deity"), Hades ("the perverse inhibition of desire"), and the crippled animal soul of Chiron. These latter figures come to be grouped under the psychological condition of *banalization,* "the death of the soul," or what Persian story-tellers would have experienced in the person of Ahriman.

Diel attempts to translate the rich, figurative language of mythical stories into "language we can comprehend" by an intellectual analysis of the elements they blend, as Robert Frost would say. Somewhere in their transit to the giddy heights of intellection, however, these mythical figures seem to slip from sight, shrivelling into concepts. Like good wine, gods and heroes do not travel well.

We are left with Zeus atop Mount Ida, privy to a cosmic panorama of clashing symbols but too far away to hear—or even see distinctly—the figures engaged in the drama on the battlefield below. Diel would "translate" the combatants—elevate, beam them up—onto the craggy Olympian slope upon which he stands, but can they draw sufficient puff in such rarefied air to keep up the fight? In their translation, gods and heroes are banalized.

Peter N. Roll (Dallas)

Homans, Peter. *Jung in Context: Modernity and the Making of a Psychology.* University of Chicago Press, 1979. 8vo, P. ix, 234. $15.00, £ 9.00.

There is a dearth (compared to studies on Freud) of studies available for those interested in the early history of Jung and Jungian psychology, so a glimpse of the title *Jung in Context* is immediately welcome. But what Professor Homans means by context hardly accommodates ordinary-language connotation of the word, *i.e.,* some insight into Jung's thought via his personal or family history, community, cultural, or intellectual traditions. Instead, we are brought, by importation of other writers, to the broadest meaning of the word context, the Laputan realms of society, modernity and culture. From these perspectives we are to view Jung. Most of these pages are filled with references to the writers through whose perspectives he attempts to see Jung (Peter Berger, sociology of knowledge; Weinstein and Platt, theory of modernity; Marthe Robert, view of two cultures; H. Kohut and J. Gedo, processes of Narcissism).

Of these perspectives, the one most thoroughly presented is his attempt to see Jung's psychobiography from the point of view of Kohut's narcissistic processes (the book could have been more honestly titled *Jung and Narcissism).* But the analysis of Jung gets swallowed by the move to wider culture. The narcissism found in Jung expands to Freud and Jung, other modern psychologies, the young people of the late 1960s and 1970s doing their own thing, to almost anyone involved in his own psychological analysis. The narcissistic process is seen everywhere, as hysteria seemed contagious in the late nineteenth century, and schizophrenia in the 20th. One comes to suspect the narcissism being seen, whether Jung's or that of the author attempting to observe him.

Scattered about in the book are several insightful summary statements on the development of Jung's religious views. Further, the author's chapter on how to read Jung is useful for newcomers to the edition and to the dating brambles created by the editors of Jung's *Collected Works*, or for those unable to unravel it for themselves in its bibliography.

By the end of the book it is disappointing to realize that we learn more about Professor Homans' imported perspectives, *i.e.*, Kohut and Marthe Robert, than we do about Jung. This is largely the fault of Homans' methodology; however suitable for professors (and students) at the University of Chicago, it is inadequate for readers seeking a clearer insight into the historical-psychological contexts of Jung and Jungian psychology. In fact Jung, whose picture appears on the dust cover and whose name in the title, is really a stalking horse for the whole shelf of Professor Homans' academic importations. One wonders whether Professor Homans has a Jung—or even any ideas at all—of his own.

How effective is Homans' secondhand analysis? Prescinding from the confusion he creates by constant reference to what seems merely a current fashion in academic analysis, let us take a look at his acknowledgedly hypothetical psycho-biography. Both Freud and Jung acknowledge in the *Freud/Jung Letters* (page 37) the presence of the 'father complex' in their relationship. Neither of them identifies this as their narcissism problem. Still Homans would have us believe that unwittingly their relationship was riddled with the psychology of narcissism, a common category of psycho-analytic psychopathology, familiar to both Freud and Jung. Can we take at face value what a writer says about himself, how he sees and experiences his personal life? Or is that writer's statement about himself simply a "manifest" expression, its "latent" meaning something which can only be revealed by the analysis of belated professors (or psychologically trained practitioners, for that matter)?

A writer who once fell victim to Professor Homans' contextual analysis said, "He robs an author of his ideas." Can we *believe* Jung when he speaks of his "father complex" in his relation to Freud or is he really talking about his narcissism problem in disguise? Nowhere in Jung's *Collected Works, Letters*, or *Memories, Dreams, and Reflections* does Jung speak of narcissism in reference to his personal psychology. Surely there is some limit to the fictions of psycho-biography? Of Robert Burton's melancholy or Alfred Adler's inferiority complex, it would be plausible to infer their respective melancholic or inferiority psychologies, because these authors wrote extensively on these subjects. Jung scarcely mentions narcissism, and in one of the few instances in a way that may be an appropriate answer to Homans. Jung is writing about the application of psychological analysis to art:

> This kind of analysis brings the work of art into the sphere of general human psychology, where many other things besides art have their origin. To explain art in these terms is just as great a platitude as the statement that "every artist is a narcissist." Every man who pursues his own goal is a "narcissist"—though one wonders how permissible it is to give such wide currency to a term specifically coined for the pathology of neurosis. The statement therefore amounts to nothing; it merely elicits the faint surprise of a bon mot. Since this kind of analysis is in no way concerned with the work of art itself, but strives like a mole to bury itself in the dirt as speedily as possible, it always ends up in the common earth that unites all mankind. Hence its explanations have the same tedious monotony as the recitals which one daily hears in the consulting room. (*CW* 15, §102)

Any reader of a book entitled *Jung in Context* could reasonably assume that its author was attracted to Jung, whatever his bias or sympathy, that in working through the Jung texts he would come up with something personal about Jung as a human being, as a man of his times, how he borrowed ideas from others, how his ideas developed, how his psychology differs from our own. No such luck. Had he put as much work into understanding Jung as into understanding his imported perspectives, this addition to Jung studies could have been more useful to those readers who do remain interested in Jung in context.

James Donat (London)

BOOK REVIEWS

Four New Works on Psychology and Creativity

Fritz, Donald W., ed. *Perspectives on Creativity and the Unconscious: Proceedings of the Jungian Conference.* Oxford, Ohio: The Old Northwest, 1980. Pp. 116. $3.

Brivic, Sheldon R. *Joyce Between Freud and Jung.* Port Washington, New York: Kennikat Press Corp., 1980. Pp. 226. $15.

Reed, Jeanette P. *Emergence.* Albuquerque: JPR Publishers, 1980. Pp. 96. $7.95.

Stacy, Don *Drawing and Painting From Imagination.* New York: Stravon Educational Press, 1980. Pp. 208. $14.95.

The many facets of a psychological understanding of creativity show in the diversity of these four books. *Perspectives* provides a good sampling of the field. The first three papers are by artists: architect Walter A. Netsch, Jr., painter Walter Darby Bannard, and critic and poet Richard Howard. Of these, especially interesting is Bannard's paper, "Art and Nonsense"; his joyful style embodies his thesis that creativity is the joyful celebration of life. The two theoretical papers in this collection—by June Singer and Silvano Arieti—find *synthesis* as a common theme in two traditionally variant approaches to creativity: creativity (Dr. Singer) as "divine inspiration" which must be synthesized with individual limits, and creativity (Dr. Arieti) as the synthesis of two different psychological modes of transforming experience—primary and secondary processes. This work concludes with a participants' colloquium, which is too limited to allow for a true exchange, so that theorists and artists find no common ground.

The problem of conflicting psychological interpretations is approached in *Joyce Between Freud and Jung.* Although valiantly attempting to view a lifetime of complex creative work from a duo of depth perspectives, the two ends of this art/psychology sandwich are too far separated by the meat to be swallowed. Brivic alternately uses a reductive psychology of the body and a teleological, mythological psychology of the spirit to flesh out the processes at work in Joyce's writings, but the two approaches never meet in the "simultaneous opposition" he desires, and the outcome does justice neither to Joyce, Jung, nor Freud.

Emergence brings the perspective of therapy to bear on the issue of creativity. In the Sand Tray therapy Ms. Reed outlines, there is a creation of "experience in miniature" through the playful manipulation of sand and small figures. This provides an opportunity for hands-on image work, using a reflection of one's life-situation that, as a creative act, is more than a conscious portrayal. Her concern with therapy and its goals leads her to focus on sequence and the interpretation of progress, revealing the story of individuation in sand.

Don Stacy's view of the creative imagination is based on artistic rather than therapeutic concerns. The development of artistic skill is not progressive, but rather involves experimentation and error; it thrives on the sustained tension of not quite knowing and yet never stopping. Throughout this instructional book, the theory implicit in the technique reveals that not only does creative artistry require coming into a relationship with the imagination, but more: the work of coming into a relationship with the imagination is itself an art, and is perhaps the locus of all our creativity.

Alan Moses (Dallas)

human relations center, inc

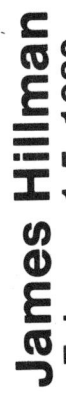

upcoming events

James Hillman
February 1-5, 1982
Revisioning Psychology: Anima Mundi
A Residential Clinical Training Symposium to be held at Casa de Maria, Santa Barbara, CA

Joseph Campbell
April 14-16, 1982
Mythology and Psychology
A Residential Symposium to be held at Casa de Maria, Santa Barbara, CA

for further information write:

Conference Coordinator, Human Relations Center, Inc.
5200 Hollister Avenue, Santa Barbara, CA 93111
or telephone (805) 967-4557

ANIMA
AN EXPERIENTIAL JOURNAL

"an unusual, thoughtful magazine, which has a meaningful, intelligent viewpoint for all who are interested in modern lifestyle."
—Bill Katz, Library Journal

"I like the ease with which you cover issues dealing with the feminine . . . your scope--the fact that you draw your readers' attention to manifestations of the feminine principle in so many different cultures, religions, art forms, and so on. Well-written articles. Stunning photographs . . .
—from a Reader's Response

"a refreshing concept — at a time when new approaches are vital.
—Gwen Frostic

We believe that a new, wholistic consciousness is emerging in our divided world, a new consciousness that incorporates the strengths of our various heritages into a new wholistic insight, and we believe that those values grow from the souls of persons enriched with the qualities traditionally labeled *feminine*. *ANIMA* keeps abreast of the implications of the latest thinking in psychology, religion, and women's studies and relates them regularly to the concerns of human wholeness.

ANIMA
1053 Wilson Avenue
Chambersburg, PA 17201

Annual Subscription $8.50

ISSN 0097-1146

JUNG and TAROT
An Archetypal Journey

by Sallie Nichols

with an introduction by Laurens van der Post

Sallie Nichols, in her profound investigation of Tarot, and her illuminated exegesis of its pattern as an authentic attempt at enlargement of the possibilities of human perceptions has... performed an immense service for analytical psychology.

Laurens van der Post

Anyone with the remotest interest or fascination with the power of the image to move the psyche will find in Sallie Nichols' Jung and Tarot: An Archetypal Journey, *just that: a journey into that realm where the image, the psyche and the soul find their source and their goal.*

Russell A. Lockhart

Sallie Nichols has returned the Tarot to modern dignity. Being completely scientific in her approach to this old card game, she reveals its depth, its symbolic meaning, and its wisdom.

James Kirsch

Hardcover (6"x9"), $24.95
ISBN 0-87728-480-6

416 pages, 22 full color illustrations, a full color fold-out chart, and 65 b & w illustrations.

Please add local state tax where applicable, plus a shipping and handling charge of $1.50 for one or two books plus 35¢ each additional book. _____ copies @ $24.95 = $_____ Plus shipping $_____ Enclosed is my check for $_____
Name _____
Address _____
City _____ State _____ Zip _____

Samuel Weiser, Inc.   740 Broadway   New York, N.Y. 10003

ELH
(English Literary History)

edited by Stephen Orgel

"ELH is *the* outstanding journal of scholarly criticism in its field."

—Louis L. Martz, Yale University

For almost a half-century, ELH has consistently published some of the finest essays on record in every field of English and American literature. Working together, prominent and imaginative editors — whose fields of expertise encompass numerous specialties — have drawn from the best of both traditional and innovative scholarship. The result is a publication that distinguished critics have proclaimed "indispensable."

The importance of historical continuity in the discipline of letters remains a central concern for ELH, but the journal does not seek to sponsor particular methods or aims. ELH keeps a balance, and it publishes superior studies from various points of view which interpret the conditions that affect major works of literature — their creation, their subsequent life, their present status.

ELH
Quarterly   March, June, Sept., Dec.

☐ 1 year, $26.00 institutions   ☐ 1 year, $12.00 individuals

NAME _____

ADDRESS _____

CITY _____ STATE _____ ZIP CODE _____

Make checks payable to: **The Johns Hopkins University Press**
ELH
Baltimore, Maryland 21218

Prepayment required. Subscriptions entered on a calendar year basis only.

EX

**Special Introductory Offer
One Year — Only $11.00**

DIACRITICS:
a review of contemporary criticism

DIACRITICS is a forum for critics writing on criticism, through evaluative reflection on important books: review articles in which contributors develop their own positions on the theses, methods, and theoretical implications of the works in question. Also included are texts representing either adventurous, innovative practical criticism or seminal theoretical activity, interviews with writers and critics, articles on film theory and film criticism, and responses to recently published articles or polemical statements.

Forthcoming issues of Diacritics will include articles by Jonathan Arac, Marc Eli Blanchard, Mary Ann Caws, Jonathan Culler, Paul de Man, Stanley Fish, Eric Gans, W. W. Holdheim, Don Marshall, Glenn Most, Sandy Petrey, Joseph Riddel, Michael Riffaterre, Marie-Laure Ryan, Michael Ryan, Gayatri Chakravorty Spivak, and Nathaniel Wing.

DIACRITICS
March, June, September, December

Please enter my one-year subscription beginning with the current issue.

☐ Institutions, $21.00   ☐ Individuals, $11.00
    (reg. $22)   (reg. $12)

Name _____

Address _____

City _____ State _____ Zip _____

Make checks payable to: **The Johns Hopkins University Press
                         Journals Division
                         Baltimore, Maryland 21218**

Prepayment required. Offer valid for new subscriptions only.

DX

American Journal of Philology

edited by Georg Luck

Nearing its centennial of publication, the *American Journal of Philology* has merited the wide acclaim of being the oldest and the best American classical journal. It features original writings in the fields of Greek and Latin antiquity, with special emphasis on literature, history, and philosophy. Published quarterly, articles range from examinations of ancient texts and presentations of comparative philology, to definitive reviews of books written on classical subjects. Contributors range across the continents, and their writings give international representation of scholars and students in the classics.

Outstanding contributors published in the *Journal* include J. Rendel Harris, A. E. Housman, M. P. Charlesworth, E. H. Sturtevant, Lily Ross Taylor, Tenney Frank, Arthur Darby Nock, Werner Jaeger, D. R. Shackleton Bailey, Lennart Håkanson, A. Hudson-Williams and Zvi Yavetz.

Subscription Order Form

_____ 1 year, $12.00 individuals

_____ 1 year, $26.00 institutions

NAME_____

ADDRESS_____

CITY_____STATE_____ZIPCODE_____

☐ Check or money order enclosed

☐ Master Charge No. _____ Exp. Date_____

☐ BankAmericard No. _____ Exp. Date_____

Signature_____

Prepayment required. Subscriptions entered on a calendar year basis only.

Make checks payable to: The Johns Hopkins University Press
AMERICAN JOURNAL OF PHILOLOGY
34th and Charles Streets
Baltimore, Maryland 21218

JOURNAL OF
HUMANISTIC PSYCHOLOGY

The official quarterly publication of the *Association for Humanistic Psychology* is concerned with the worth and dignity of the individual and with the conditions of human experience and growth.

Topics of Special Interest

authenticity, encounter, self-actualization, self-transcendence, search for meaning, creativity, personal growth, psychological health, being motivation, values, identity, love

Selected Articles

Transpersonal Perspectives in Psychotherapy	Frances Vaughan Clark
Psychic Healing in the Philippines	Stanley Krippner
Gregory Bateson and Humanistic Psychology	Rollo May
Aiming at the Self: A Paradox	Maurice Friedman
Humanistic Education	Abraham Maslow
Humanistic Psychology as a Personal Experience	Charlotte Bühler
Castaneda: Humanist and/or Mystic	Barbara Forisha
The Vertical: An Experiential Side to Human Potential	Ida P. Rolf

Order from:
JHP Circulation Office
325 Ninth Street
San Francisco, CA 94103

Editor:
Thomas C. Greening
1314 Westwood Blvd.
Los Angeles, CA 90024

ORDER FORM

Please enter the following subscription to JHP for _____ year(s) (four quarterly issues) starting with the next issue:

- ☐ Individual $12
- ☐ Institutional $18
- ☐ APA member $11
- ☐ APA Div. 32 member $10
- ☐ Payment enclosed ☐ Bill me
- ☐ Send table of contents 1961-1979 and order form for back issues
- ☐ Send information about AHP

Name _____
Address _____
City/State _____ Zip _____

LIMITED EDITION PAPERBACKS

All prices substantially reduced

Marie-Louise von Franz, Honorary Patron

Studies in Jungian Psychology by Jungian Analysts

1. **The Secret Raven: Conflict and Transformation in the Life of Franz Kafka.**
Daryl Sharp. ISBN 0-919123-00-7. Reduced to $8.00.
The best-selling depth analysis of artistic despair. Sympathetic, perceptive, and concise. Directly relevant to anyone who has experienced the uncompromising demands of the instincts versus the spiritual quest, the conflict between love and sex, or the individual versus society dilemma. Illustrated. Index. 128 pages.

2. **The Psychological Meaning of Redemption Motifs in Fairytales.**
Marie-Louise von Franz. ISBN 0-919123-01-5. Reduced to $8.00.
A unique account of the significance of fairytales for an understanding of the purpose of personal conflicts. Especially helpful for its clear description of projection and active imagination, and for its symbolic, non-linear approach to the meaning of typical dream motifs (bathing, beating, animals, etc.). Index. 128 pages.

3. **On Divination and Synchronicity: The Psychology of Meaningful Chance.**
Marie-Louise von Franz. ISBN 0-919123-02-3. Reduced to $10.00.
A penetrating study of the meaning of the irrational. Examines time, number, and methods of divining fate such as the I Ching, astrology, palmistry, dice, Tarot cards, etc. Explains synchronicity, contrasting Western scientific attitudes with those of the Chinese and so-called primitives. Illustrated. Index. 128 pages.

4. **The Owl Was a Baker's Daughter: Obesity, Anorexia Nervosa, and the Repressed Feminine.**
Marion Woodman. ISBN 0-919123-03-1. Reduced to $10.00.
An illuminating work on feminine psychology, with particular attention to the body as mirror of the psyche in eating disorders and weight disturbances. Explores the loss and rediscovery of the feminine principle through Jung's Association Experiment, case studies, dreams, and mythology. Illustrated. Index. 144 pages.

5. **Alchemy: An Introduction to the Symbolism and the Psychology.**
Marie-Louise von Franz. ISBN 0-919123-04-X. Reduced to $15.00.
A lucid and practical guide to what the alchemists were really looking for — emotional balance and wholeness. Indispensable for an understanding of images and motifs in modern dreams and drawings. Invaluable for anyone interested in relationships and communication between the sexes. 84 Illustrations. Index. 288 pages.

6. **Descent to the Goddess: A Way of Initiation for Women.**
Sylvia Brinton Perera. ISBN 0-919123-05-8. *New Title.* $9.00.
A highly original and provocative study of women's freedom and the need for an inner, female authority in a masculine-oriented society. Based on the Sumerian goddess Inanna/Ishtar's journey to the underworld and her return. Rich in insights from dreams and the author's experience as a therapist. Index. 128 pages.

INNER CITY BOOKS *was founded in 1980 to promote the understanding and practical application of the work of C.G. Jung. We are grateful to our original buyers, whose generous response has made price reductions possible.*

TERMS OF SALE

Prices quoted are in U.S. dollars, except for Canadian orders
Orders from outside Canada pay in U.S.funds
PREPAID ORDERS ONLY (except Libraries and Booksellers)
Add 60¢/book for postage and handling, *or* $2.00/book overseas airmail

DISCOUNTS

Retail Booksellers: 40% (postfree / net 60 days)
Wholesalers: 50% (postfree / net 60 days)
Libraries (direct orders only): 20% (postfree / net 60 days)

INNER CITY BOOKS   Box 1271, Station Q, Toronto, Canada M4T 2P4   (416) 484-4562

BOUNDARY 2, a journal of postmodern literature

announces a special issue:

Why Nietzsche Now?
Winter 1981 (IX/2)

DAVID ALLISON,   on *The Birth of Tragedy*
J. HILLIS MILLER,   on Truth and Lie in the Ultra Moral Sense
MARTIN HEIDEGGER,   on "The Vision and the Riddle": The Eternal Return in *Thus Spoke Zarathustra* (previously untranslated)
STANLEY CORNGOLD,   on *The Genealogy of Morals*
RUDOLPH GASCHÉ,   on *Ecce Homo* as Autobiography
DAVID KRELL,   on The Figure of the Mole in Kant, Hegel, and Nietzsche
R.E. KUENZLI,   on *Zarathustra* and Deconstruction
JOSEPH RIDDELL,   on Nietzsche and the Deconstructive Project of Modern American Poetics (from Poe to Olson)
PAUL BOVÉ,   on Nietzschean Influences in Foucault and Said
DAVID HOY,   on *The Will to Power*
CHARLES ALTIERI,   on *Ecce Homo* and the Criticism of Narcissism
JONATHAN ARAC,   on The Use and Abuse of Nietzsche in Recent American Criticism: de Man and Donadio
and others

Still Available:
  Robert Creeley Spring/Fall 1978 (second printing)
  Revisions of the Anglo-American Tradition: Part II
  Robert Duncan, Winter 1980
  Supplement on Irony, Fall 1980   and other issues

boundary 2, SUNY-Binghamton, Binghamton, NY 13901
Subscriptions (three issues): $13 individuals, $10 students, $20 institutions, $5 single issues; add $1 overseas postage

---

BOUNDARY 2 a journal of postmodern literature,

announces the forthcoming issue:

Peter Szondi
Spring 1981 (IX/3)

MANFRED FRANK,   The Text and its Style: Schleiermacher's Speech Theory
RAINER NAEGELE,   Text, History, and the Critical Subject: Notes on Peter Szondi's Theory and Praxis of Hermeneutics
MICHAEL HAYS,   Drama and the Dramatic Theory: Peter Szondi and the Modern Theater
WOLFGANG FIETKAU,   Peter Szondi, Walter Benjamin, and the Poetics and Philosophy of Tragedy
GERD MATTENKLOTT,   On the Meaning of Texts in Drama: Some Reflections on Szondi's Sociology of Dramatic Forms
THOMAS FRIES,   Defense of the Word: Peter Szondi's "Studies on Celan"
BERNARD BÖSCHENSTEIN,   "Studies on Hölderlin": Exemplarity of a Path
KARL GROB,   The Theory and Practice of Philology: Reflections on the Public Responses of Peter Szondi
TIMOTHY BAHTI,   Reading German Romantic Genre Theory

Still Available:
  Why Nietzsche Now, Winter 1981 (IX/2)
  Supplement on Irony, Fall 1980 (IX/1)
  Duncan issue, Winter 1980 (VIII/2)
  Robert Creeley: A Gathering, Spring/Fall 1978 (second printing)

  and other issues

boundary 2, SUNY-Binghamton, Binghamton, NY 13901
Subscriptions (three issues): $13 individuals, $10 students, $20 institutions, $5 single issues (Creeley $8); add $1 overseas

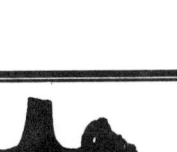

Read not the Times, read the Eternities.

——— Henry David Thoreau

If Thoreau were alive today, he'd probably be a reader of PARABOLA, with its rich store of knowledge from ancient myth and folklore. He'd also delight in our writers and artists who address the important issues of the day with a depth that only the timeless traditions can provide. Won't you become a reader too?

BACK ISSUES FROM PARABOLA

—Volume I, No. 1 **The Hero** Mircea Eliade, Barbara G. Myerhoff, Barre Toelken, P.L. Travers, Jacob Needleman, Edward Edinger, Minor White, Huston Smith interview. *(Reprint)*
—Volume I, No. 2 **Magic** Barbara G. Myerhoff, Daniel Noel, Robert Ellwood, Jacob Needleman, Victor Turner, Thomas Moore, Christmas Humphreys, Joseph Campbell interview.
—Volume I, No. 3 **Initiation** Sam Gill, Janwillem van de Wetering, Arthur Amiotte, Evelyn Eaton, Fernando Llosa Porras, Mircea Eliade interview.
—Volume I, No. 4 **Rites of Passage** Frederick Franck, James Wolfe, Ursula K. Le Guin, D.M. Dooling, Robert E. Meagher, William Irwin Thompson interview. *(Reprint)*
—Volume II, No. 1 **Death** P.L. Travers, Conrad Hyers, Isaac Bashevis Singer, Brother David Steindl-Rast, William Doty, William Burke Jr., interview with Tibetan Lamas.*(Reprint)*
—Volume II, No. 2 **Creation** Sam Gill, P.L. Travers, David Rosenberg, David Johnson, Jane Yolen, John Fentress Gardner, Daniel Whitman, Kenneth Phillips, Zalman Schachter interview. *(Reprint)*
—Volume II, No. 3 **Cosmology** Brother David Steindl-Rast, Ursula K. Le Guin, Schwaller de Lubicz, Lorel Desjardins, Elaine Jahner, Jean Toomer, Anne Bevan, Harry Remde, Lloyd Motz interview. *(Reprint)*
—Volume II, No. 4 **Relationships** Frederick Franck, Robert E. Meagher, Shems Friedlander, Lizelle Reymond, Jean Toomer, Barre Toelken, Jane Yolen, Diane Wolkstein interview.

—Volume III, No. 1 **Sacred Space** Ananda K. Coomaraswamy, Barbara Stoler Miller, Robert Lawlor, Irving Friedman, Richard Smithies, Andrew L. March, Thomas Bridges, Pablo Neruda, Helene Fleury, P.L. Travers and Michael Dames interview.
—Volume III, No. 2 **Sacrifice and Transformation** Annemarie Schimmel, Joseph Epes Brown, Ivan Morris, Father Alexander Schmemann, Christopher Fremantle, Robert A.F. Thurman, photographic sequence with Minor White and others, Rabbi Adin Steinsaltz interview.
—Volume III, No. 3 **Inner Alchemy** Mircea Eliade, D.M. Dooling, Harry Remde, Jacob Needleman, Elemire Zolla.
—Volume III, No. 4 **Androgyny** Elaine H. Pagels, Titus Burckhardt, Keith Critchlow, P.L. Travers, Barbara G. Myerhoff, Lobsang Lhalungpa interview.
—Volume IV, No. 1 **The Trickster** Emory Sekaquaptewa, Michel Waldberg, Lynda Sexson, Barbara Tedlock, P.L. Travers, David Leeming, Joseph Epes Brown interview.
—Volume IV, No. 2 **Sacred Dance** Elaine H. Pagels, Rosemary Jeanes, David P. McAllester, Anita Daniel, Fritjof Capra, William L. Prensky, Annemarie Schimmel, Peter Brook interview.
—Volume IV, No. 3 **The Child** Don Talayesva, Richard Lewis, Frederick Franck, Lynda Sexson, Lobsang Lhalungpa, art and stories by children.
—Volume IV, No. 4 **Storytelling and Education** Sr. Marie Jose Hobday, Richard Lewis, Abraham Menashe, Thomas Buckley, James Hillman, Maria Dermout, Robin Ridington, Sam Gill, Wilbur and Paul Jordan-Smith, interviews with Anne Charles, Richard Lewis, Nancy Rambusch; I Wayan Wija and Diane Wolkstein.

—Volume V, No. 1 **The Old Ones** Keith Critchlow, Agnes Vanderburg, Frederick Franck, J. Stephen Lansing, Joy Elvey Bannerman, Megan Biesele, Lobsang Lhalungpa, Jonathan Chaves, Barbara G. Myerhoff, Robert Bly, Rolf Jacobsen, Gary Snyder; interviews with Deshung Rinpoche and Joseph Campbell.
—Volume V, No. 2 **Music Sound Silence** Herbert Whone, Tomas Transtromer, David A. Lavery, Peyton Houston, Tom Moore, David P. McAllester, Howard Schwartz, Robert Lawlor, Steve Reich interview.
—Volume V, No. 3 **Obstacles** Al Young, David Malouf, Jacques Lusseyran, Abraham Menashe, Brother David Steindl-Rast, Jonathan Omer-Man, Italo Calvino; interviews with Mohawk Chiefs at Akwesasne and H.H. the Dalai Lama.
—Volume V, No. 4 **Women** P.L. Travers, Helen M. Luke, Seonaid Robertson, Heinrich Zimmer, Ursula K. Le Guin, Barbara Rohde, Joseph Campbell, Diane Wolkstein, Samuel Noah Kramer, Judy Swamp interview.
—Volume VI, No. 1 **Earth and Spirit** Peter Matthiessen, David Guss, Victor Perera, Peter Nabokov, Robert Bly, Paul Caponigro, P.L. Travers, John Kastan, D.M. Dooling, Peter Heinegg, Thomas Buckley, Oren Lyons, Dr. Firoze M. Kotwal interview.
—Volume VI, No. 2 **The Dream of Progress** Kathleen Raine, David Price, David Malouf, Dino Buzzati, Seyyed Hossein Nasr, David Leeming, Paolo Soleri, Scott Eastham, interviews with Chinua Achebe and Jonathan Cott; Jacob Needleman and John Loudon.

Each issue is a handsome, readable paperback of 128 pages with careful attention to graphic design featuring original artwork and photographs.

Back issues are available at $7.00 per copy and; for orders of twelve or more, at $6.00 per copy. Please circle your selections below. Prepaid orders only.

Vol. I	No. 1	No. 2	No. 3	No. 4
Vol. II	No. 1	No. 2	No. 3	No. 4
Vol. III	No. 1	No. 2	No. 3	No. 4
Vol. IV	No. 1	No. 2	No. 3	No. 4
Vol. V	No. 1	No. 2	No. 3	No. 4
Vol. VI	No. 1	No. 2		

A subscription to PARABOLA for current and future issues is $16.00 for one year. We will be exploring Masks, Demons, Sleep, Dreams, and Ceremonies.

I enclose $_____ for _____ back issues.
_____ I enclose $16 for a one year subscription.
Total enclosed $_____ U.S. Dollars only.

Name_____

Address_____

City/State/Zip_____

Send to PARABOLA
150 Fifth Ave., New York, NY 10011   SZ

PARABOLA • The Quarterly Magazine of Myth and Tradition

LAPIS: An annual journal published by LAPIS Educational Association, Inc., a non-profit organization for the integration of Jungian and archetypal studies with literature, depth psychology, philosophy, art, cultural and spiritual studies.

LAPIS means Stone in Latin, and represents the Philosopher's Stone, which is an agent of transformation and a symbol of the Self in Jungian psychology.

LAPIS is a member-supported publishing effort and association of like-minded individuals. LAPIS is seeking papers and articles featuring: Studies of symbol-systems from a Jungian, archetypal, or psychotherapeutic viewpoint; articles focusing on an archetypal theme such as the Shadow, the Great Mother, the Dark Night, Initiatory Voyages.... LAPIS also publishes visionary/archetypal poetry, and some personal experiences of growth through symbolic understanding.

LAPIS returns the copyright to authors after publication.

A copy of the current issue of LAPIS is $4.00—$5.00 outside of the USA. If the current issue is unavailable, your order will be applied to the forthcoming issue. Some back issues are available for a lower price. Special prices on large orders.

A two-year subscription (two issues) is $10.00—$12.00 outside of the USA. Postage is included in the prices.

For information about memberships, subscriptions, price lists, editorial guidelines, please send a self-addressed-stamped-envelope to: LAPIS Educational Association, Inc. c/o Karen Degenhart, Editor, 18420 Klimm Avenue, Homewood, Illinois 60430. USA.

THE CLASSICAL WORLD

Published seven times yearly (from September to May). Each volume contains approximately 450 pages. Paid international circulation of more than 3,000.

Since 1907 *CW* has provided a combination of services and features which make the journal an indispensable tool for teaching and research in the Classics.

Each volume of *The Classical World* contains

ARTICLES...
 of scholarly and general interest to students of Graeco-Roman culture and its aftermath.

SURVEYS...
 complete and annotated bibliographical surveys of scholarship on authors, genres, special areas. For example:

- 1976: D.E. Gerber, "Studies in Greek Lyric Poetry: 1967-1975"
- 1977: H.W. Benario, "Recent Work on Tacitus: 1969-1973"
- 1978: R.J. Rowland, Jr., "A Survey of Selected Ciceronan Bibliography (1965-1974)"
- 1979: D.G. Brearley, "Texts and Studies in Latin Orthography"
  J.P. Holoka, "Homer Studies 1971-1977"
- 1980: J.H. Dee, "A Survey of Recent Bibliographies of Classical Literature"
  A.G. Elliot: "Ovid's *Metamorphosis:* A Bibliography, 1968-1978"

Also: annual lists and editions for teaching Greek and Latin authors and languages, and A-V materials for the teaching of Classics.

REVIEWS...
 CW specializes in the *early, brief* (500-1000 words) and *expert* review of new books in *all* areas of Classical Antiquity and related subjects (*yearly average* of 175 books)

BOOKS RECEIVED...
 extensive and *immediate* listing of *all* books received from publishers around the world with complete bibliographical information (*yearly average* of 250-300 items)

PLUS... other features of interest to the teacher/scholar

For a free sample copy of *CW* and subscription blank write to

The Classical World
Department of Classics
Duquesne University
Pittsburgh, PA 15219